Dictionary of Hermeneutics

A Concise Guide to Terms, Names, Methods, and Expressions

James D. Hernando

GPH
Gospel Publishing House
Springfield, Missouri
02-0453

First edition

ISBN: 0-88243-086-6

Printed in the United States of America

Table of Contents

Preface

During twenty-two years of teaching hermeneutics, I have encountered innumerable students who have had difficulty reading their textbooks. They encounter many terms or concepts which are either totally foreign to them or used in an entirely different sense.[1] These students are by and large extremely intelligent, but many come from other disciplines or are second career people without a formal biblical or theological education.[2] For them reading comprehension suffers due to a lack of foundational knowledge and background.

Over the years, with the help of my students, I have identified and compiled a list of terms, names, concepts, and expressions that routinely appear in hermeneutics texts and create problems in comprehension. The authors are not trying to be obtuse but due to the economy of space sometimes do not adequately define or discuss these terms so that the "uninitiated" can understand the content. For example, R. H. Soulen's *Handbook of Biblical Criticism* contains many hermeneutical terms but is written for more advanced students who have a grasp not only of hermeneutics but the history of hermeneutical theory, plus some familiarity with a wide range of disciplines within biblical criticism. Consequently, the learning curve is incredibly steep—and unnecessarily so—for students who are encountering hermeneutics for the first time.

This book is primarily devoted to hermeneutical terms, names, and expressions. Chapter 7 was added as a supplemental chapter. My colleagues

[1] For example, first year students will undoubtedly run across the term "dogmatic" as in the expression "dogmatic exegesis." Most will not understand that the author is not talking about a somewhat arrogant assertion in biblical interpretation based on less than sufficient evidence. Rather he or she needs to know that such refers to biblical interpretation done with the framework of a theological system or confession of faith to which the interpreter is committed.

[2] The seminary where I teach typically has about 35–40% of its incoming students in that category.

at Global University challenged me to include "Related Terms from Other Disciplines" that often appear in texts in biblical and theological studies but are seldom adequately defined. Students who are new to the fields of hermeneutics and biblical studies should find this book a helpful and handy reference volume when reading their main textbooks, supplemental texts, and research articles. The intended goals, then, are to 1) lessen the learning curve for students new to the field of hermeneutics; 2) minimize the frustration of reading material without adequate comprehension due to a deficiency of background; and 3) provide a useful reference tool for further study and interpretation of the Bible.

If the above goals are met with even a modicum of success, I will rejoice both in and out of the classroom and be grateful to God for the chance to facilitate the learning of His chosen servants.

Acknowledgements

I want to begin by giving praise and thanksgiving to the Lord for calling and gifting me to be a teacher in His Church. Teachers are often blessed by their students who inspire them to continue learning and become better teachers. That is true in my case. The students listed below wrote papers and projects that helped me identify so many of the terms contained in this book.

I certainly want to express my appreciation to The Assemblies of God Theological Seminary for granting me a sabbatical leave to write this book and to my faculty colleagues who cheered me on to completion.

My heartfelt thanks goes out to Dr. Dilla Dawson of Global University who encouraged me in this writing project and Dr. Quentin McGhee and Dr. Willard Teague who saw a broader application for this book and provided a list of terms that are included in Chapter 7.

Finally, I would like to acknowledge a debt to my wife, Moira, not only for her invaluable editorial assistance, but for being an unwavering source of love, encouragement, and constructive criticism. I could not have finished the project without her.

I would like to express thanks and appreciation to the following students whose course projects provided invaluable guidance in choosing terms included in this book: Jeanette Collins, Mary Beth Godard, Brian Jenkins, Irma Juarez, Heidi Jumper, Randy Jumper, Jason Loper, Derrick Miller, Jeanine Schreiner, UnYong Statwick, Brandon Slifka, Greg Stone, Jared Stoner, Jeff Williams, and James Wright

Introduction

Dictionary of Hermeneutics: A Concise Guide to Terms, Names, Methods, and Expressions was written to serve as a primer and resource book for entry-level graduate students studying hermeneutics for the first time.[1] The book is comprised of short articles[2] on terms, expressions, and people related to the field of biblical hermeneutics, its presuppositions, theory, and praxis. The nature and purpose of the book is such that brevity is prized, yet without compromising accuracy. Undoubtedly, much more could be written on every term included. To some what is not said or left out is essential to an accurate understanding of the term. This author has labored to provide the necessary information that will yield an adequate understanding, if not a complete one. Of course, readers will disagree over what is and what is not adequate and essential information.

Again it will be helpful to describe the strategy of this volume. It consists of a threefold objective: 1) To write short, clear definitions that avoid the use of technical jargon and assume virtually nothing in terms of prior knowledge of the field.[3] For many of the terms there are call-out boxes with a biblical text that provides an example or illustration of the term defined. Again, the goal is to provide need-to-know information for comprehension of entry level texts; 2) Where applicable, to write a description of the relevance of the term (phrase, name, etc.) to broader issues or topics within the field

---

[1] For the last nine years I have asked students in my hermeneutics classes to note what terms they have encountered that they felt were not adequately defined or discussed. I have kept and compiled a list of these terms and added many of my own. Although my primary audience are those first-year seminary students without prior biblical or theological education, this book would also serve students on the undergraduate level as well.

[2] Note that I am using the term "article" and not "definition" since more than simple definitions are usually given, although for some terms little more than a definition is needed.

[3] Where it is necessary to mention an "insider" term, the word has been set off in Small Caps, indicating that this has an article elsewhere in the book. The student can then go to the Subject Index and find the page number where that term can be found.

of hermeneutics[4]; 3) Each article has built-in documentation in the parenthetical reference style. This format has the advantage of presenting a more casual, less technical format. However, where additional clarifying content is needed or deemed helpful, supplemental footnotes are provided. The author has written as an evangelical Pentecostal, but where deemed appropriate, the divergent definitions and understandings of other traditions are presented.

4 For example, after defining a technical term like *usus loquendi,* we would add an explanation that this Latin term ("common use") is somewhat antiquated and refers to the ordinary designation of a word in a given cultural-historical context. We would also supply a conceptual link to other articles, for example, Cf. *Sensus literalis.*

Abbreviations

Reference Works

BDAG Danker, Frederick William, ed. *A Greek-English Lexicon of the New Testament and Other Early Christian Literature.* 3d ed. Chicago: University of Chicago Press, 2000.

BDF Blass, F., A. Debrunner, and Robert W. Funk. *A Greek Grammar of the New Testament and Other Early Christian Literature.* Chicago: University of Chicago Press, 1961, rep., 1975.

BDT Taylor, Richard, ed. *Beacon Dictionary of Theology.* Kansas City, Mo.: Beacon Hill Press, 1983.

BDOT Harrison, E., G. W. Bromiley and Carl F. H. Henry. *Baker's Dictionary of Theology.* Grand Rapids: Baker Book House, 1978.

DPCM Burgess, Stanley M., and Gary B. McGee, eds. *Dictionary of Pentecostal and Charismatic Movements.* Grand Rapids: Zondervan, 1988.

ENT Elwell, Walter A., ed. *Evangelical Dictionary of Theology.* Grand Rapids, Mich.: Baker Book House, 1984.

HHBI McKim, Donald K. *Historical Handbook of Major Biblical Interpreters.* Downers Grove, Ill.: InterVarsity Press, 1998.

NBD Douglas, J. D., ed. *The New Bible Dictionary.* Grand Rapids: Wm. B. Eerdmans, 1962. Reprint, 1978.

NTI Marshall, I. Howard, ed. *New Testament Interpretation: Essays on Principles and Methods.* Grand Rapids: Wm. B. Eerdmans, 1977.

NDBT Alexander, T. D. and Brian S. Rosner, eds. *New Dictionary of Biblical Theology.* Downers Grove, Ill.: InterVarsity Press, 2000.

PDTT Grenz, Stanley, David Guretzki, and Cherith Fee Nordling. *Pocket Dictionary of Theological Terms.* Downers Grove, Ill.: InterVarsity Press, 1999.

PDBS Patzia, Arthur G., and Anthony J. Petrotta. *Pocket Dictionary of Biblical Studies.* Downers Grove, Ill.: InterVarsity Press, 2002.

PDAP Evans, C. Stephen. *Pocket Dictionary of Apologetics and Philosophy of Religion.* Downers Grove, Ill.: InterVarsity Press, 2002.

Books of the Bible

Old Testament

Genesis	Gen.
Exodus	Ex.
Leviticus	Lev.
Numbers	Num.
Deuteronomy	Deut.
Joshua	Josh.
Judges	Jud.
Ruth	Ruth
1 Samuel	1 Sam.
2 Samuel	2 Sam.
1 Kings	1 Kings
2 Kings	2 Kings
1 Chronicles	1 Chron.
2 Chronicles	2 Chron.
Ezra	Ezra
Nehemiah	Neh.
Esther	Est.
Job	Job
Psalms	Ps.
Proverbs	Prov.
Ecclesiastes	Ecc.
Song of Solomon	S. of Sol.
Isaiah	Isa.
Jeremiah	Jer.
Lamentations	Lam.
Ezekiel	Ezek.
Daniel	Dan.
Hosea	Hosea
Joel	Joel
Amos	Amos
Obadiah	Oba.
Jonah	Jonah
Micah	Micah
Nahum	Nahum
Habbakuk	Hab.
Zephaniah	Zeph.
Haggai	Hag.
Zechariah	Zech.
Malachi	Mal.

New Testament

Matthew	Matt.
Mark	Mark
Luke	Luke
John	John
Acts of the Apostles	Acts
Romans	Rom.
1 Corinthians	1 Cor.
2 Corinthians	2 Cor.
Galatians	Gal.
Ephesians	Eph.
Philippians	Phil.
Colossians	Col.
1 Thessalonians	1 Thess.
2 Thessalonians	2 Thess.
1 Timothy	1 Tim.
2 Timothy	2 Tim.
Titus	Titus
Philemon	Phile.
Hebrews	Heb.
James	James
1 Peter	1 Peter
2 Peter	2 Peter
1 John	1 John
2 John	2 John
3 John	3 John
Jude	Jude
Revelation	Rev.

1

Terms and Expressions

Allegorize

To interpret a text as if it were an allegory or as if allegorical. Cf. ALLEGORY, ALEXANDRIAN SCHOOL, and ALLEGORICAL INTERPRETATION.

Allegory

> "Drink water from your own cistern, running water from your own well" (Prov. 5:15) is an allegory admonishing marital fidelity.

A metaphor extended into a story (Kaiser and Silva, 94). The elements of the story take on meanings that are quite different from the ordinary literal sense of the words.[1] With this definition parables in the OT and NT would qualify as allegory (Duvall and Hays, 179).[2] Most scholars make a distinction between admitting the existence of allegory in Scripture and the allegorization (see ALLEGORIZE) of the Scriptures themselves (Ryken, 145–48). Those who use the allegorical approach usually identify it with eliciting Scripture's so-called deeper spiritual meaning (McQuilken, 38–40).[3] Cf. TYPOLOGICAL INTERPRETATION.

---

[1] A famous allegory is John Bunyan's *Pilgrim's Progress,* in which the story of a traveler and his experiences are told to convey truth about the spiritual journey of faith in a Christian's life.

[2] There is continual debate over whether parables should be treated as allegories. Biblical scholars have long resisted the identification, cautioned by the testimony of history to arbitrary and fanciful interpretation. Leland Ryken makes an effort to answer the objections to this identification in *How to Read the Bible as Literature* (Grand Rapids: Zondervan, 1984), 199–203.

[3] In the history of biblical interpretation, both Jewish and Christian, the allegorical approach was very common. It is often paired with "typology," which also has a comparative element ("this" represents "that"). However, whereas typology is grounded in history and the analogies are more natural and suggestive (e.g., Moses' lifting of the bronze serpent [Num. 21:4–9] and the crucifixion of Jesus [John 3:14f]), the analogous connections made by allegory are remote and often strange. Thus, Philo of Alexandria could see in the description of the four rivers of Eden (Gen. 2:10–14) a discourse on four virtues. Similarly, Clement of Alexandria saw Moses' prohibition against eating unclean animals a warning to shun various

Analogy of faith (Lat. *analogia fidei*)

> "What you heard from me, keep as *the pattern of sound teaching,* with faith and love in Christ Jesus." –2 Tim. 1:13

To interpret Scripture in consultation with a recognized standard or expression of Christian orthodoxy. Early church fathers referred to that standard as the "rule of faith" (Lat. *regula fidei*), which could be identified with apostolic teaching (oral or written), the Scriptures, or creedal statements of faith. The Protestant Reformers argued that "Scripture alone" (*sola Scriptura*) was that authoritative standard, and that interpretation is best done by comparing Scripture with Scripture. Roman Catholicism, on the other hand, maintains that Scripture and various forms of church tradition (creeds, writings of church fathers, the decisions of church councils) must be consulted when determining matters of faith and doctrine (Ramm 1970, 36, 55f; Kaiser 1981, 134f).

Analogy of Scripture

A corollary principle to the Analogy of faith. The Reformers argued that the Bible was its own best interpreter. Luther held that the Scriptures possessed sufficient clarity so that the devout and competent believer could understand its meaning without consulting outside sources of tradition. When confronted with an obscure passage, priority should be given to the passage that is clear. Thus, "Scripture interprets Scripture" is a statement of the priority given to the Bible in determining matters of faith and practice.

Application

Refers to that part of the hermeneutical task which seeks to explain how the meaning of the text (derived through Exegesis) can become "meaningful," i.e., impact the reader-interpreter's present situation. Cf. Significance.

Authorial intent

Refers to what an author intended to say when he wrote a text. The expression raises the hermeneutical question of where meaning is to be found. The three proposed locations are the author, the text, and the reader.[4] Cf. Revelation.

---

vices. Good discussions of the historical origins of allegorical interpretation can be found in Milton S. Terry, *Biblical Hermeneutics: A Treatise on the Interpretation of the Old and New Testaments* (New York: Hunt and Eaton, 1890), 58–60, and Bernard Ramm, *Protestant Biblical Interpretation,* 3rd ed. (Grand Rapids: Baker Book House, 1970), 24–45.

[4] For a well-reasoned defense of locating the meaning of text with authorial intent see Robert H. Stein, "The Benefits of an Author-Oriented Approach to Hermeneutics," *Journal of the Evangelical Theological Society* 44, no. 3 (September 2001): 451–66.

Authoritative (See also Canon, Canonical)

In biblical studies or hermeneutics refers to something that has authority and establishes a norm that is binding on a particular community. For example, the authoritative writings of the Christian church are the Scriptures, or Bible.

Canon (Gk. *kanon*)

Is most often used to designate the collection of biblical books that Christians accept as uniquely authoritative for defining Christian faith and practice. From the literal meaning of "reed" the term took on the figurative sense of a measuring rod, or ruler, to the general sense of a norm, or standard. In the Early Church, the term was used to refer to the doctrinal and ethical teachings of the apostles that defined the Christian faith. It was not applied to the OT and NT until the fourth century (Dunbar, 300). Thus "canon" designates the boundaries of God's inspired Word or written revelation (Klein, Blomberg, and Hubbard, 92), which are not the same for all Christian traditions.[5] (See Apocrypha below.)

While the term raises a host of issues about what various church traditions regard as authoritative in defining their faith,[6] the application to hermeneutics is foundational. Biblical hermeneutics seeks to interpret only those Scriptures regarded as canon. Some scholars like Brevard Childs argue that the canon should shape our interpretation of the Scriptures and is the most appropriate context for doing biblical theology.

Apocrypha

Derived from the Greek word meaning "hidden," refers to a collection of books in the Septuagint (Gk. version of the OT) and the Latin Vulgate. They are accepted as canonical Scripture by Roman Catholicism and Eastern Orthodoxy. However, they are rejected as noncanonical and omitted from the Protestant and Jewish canons of Scripture.

---

[5] Most notably Roman Catholicism and Eastern Orthodoxy accept the books of the Apocrypha as part of the inspired Canon of Scripture.

[6] "For example, Roman Catholicism sees various expressions (both oral and written) of church tradition as authoritative. Among these would be the creeds and decisions of the *Magisterium*, the teaching office of the Church. Eastern Orthodoxy recognizes that liturgy and worship hold an authoritative role in defining orthodoxy. Methodism's *quadrilateral* doctrine recognizes that along with the Bible, tradition, reason, and experience must be consulted." For a broader discussion of these traditions, see J. D. Woodbridge and T. E. McComiskey, *Doing Theology in Today's World* (Grand Rapids: Zondervan, 1991).

Canonical

Designates those biblical writings recognized by the Christian church as the inspired canon of Scripture. Scholars writing on the history of the formation of the biblical canon will apply the word in one of three ways: (1) to the character, or quality, that expresses the orthodoxy of the apostolic faith; (2) to the authoritative status a writing held in the Early Church; (3) to the inclusion of a writing in the delimited list of OT or NT Scripture.[7]

Commissive language

> From now on let no one cause trouble for me, *for I bear on my body the brand-marks of Jesus.* —Gal. 6:17, NASB

Refers to language the goal of which is motivation to action or decision, to express emotions, or to evoke an emotional response. It is usually placed over against "referential language," which is used to dispassionately describe something by conveying information (Stein 1994, 73).[8] See Referential Meaning.

Conceptual parallel

> But [He] emptied Himself, taking the form of a bond-servant, and being made in the likeness of men. —Phil. 2:7, NASB
> Since the children share in flesh and blood, He Himself likewise also partook of the same. —Heb. 2:14, NASB

Occurs when two or more passages or verses address the same subject, concept, or idea without using the same words. For example, Philippians 2:7,8 and Hebrews 2:9–15 both describe the incarnation of Christ, but with different terminology.

Connotative meaning

> "And with his stripes we are healed" (Isa. 53:5, KJV), i.e., the wounds and marks of Christ's sufferings on the cross.

Refers to verbal meaning that is a departure from the ordinary literal sense of a word to a special use or application of that word in a specific context or association. See Contextual meaning and Denotative meaning.

---

[7] For an excellent survey of this issue, see Theodore Donner, "Some Thoughts on the History of the New Testament Canon," *Themelios* 7 (1982): 23–27.

[8] The two terms are not mutually exclusive, for people can pass along information while using "commissive language" and the information conveyed by "referential language" can stir up an emotional response. See Robert H. Stein, *A Basic Guide to Interpreting the Bible: Playing by the Rules* (Grand Rapids: Baker Book House, 1994), 74.

Contextual meaning

The meaning of a word, phrase, sentence, paragraph, passage, etc., as it stands in relationship to the larger literary context, from a sentence to the entire book of the Bible. For example, words often have a range of meaning (see SEMANTIC RANGE). The interpreter chooses which meaning best fits the verbal or literary context in which the word is found.

Contextualization

Is the task of making the message or truth claims of Scripture both intelligible and relevant to a receptor audience or culture.[9] See ETHNOHERMENEUTICS (ch. 4).

Criticism

In association with biblical interpretation, "criticism" refers to the scientific investigation of literary documents (e.g., the Bible) in regard to such matters as origin, formation of the text, composition, analysis of content, and historical background.

Cultural-historical context

Refers to the placement of a text against the cultural and historical background of its author and its first readers. The goal of such placement is to more accurately determine what the biblical author intended to communicate to them by his choice of words and literary devices.

Cultural relativism

Holds that the truth value of any idea is dependent on the culture that produced it. When applied to the moral or theological content of Scripture it becomes problematic, because it denies the divine authorship of Scripture and therefore rejects the notion that the Bible contains any truth that is eternal and transcultural in its relevance or authority (McQuilkin, 32–34).

Culture

Refers to all expressions of human life in a particular time and place. It is a comprehensive term, and so we can talk about material culture (seen in the

---

[9] David J. Hasselgrave addresses the challenge of contextualization in view of religious pluralism and the varieties of EPISTEMOLOGY that attend modern approaches to hermeneutics. See "Contextualization and Revelational Epistemology" in *Hermeneutics, Inerrancy and the Bible*, ed. E. D. Radmacher and R. D. Preus (Grand Rapids: Zondervan, 1984), 691–738. D. A. Carson provides "A Sketch of the Factors Determining Current Hermeneutical Debate in Cross-Cultural Contexts" in *Biblical Interpretation and the Church: The Problem of Contextualization*, ed. D. A. Carson (Nashville: Thomas Nelson, 1984), 11–29.

physical artifacts and remains of culture) or culture with respect to a variety of different contexts: social, political, economic, religious, literary, artistic, technological, etc.

Examination of the cultural context of a passage is an integral part of interpretation, or Exegesis, as it seeks to understand the words of Scripture in their native setting framed by time, geography, and culture (Virkler, 79–81; Ramm 1970, 133f).

Deductive reasoning

The kind of logical thought that draws a conclusion about particulars from a general conclusion. E.g., a person, having concluded that God possesses a perfectly righteous and holy nature might deduce (or infer) that in all His earthly acts Jesus, the Son of God, was sinless and blameless before God.

Deliberative (See Rhetorical criticism, ch. 4)

Denotative meaning

Refers to the actual thing(s) behind the literal sense of a word, distinct from that which might be implied, suggested by special association or metaphorical use. For example, the denotative meaning of "sword" in Jesus' words, "'Put your sword back in its place'" (Matt. 26:52) refers to the literal weapon. However, the Connotative meaning of sword—e.g., "'The sword will never depart from your house'" (2 Sam. 12:10)—refers to violent conflict rather than a literal sword.

Didactic

Means designed or intended to teach. While in one sense all Scripture can be said to teach (2 Tim. 3:16), this term is used to describe literary genres (e.g., Proverbs, Epistles) whose primary purpose is to give instruction.

Distantiation

Refers to the interpreter's realization of how wide the gap is that separates his or her understanding of the text and the world (or Horizon) of the text (Carson 1984a, 20–22). The awareness of that gap helps to see one's own Presuppositions and the influence they have on one's understanding of the text.

Dogmatic (See DOGMATIC APPROACH, ch. 4)

Of or relating to dogma (doctrine or a set of doctrines). For example, dogmatic exegesis occurs when biblical interpretation is carried out by someone committed to a particular theological system or confession of faith who consciously consults that system in measuring the accuracy of his or her interpretation. This raises debate over the role (and the extent) a theological system should play in shaping or controlling one's interpretation of Scripture.[10]

Dynamic equivalence (Also called "functional equivalence")

Thought-for-thought equivalency in translation, with the goal of having the same effect on the modern readers as the original text had on its readers. This strategy of translation is less concerned with closely following the Greek or Hebrew syntax and grammar in a literal word-for-word translation (known as "formal equivalence") as long as the thoughts are equivalent (Klein, Blomberg, and Hubbard, 74).

Eisegesis

Literally, "to draw or lead into" and refers to the interpretive error of reading into a text one's own presupposed or preconceived ideas as a substitute for careful EXEGESIS to determine what the author meant to say. Eisegesis has many motivations and expressions, but a common assumption is that a text has many meanings, not just one.[11] See POLYSEMY.

---

[10] Moisés Silva and Walter C. Kaiser Jr. carry on a collegial debate within their coauthored volume *An Introduction to Biblical Hermeneutics: The Search for Meaning* (Grand Rapids: Zondervan, 1994). Silva (259–64) argues not only that it is impossible to separate exegesis and theology but that exegesis profits from consciously interpreting Scripture within a theological framework. Kaiser, on the other hand (202–6), maintains that "exegesis is prior to any system of theology" and must remain so if Scripture is to function as an independent and autonomous authority over human theological systems or doctrinal formulations.

[11] Walter C. Kaiser Jr. cites the views of Vern S. Poythress as a disturbing example of the legitimatization of plural meanings. In addition to the speaker's meaning, Poythress speaks of the meaning determined by the audience's reaction and the "discourse" meaning which is established by "competent judges" knowledgeable in linguistic and historical backgrounds. See Vern S. Poythress, "Analysing a Biblical Text: Some Important Linguistic Distinctions," *Scottish Journal of Theology* 32 (1979): 113, 126. But Kaiser's criticism is worth noting. Even if "competent judges" determine discourse meaning ("meanings" is more realistic), it still leaves the problem of determining which is to be considered the CANONICAL meaning. See Kaiser, *Toward an Exegetical Theology: Biblical Exegesis for Preaching and Teaching* (Grand Rapids: Baker Book House, 1981), 47–48.

Epistemology

Refers to that branch of philosophy that investigates the nature, sources, and acquisition of knowledge. Its importance for hermeneutics lies with the fact that epistemological assumptions lie behind every approach to interpretation. Answers to questions such as "What is truth?" and "How can I know it?" are central to the concerns of epistemology. "What kind of truth is contained in the Scriptures?" and "How does Scripture convey truth?" are questions that bring the two disciplines face-to-face.

Etymology

Is the study of the origin and historical development of words, their forms, and meanings. This is done by tracing the development of a word from its earliest recorded occurrence in the language of its origin. Especially noted are the changes that occur in the form of the word and its meaning as a result of the influence of other languages, cultures, and literary genres.

Popular use of etymology often results in the error of defining a word by combining the meanings of its linguistic parts (Carson 1984a, 27–32). For example, in the same way "awful" no longer means "full of awe," the NT word *homologeō* does not mean "to say the same" or "to agree" (Gk. *legein,* "to say," and *homos,* "same") but rather "to profess, confess, or declare publicly." A helpful rule to remember: Usage and context, not etymology, determine the meaning of a word.

Exegesis

Literally means a "drawing out" and refers to the analysis and explanation of a text to determine the meaning intended by the author and understood by the first readers. Confusion arises when the term is used interchangeably with Hermeneutics (Virkler, 18) and Interpretation (Silva, 31) without qualification or differentiation. One more or less common distinction is that whereas "hermeneutics" investigates the principles and methods used in interpretation, "exegesis" is the actual use and application of those principles and methods to the text (Kaiser and Silva, 285). More modern approaches to hermeneutics have stressed the task of drawing out the relevance of interpretation for the contemporary reader (Tate, xv).

Existentialism

A school of philosophy that defines human life in terms of "being," or existence.[12] Existentialism is sometimes characterized by the expression "Being

[12] Existentialism is a philosophy with many faces, or expressions, which are not at all compatible in their conclusions. For example, the origins of existentialism have been traced to both the Danish philosopher Søren Kierkegaard, a committed Christian, and the avowed German atheist Friedrich Nietzsche. In the twentieth century it is associated with the philosophical

precedes essence." This states the conviction that people are human beings not because they possess some special nature or essence, but because they exist and choose to live in a particular way. Human existence becomes authentic and is meaningfully expressed when an individual passionately engages life through free acts of the will. Thus, the "existential approach" to biblical interpretation is subjective and tends to focus on the interpreter as the determiner of meaning (Dockery, 165). It emphasizes not the rational comprehension of Scripture (i.e., an objective textual meaning), but the interpreter's personal encounter with and response to the message of the text.[13] See Christian existentialism.

Exposition (Lat. *exponere,* "to explain")

The explaining or setting forth of the meaning of a text. It is commonly distinguished from Exegesis,[14] especially to differentiate interpreting a text to arrive at its historical sense, from the task of expounding that meaning to show its relevance for today (Soulen 1981, 70). When applied to the field of Homiletics, expository preaching builds on the labor of exegesis. An expository sermon that expounds, or explains, a biblical text for a contemporary hearer should first determine what the text meant to the author and its first readers (Virkler, 234f).[15]

---

writings of Martin Heidegger, the theologies of Karl Barth, Emil Brunner, and Rudolf Bultmann, and the literary exploits of Jean-Paul Sartre and Albert Camus. What unites these divergent expressions of existentialism is the emphasis on the personal and subjective discovery of truth or meaning, whether such meaning is affirmed within a Christian/theistic worldview, or denied within a nihilistic (i.e., life has no meaning) and atheistic framework. For a brief but insightful introduction to existentialism, see Colin Brown, "Existentialism," in the *Evangelical Dictionary of Theology,* ed. Walter A. Elwell (Grand Rapids: Baker Book House, 1984), 395–97.

[13] In particular, the emphasis is on how the reader-interpreter is made aware of the possibilities of understanding human existence through the message of the text. See David S. Dockery, *Biblical Interpretation Then and Now: Contemporary Hermeneutics in the Light of the Early Church* (Grand Rapids: Baker Book House, 1992), 166–68.

[14] This is so despite the fact that linguistically the terms are virtually synonymous ("exegesis" is a "drawing out," and "exposition" a "setting out" of the meaning). Writers often use both terms to denote the Interpretation of a biblical text. For example, J. I. Packer equates the expositional labors of the Reformers with exegesis. See *Fundamentalism and the Word of God* (InterVarsity Press, 1958; Grand Rapids: Wm. B. Eerdmans, n.d.), 19. Moisés Silva, in *Introduction to Biblical Hermeneutics,* 19, remarks that exegesis is just a "fancy" way of referring to interpretation.

[15] A. Berkeley Mickelsen argues both for the distinction of exegesis and exposition and for their inseparability if true interpretation is to be done. See *Interpreting the Bible* (1963; Grand Rapids: Wm B. Eerdmans, 1974).

External evidence

Broadly applied to the evidence that comes from literary sources other than the one being considered.[16] The term often appears in works dealing with TEXTUAL CRITICISM (see ch. 4), which attempts to determine the original form of an ancient text for which there are numerous copies. External evidence examines the manuscripts in support of or at variance with a particular textual reading, or VARIANT (Fee and Stuart 1982, 131). See INTERNAL EVIDENCE.

Figurative language

"That hermeneutics exam was a *bear.*" Figuratively speaking it was an *unmanageable beast* or a *killer* of a test.

Refers to all uses of words that are metaphorical or symbolic in nature, conveying a meaning different from their common, literal sense. In biblical interpretation, understanding the meaning of figurative language often involves the study of its cultural, historical, and literary contexts (McQuilken, 165–84).[17] Cf. DENOTATIVE MEANING.

Genre (see Genre, ch. 5)

Refers to a group of texts that share common traits (Longman, 76). The term is applied to any literary type characterized by a particular form (style), function (purpose), and content. In biblical interpretation, genre analysis belongs to the category of SPECIAL HERMENEUTICS, which deals with these features and asks what perspectives, considerations, rules, or principles should be kept in mind as we interpret a particular literary genre. Understanding how a genre works or communicates can help us avoid misinterpretation (Ryken, 25). When we bridge this cultural-literary gap we enter the author's world. We gain access not only to a manner of expression, but a way of thinking. Consequently, we are in a better position to understand what he was trying to communicate to his first readers (Johnson, 1–4).

Hapaxlegomena (Gk., "spoken once")

In TEXTUAL CRITICISM a term used most often of words that appear only once in the biblical text. When one encounters such a word it is necessary to

---

[16] For example, the external evidence for the development of the New Testament CANON would include the writings of the Apostolic Fathers, the church fathers from the second through the fourth centuries, and noncanonical writings from the same period that might quote or allude to passages from the NT.

[17] For an excellent discussion of the function of figurative language and how to recognize its use, see Robertson McQuilken, *Understanding and Applying the Bible*, rev. ed. (Chicago: Moody Press, 1992), 165–183.

consult lexicons that survey extrabiblical literature contemporaneous with the Bible. It can also be applied to a word that appears only once in the writings of a particular author.

Hermeneutics (Gk. *hermēneuō,* "to interpret")

The discipline that studies the theory, principles, and methods used to interpret texts, especially ancient ones such as the sacred Scriptures. Traditional hermeneutics focuses primarily on the discovery of the historical meaning as intended by the author and understood by the original audience. Modern approaches to hermeneutics often stress the role of the reader in creatively engaging the text in the discovery of its SIGNIFICANCE for today.

Hermeneutic

Refers to a particular system of interpretation organized around an established frame of reference having an acknowledged set of presuppositions, values, or beliefs, which guides or controls the interpretation of texts.[18]

The term is associated with the work of H-G. Gadamer, who viewed hermeneutics not as a method of interpretation but as a description of how one comes to understanding through a text. See GADAMER, HANS-GEORG (ch. 3).

General hermeneutics

Refers to those rules and principles that pertain to the interpretation of any text, irrespective of literary genre.

Special hermeneutics

Refers to those distinctive rules and principles that pertain to the interpretation of a particular text, or group of texts, usually in relation to a specific genre or literary category.

Historical-critical method, the (HCM)

An approach to biblical interpretation sometimes known as "historical criticism" (Soulen 1981, 87).[19] However, strictly speaking, the HCM refers to a kind

[18] It often is associated with a comprehensive ideology that governs how one views the process of understanding as it is mediated through the text. That ideology may be either philosophical (e.g., an existential hermeneutic), sociopolitical (e.g., liberation hermeneutic), or cultural (e.g., African, Asian, Latin American, etc., hermeneutic).

[19] Soulen points out that the term is somewhat erroneously used to designate the whole range of methodologies related to biblical criticism. Instead, it more correctly designates "that underlying principle of historical reasoning which came to flower in the 19th century."

of philosophy of history that became preeminent in the 19th century under the influence of the social scientist Ernst Troeltsch (1865–1923). In a published work in 1922 he wrote a chapter called "Historical and Dogmatic Method in Theology." In it he outlined and expounded a method of doing historical investigation that was grounded in axioms and presuppositions *not only about history but all human experience.* The problem for hermeneutics stems from the fact that these presuppositions are at odds with the biblical worldview held by the authors of Scripture.[20] See Historical criticism (ch. 4).

Homiletics

The science and art of sermon preparation and preaching. Homiletics is often regarded as an integral part of the interpretative process that transforms the results of biblical exegesis into an intelligible and relevant message for today.

Horizon(s) (See Gadamer, Hans-Georg)

Idiom

"Amen, I say to you . . ." i.e., "I tell you the truth" or "Indeed/Truly I say to you . . ."

An expression or use of words that is peculiar to a particular language, either grammatically (e.g., the double negative used for emphasis in some languages) or having a meaning that is something other than the sum of its linguistic parts (e.g., "Go ahead, back up!").

[20] Troeltsch's proposed method of historiography (i.e., doing history) included the following principles: (1) The Principle of Criticism (or "Methodological Doubt")—All historical knowledge is historically conditioned (i.e., it is written by people who are tied to their time and limited by it), and as such is open to continual verification and correction by a reexamination of the evidence. (2) The Principle of Analogy—There is a fundamental homogeneity to all human experience. That is, all historical phenomena falls within a standard range of human experience. Because a comparative relationship exists between all such experience past and present, mankind's present experience can provide objective criteria by which we can judge *what could or could not have happened in the past.* Thus, historical research yields only *probabilities not certainties.* (3) The Principle of Causation—Every historical event is the product of a known law of cause and effect. Proof of a historical fact must include an explanation according to these laws. E.g., Bultmann regarded history as a closed continuum of cause and effect. History is the interpretation of events according to those laws of causation: physical, social, psychological, etc. See Edgar Krentz, *The Historical Critical Method* (Philadelphia: Fortress Press, 1975), 56–61. What is clear is that these axioms are at the core rationalistic and naturalistic, making the supernatural content and claims of Scripture inadmissible.

Illumination

Refers to the action of the Holy Spirit in imparting insight and understanding to the individual reader (or hearer) of the Scripture so that the truth is comprehended and its implications are understood as regards to an appropriate response of faith (Stein 1994, 65–71).[21] Furthermore, the illuminating work of the Spirit brings about a spiritual understanding (1 Cor. 2:14) that transcends the rational or cognitive dimension of human intelligence.[22]

> *I pray that the eyes of your heart may be enlightened, so that you will know* what is the hope of His calling, what are the riches of the glory of His inheritance in the saints, and what is the surpassing greatness of His power toward us who believe. –Eph. 1:18,19, NASB

Inductive (reasoning)

The kind of logical thought that draws a general conclusion based on observing and analyzing particular facts. E.g., a person might "induce" (infer) from all the sayings of Jesus that He clearly understood himself as the Messiah and Son of God.

---

[21] One perennial question related to this term is "What is the role of the Holy Spirit in the interpretation of Scripture?" A follow-up question might be "Can an unbeliever, who does not have the indwelling of the Holy Spirit, truly understand the Scriptures?" During the Reformation, Luther and Calvin both stressed the necessity of illumination and faith for interpretation. That the Holy Spirit is vital to that process is clear (1 Cor. 2:11–14). However, the exact nature of the Spirit's work is vague and not clear from Scripture. Although we cannot solve the problem in a footnote, one observation seems clear: Unbelievers can arrive at the exegetical meaning of Scripture. That is, by using the exegetical method, they can determine the textual meaning as intended by the historical author. However, there is a level of "knowing," or understanding, that transcends the rational or cognitive apprehension. One can understand what Moses, the Prophets, Jesus, or Paul said, meant, and taught without believing their teachings or responding in faith. Whatever else the Spirit does for us in our encounter with Scripture, He moves us toward this second level of apprehension and response. See Kaiser and Silva, *Introduction to Biblical Hermeneutics,* 167–68.

[22] Both Pentecostals/Charismatics and Evangelicals acknowledge the Holy Spirit's role in the illumination of Scripture. See F. L. Arrington, "Hermeneutics," in the *Dictionary of Pentecostal and Charismatic Movements,* ed. Stanley M. Burgess and Gary B. McGee (Grand Rapids: Zondervan, 1988), 382–87; Roger Stronstad, *Spirit, Scripture and Theology: A Pentecostal Perspective* (Bagio City, Philippines: APTS Press, 1995), 73–74. Cf. Kaiser and Silva, *Introduction to Biblical Hermeneutics,* 167–68. However, debate exists whether Pentecostals and Charismatics have an interpretative edge or understand the Scriptures differently than do Evangelicals or non-Pentecostals/Charismatics. Gordon Anderson, a classical Pentecostal, cautions against a claim to the uniqueness of a Pentecostal hermeneutic, which not only sounds elitist but also flounders when pressed to explain how the meanings derived by Holy Spirit-illuminated, Pentecostal interpreters differ from those of non-Pentecostals. See Gordon L. Anderson, "Pentecostal Hermeneutics," in the Conference Papers, vol. 2 of the 22nd Annual Meeting of the Society for Pentecostal Studies (Springfield, Mo., November 12–14, 1992), 5–7.

Inspiration

Designates the supernatural work of the Holy Spirit that enabled and motivated the human authors of Scripture to produce an accurate record and revelation of God's redemptive will, purpose, and activity (*PDTT,* 66; Erickson, 199).[23]

Intentional fallacy

That is to say, the so-called fallacy of assuming one can know the intention of an author. It is the objection to locating the meaning of a text with what the author intended to say because no one can know all that the author was thinking or feeling during the act of writing. Furthermore, authors may choose words that do not adequately say what they intend (Stein 1994, 23, 204). A common criticism of this view is that it removes the possibility of objective textual meaning and serves to undermine the validity of all meaningful verbal communication.[24]

Internal evidence

In Textual criticism, refers to the evidence supporting a particular textual reading (or Variant) from within the literary work itself. It concerns the particulars of how a text was written, what copyists would have done, how and what authors would most likely have written given their known literary style and way of thinking.

Interpretation

The act or process of explaining the meaning of verbal communication, either oral or written. It is the goal of Hermeneutics and Exegesis. Hermeneutical debate continues over whether the term should include the task of drawing out Significance for the contemporary reader. Further debate concerns whether the meaning of the text is the one intended by the author,

---

[23] Note that this definition of the term is distinctively theological. Keep in mind that "inspiration" is often used in a humanistic sense, i.e., to refer to an inspiring experience that has awakened or provoked deep religious feelings.

[24] The objection fails to distinguish between the author's intended meaning and his internal thought processes and experience when he wrote the text. The latter is exhaustive knowledge of the author and is inaccessible. The former is limited by his selection and arrangement of words and is accessible through and located in the text. While it is true that authors often fail to express themselves clearly, the biblical authors were not left unaided. The doctrine of Inspiration contends that they had the enablement of the Holy Spirit (2 Peter 1:21). For a lucid though introductory discussion of the "intentional fallacy," see Robert H. Stein, "Who Makes Up the Rules," in *Rightly Divided: Readings in Biblical Hermeneutics,* ed. Roy B. Zuck (Grand Rapids: Kregel Publications, 1996), 35–37.

the one conveyed by the text itself (independent of what the author wanted to say), or the meaning the reader gets out of the text.[25]

Latinism

A word or expression that shows the influence of Latin on the text of the NT. This appears mostly in the use of terminology related to the Roman military establishment, legal administration, measurement, and coins (Soulen 1981, 106).

> And a poor widow came and put in two small copper coins, (Gk. *lepta*) which amount to a cent (Latin *kodrantes*) –Mark 12:42, NASB

Leitwort (Ger., "leading word")

Refers to a term or group of words that appears frequently in a particular text, reflecting a prominent theme. By identifying such a thematic emphasis of the author, the interpreter is given a conceptual clue as to what the text means (Kaiser and Silva, 285). See STICHWORT (Ger., "key word").

Linguistics

The formal study of human language, particularly as speech. This includes units of speech, the nature and function of language itself, its structure, and how language changes. It has become a complex and comprehensive term encompassing a whole range of language-related disciplines. The traditional subdivisions of linguistics are phonetics (speech sounds and pronunciation), phonology (history and theory of the changes in speech sounds), morphology (the formation of words), syntax (arrangement of words into meaningful expressions of thought), grammar (rules governing linguistic expression), semantics (history and theory of the development of word meaning), pragmatics (study of the relationship of words and sentences to their contextual usage). See SEMIOTICS.

Literal translation

A translation that tries to stay as close as possible to the exact wording and phrasing of the original biblical language and still make sense in the language of the intended audience. See RECEPTOR LANGUAGE (Fee and Stuart 1982, 35).[26]

---

[25] For a survey and helpful discussion of the three locations of meaning, see Stein, *Interpreting the Bible*, 17–36.

[26] Gordon D. Fee and Douglas Stuart present a clear and helpful discussion of the science of translation and what constitutes "a good translation" in *How to Read the Bible for All Its Worth* (Grand Rapids: Zondervan, 1982), 29–42.

Literary context

The text that surrounds the text to be interpreted. There are various circles of context that the interpreter must consider. These include the verses immediately preceding and following the text, a paragraph, chapter, section, book, testament, and even the entire canon of Scripture.

Meaning

Here is a word that is used differently by scholars in their various approaches to interpretation.[27] From an evangelical perspective it seems wise to adopt the position that the meaning of a text is inextricably tied to the truth-intention of the inspired author represented in the text of Scripture. All subsequent "implications" or APPLICATIONS derived from interpretation seem best identified with the SIGNIFICANCE that the text has to a particular reader.[28]

Mechanical layout (Also called "syntactical analysis")

```
I thank my God
    in all my remembrance of you,
    always offering prayer
                with joy
    in my every prayer
                for you all,
    in view of your participation
                    in the gospel
                    from the first day
                    until now.
                    —Phil. 1:3-5, NASB
```

A display of a text of Scripture in such a way that the reader can discern the relationship of subordinate clauses or phrases to the main clauses which they qualify or modify.[29] Such an arrangement of the text helps the reader to understand the author's propositional flow of thought. Scholars use a variety of formats, but usually have in common the indentation of subordinate clauses and phrases under the word that is being modified.

---

[27] Kaiser provides an insightful discussion of "the meaning of meaning" in Kaiser and Silva, *Introduction to Biblical Hermeneutics,* 27–45.

[28] E. D. Hirsch Jr., whose distinction is cited by many Evangelicals, writes, "*Meaning* is that which is represented by the text; it is what the author meant by his use of a particular sign sequence; it is what the signs represent. *Significance,* on the other hand, names a relationship between that meaning and a person, or a conception, or a situation, or indeed anything imaginable." See *Validity in Interpretation* (New Haven, Conn.: Yale University Press, 1967), 8, cited by Kaiser and Silva, *Introduction to Biblical Hermeneutics,* 41. To Hirsch, textual meaning is fixed and unchanging, whereas its significance is always changing. However, "[t]o banish the original author as the determiner of meaning [is] to reject the only compelling normative principle that could lend validity to an interpretation."

[29] For example, in our text box the main clause is modified adverbially by the phrases and clauses indented below the word "thank." They tell us, among other things, when, why, and how Paul thanks God.

Metaphysics / Metaphysical

The division of philosophy that concerns itself with the fundamental nature of reality and being. Something is metaphysical if it involves reality or things that go beyond, or transcend, what our physical senses can perceive, i.e., reality that is supernatural. The doctrines of God, the incarnation, sin, salvation, etc., involve the theologian in metaphysical discussions.

Methodology

When referring to hermeneutics, the process or procedure taken in interpretation. It includes the rules, principles, and presuppositions that guide and direct the process of interpreting a written text.

Morphology

The study and description of word formation in language. In those languages that rely on changes in the form of the words (i.e., inflections—changes at the beginning, middle, and end of words)[30] to identify and determine their grammatical or syntactical function, morphology is particularly important for both translation and interpretation.

Occasional (writing)

When biblical scholars refer to a writing as being "occasional," they mean that it arose out of and in response to a concrete set of historical circumstances, or occasion. Understanding the occasional nature of, for example, an Epistle means identifying the historical context of both its author and its original recipients (Fee and Stuart 1982, 45f). See *Sitz im Leben*.

Ontology / Ontological

A branch of Metaphysics that studies the nature of being, or existence. An ontological discussion of God is one focused on understanding the essential nature of God in His very being as God.

Orthodoxy (or "orthodox")

I felt the necessity to write to you appealing that you contend earnestly for the *faith which was once for all handed down to the saints.* –Jude 1:3, NASB

The state or quality of conforming to an established doctrine or set of doctrines, especially in religion. In popular speech it simply

[30] Such languages are called "synthetic" or "agglutinative" languages, whereas languages that depend largely on word order to determine meaning (like English) are called "analytic" languages. See Ramm, *Protestant Biblical Interpretation,* 136–37.

means correct belief, with the criteria for judging its correctness inferred or understood. Christian orthodoxy, then, refers to those basic teachings that the Church has always preached and taught.[31] See Tradition.

Orthopraxy

Refers to the correct practice, or conduct, within a given sphere. With regard to Christianity, it would denote a moral or ethical conduct that is inherently spiritual (Gal. 5:16–26). It is the manner of life that conforms to and expresses one's faith and commitment to Christ and His teachings.

Parallel passage

> Only *conduct yourselves in a manner worthy* of the gospel of Christ. –Phil. 1:27, NASB
>
> I . . . implore you to *walk in a manner worthy* of the calling with which you have been called. –Eph. 4:1, NASB

Parallel passages are two or more passages that record the same event or teaching (McQuilken, 210). For example two or more Gospels that record a particular discourse or miracle of Jesus would be regarded as parallel passages.

Parallelism (See ch. 6, "Literary Devices")

Parallelomania, verbal

A pejorative term for the practice of listing verbal parallels from two bodies of literature as evidence that they share similar ideas and therefore may be dependent on one another[32] (Carson 1984a, 43). A classic example is the allegation that Paul in Colossians is somehow indebted to Gnostic writers because he uses a number of terms that appear frequently in Gnostic writings.[33]

---

[31] Often a sectarian modifier might be added. When it is, a creedal standard is understood. For example, *Presbyterian* orthodoxy is usually measured against the Westminster Confession, *Lutheran* orthodoxy against the Augsburg Confession, and *Catholic* orthodoxy against the Council of Trent.

[32] The term was coined by Samuel Sandmel in "Parallelomania," *Journal of Biblical Literature* 81 (1962): 2–13.

[33] Interpreters should note that dependence can be construed from both ends. Since the Gnostic writings where this terminology appears are much later than the NT, it is entirely reasonable to suggest their dependence on Paul. Furthermore, one has to ask also how a particular word is being used in both pieces of literature and what it was referring to. For an excellent work on the alleged dependence of the NT on the religious thought of the Greco-Roman world, see Ronald H. Nash, *Christianity and the Hellenistic World* (Grand Rapids: Zondervan, 1984), 203–24.

Paraphrase

To restate a text or passage of Scripture using different wording or literary forms. The usual reason for paraphrasing a text is to make clear or relevant its meaning, when the meaning of the text is somewhat unclear from a literal translation. The challenge of paraphrasing is to retain the sense the author intended in words that are understood by the contemporary reader.

> And do not be conformed to this world. –Rom. 12:2, NASB
>
> Don't let the world around you squeeze you into its own mould. –Rom. 12:2, *Phillips*

Pericope

Commonly refers to a selected portion of a book chosen for liturgical reading. The term is used to designate a specific paragraph or a section of Scripture that addresses a particular subject (Kaiser and Silva, 285). In Form criticism (see ch. 4) the term refers to self-contained units of gospel tradition, containing stories or teachings of Jesus. They are thought to have circulated first in oral form before being collected and written down (Efird, 91). It should be noted that traditional paragraph divisions found in the Bible do not always mark the limits of a pericope.

Perspicuity (as in "perspicuity of Scripture")

The belief that the words of Scripture are sufficiently clear (perspicuous) so that the competent Christian can read and understand its redemptive message without the need for church tradition as an official guide. Martin Luther was a strong proponent of this view, which was tied to his belief in the "priesthood of all believers" and the Reformation doctrine of *sola Scriptura* (Ramm 1970, 55; Kaiser and Silva, 165).

This view does not ignore the fact that many passages are obscure and difficult to interpret. Neither is it a denial of the need for accurate translation, diligent study, and careful Exegesis.

Phenomenal language

Descriptive language that speaks of things as they appear from a finite human and historically conditioned perspective. Such language is often not intended to be taken literally. For example, the description of the mustard seed as "'the smallest seed you plant in the ground'" (Mark 4:31) is phenomenal language because among the people addressed it was regarded/seen as the smallest of seeds (Ramm 1970, 210–11; McQuilken, 245; Virkler, 84–86).

Philology (or "philological")

Narrowly refers to the historical and comparative study of words and is often used to refer to the field of linguistics. However, it also has an application to the study of literary works with reference to their historical, cultural, and literary aspects. When used in this broader sense to refer to the "philological method" of interpretation, it is roughly equivalent to the Grammatical-historical method (ch. 4).

Philosophy

Generally the term refers to a worldview of a person or group that attempts to construct a coherent view of all knowledge about the universe and one's experience in it. It can also be understood as the intellectual search for truth and meaning by addressing fundamental questions in life. These questions fall into the categories of Metaphysics (What is reality or the nature of being?), Epistemology (What is knowledge?), and Ethics (What is good ?). To understand the biblical text accurately, interpreters must consider the worldviews held by both the author of a text and its intended audience as well as compare or contrast them with their own (Evans, 92).

Polysemy

Having multiple meanings. Words normally have more than one meaning, which make up their Semantic range. A hermeneutical problem exists when texts are viewed as having many meanings, none regarded as objectively true or correct. Instead, all meanings are seen as valid or invalid based on their effect on the interpreter (Osborne, 84; Carson 1984a, 129) or, in some approaches, how the interpretive community understands it (Carson 1996, 75–76).[34] This results in relativity and subjectivity that denies an objective meaning to a text.[35]

An evangelical version of polysemy would argue for levels of meaning, carefully determined by competent judges (i.e., scholars) who are historically and linguistically informed (Poythress, 113). Again it can be asked whether these

---

[34] Carson cites as example and illustration the work of the deconstructionist Stanley Fish in "Is There a Text in This Class?" (Cambridge: Harvard University Press, 1980), 326–27.

[35] This posture is identified with the hermeneutical heirs of the New Hermeneutic, and many of the postmodern literary approaches (e.g., Deconstruction). See Luiz Gustavo da Silva Goncalves, "The Deconstructing of the American Mind: An Analysis of the Hermeneutical Implications of Postmodernism," in *Evangelical Hermeneutics,* ed. Michael Bauman and David Hall (Camp Hill, Pa.: Christian Publications, 1995), 233–61. One obvious problem is that such an approach to interpretation is self-defeating. A colleague of this author once asked an advocate of the New Hermeneutic if he wanted his contract to be interpreted in that way. A nervous laugh was the only response he received.

"levels of meaning" are not being confused with various forms of Significance. Furthermore, this approach, fails to determine which of the meanings should be given authoritative Canonical status (Kaiser 1981,46).

Presuppositions

The first principles or assumptions held about a certain subject matter prior to investigation or development of an argument or viewpoint and out of which that viewpoint is derived (McKim 1996, 219). One's presuppositions affect how we interpret the Bible by shaping how we approach the text, to a large extent determining both the questions we ask and the answers we anticipate. Presuppositions fall into a number of categories. Those most influential for hermeneutics are "theological" (our doctrinal commitments), "epistemological" (how we understand the acquisition of knowledge or truth), and "methodological" (how we view the task of interpretation). See Pre-understanding.

Pre-understanding

Refers to a body of assumptions, attitudes, and biases brought from one's historical background and experience to the interpretation of reality or any expression of it, including Scripture (D. Ferguson, 6). A person's pre-understanding is made up of a set of Presuppositions that focus on specific subject matter. Recognition of our pre-understanding and how it colors our interpretation is important to achieving objectivity in the interpretive process, muting the clamor of our presuppositions enough to hear the message intended by the biblical author to the original recipients (Klein, Blomberg, and Hubbard, 7–8).[36]

Principalization

To "principalize" Scripture is to take what the biblical author intended to teach or convey and restate it in the form of timeless and abiding truths that can be readily applied to the contemporary Church (Kaiser 1981, 152).[37]

---

[36] Duncan Ferguson explores the role of pre-understanding in the Interpretation of Scripture. He concludes that one's pre-understanding is inescapable, but that the interpreter is not slavishly bound by it. Rather, the interpreter has intelligence and freedom in consciously endorsing assumptions and attitudes within his pre-understanding. See *Biblical Hermeneutics: An Introduction* (Atlanta, Ga.: John Knox Press, 1986), 6–12. It should be noted that the interpreter is also free to reject or alter his Presuppositions in favor of those discovered in the text through Exegesis.

[37] The difficulty in "principalization" is most often exegetical—determining what the author intended to teach or convey as abiding truth. Kaiser sees principalization as integral to the task of expository preaching that draws out the theology of the text and makes it relevant to our day. See *Toward an Exegetical Theology,* 149–63.

Generic principle

Pertains to the application of scriptural truth. It refers to the statement of a biblical norm, or standard, that can be applied to a wide range of situations. The proper Christian response to such principles is in one sense always the same—faith and obedience. However, the manner in which faith and obedience are expressed depends on two main variables: (1) whether the principle is explicit or implied and (2) whether the situation described in the principle has an application to contemporary life (McQuilken, 300–315).

Progressive revelation

> God, after He spoke long ago to the fathers in the prophets in many portions and in many ways, in these last days has spoken to us in His Son. –Heb. 1:1,2, NASB

Expresses the belief that God's revelation of himself and His plan of salvation is progressive and incremental as recorded in Scripture. Thus, the interpreter of the Bible who recognizes this dynamic process will regard *later* revelation as being more complete than earlier revelation. For example, what God reveals about himself through the person of Christ in the NT is seen as a clearer, more complete picture than what can be found in the OT writings. Consequently, the NT writings are given greater weight when formulating doctrine or when comparing Scripture with Scripture for the purpose of interpretation (Erickson, 132–34; *PDTT,* 96).

Propositional revelation

> Now we have received, not the spirit of the world, but the Spirit who is from God, so that we may know the things freely given to us by God, which things we also speak, not in words taught by human wisdom, but in those taught by the Spirit, combining spiritual *thoughts* with spiritual *words.* –1 Cor. 2:12,13, NASB

The view that the revealed truth of Scripture can be logically presented in coherent statements, or propositions. It is related to verbal inspiration (meaning that inspiration extends to the *words* of Scripture and not just the ideas), which views the Scriptures as a mode and repository of divine revelation. Propositional revelation is a presupposition not only of theology but also of all public communication of biblical interpretation[38] (Silva 1996, 214–15; Erickson, 216).[39]

---

[38] When someone asks, "What does that Scripture mean?" or "What does the Bible teach?" the assumption is that the meaning or teaching can be intelligibly reduced to propositional statements. Those who argue that the revelatory truth of Scripture is more than rational cognition are correct, but it is not less than the propositional truth that the inspired authors wanted to express.

[39] The debate over whether Revelation is propositional or personal is long-standing, that is,

Rationalism

A belief system that regards the human mind as (1) an independent, autonomous authority (2) capable of determining truth. Rationalism had its seedbed in the Renaissance and its cultivation in the Enlightenment, during which reason was used to challenge the authority of the Church and the teachings of Scripture (Klein, Blomberg, and Hubbard, 43). John Locke, for example, elevated reason above the REVELATION of Scripture. Reason was to evaluate the teachings of Scripture as being according to, above, or contrary to reason.[40] Thus, human reason operating through experience is viewed as the final authority.

Interpretive approaches that are rationalistic bring along a naturalistic worldview that rejects the supernatural as being contrary to reason and experience. Rationalism carries the presupposition that the ideas (doctrines) of Scripture can be regarded as merely human in origin.[41]

Receptor language (Also called "target language")

A term used in connection with Bible translation. It refers to the language the Scriptures are being translated into (Fee and Stuart 1982, 35), as opposed to the original biblical language, which is referred to as the source language.

Referent

The "thing" (whether person, event, object, etc.) a word or expression is directed to (Kaiser and Silva, 34). The referent is often determined by the larger literary context and not by the isolated word itself. For example, John refers to "the Jews" as those seeking to kill Jesus (John 5:18; 7:1). Careful examination of John's Gospel reveals that the term does not always designate the Jewish people in general but sometimes the Jewish religious leaders in particular (cf. 7:13,25; 8:40; cf. 8:13).

---

whether REVELATION can be equated with the truth revealed in Scripture and articulated in doctrinal or theological statements or only as personal encounter of God himself (see NEOORTHODOXY). See Millard Erickson, *Christian Theology,* 2nd ed. (Grand Rapids: Baker Book House, 1999), 216–23.

[40] See John Locke, "An Essay on Human Understanding," Book IV, Chapter 17, cited in James C. Livingston, *Modern Christian Thought from the Enlightenment to Vatican II* (New York: Macmillan, 1971), 16–17.

[41] The implication for hermeneutics, which aims at understanding the ideas of Scripture transmitted through language, is clear. The ideas and teachings of Scripture are no longer to be regarded as REVELATION (i.e., having a transcendent and divine origin), or universally valid truths, but simply ideas that are derived solely from human religious experience that are culturally relative and historically specific.

Referential meaning

Designates the thing or reality a word or text refers to. It is the meaning that completes the sense of the word(s) used, usually in light of a broader unknown or unfamiliar context. Thus, Nicodemus heard the words of Jesus (in John 3:5–8) and understood the words themselves but not the spiritual reality they referred to. See also the Samaritan woman's similar confusion over the literal sense of the word "water" in John 4:10–15 (Kaiser and Silva, 34–35) and its spiritual REFERENT.

Scholars will refer to referential language as that which is used to convey information, contrasted with COMMISSIVE LANGUAGE, which is used to express, convey, or evoke emotions.

Revelation

"In the past *God spoke* to our forefathers through the prophets at many times and in various ways, but in these last days *he has spoken to us by his Son,* whom he appointed heir of all things, and through whom he made the universe" (Heb 1:1,2) is an example of "special revelation."

The disclosure of something previously unknown. In theology it usually refers to God's disclosure of some aspect of himself or His divine will to mortals. Revelation is seen in two categories: (1) natural revelation, which is located in nature, history, and conscience (cf. Rom. 1:19,20), and (2) special revelation, which is located in God's revelatory deeds and Word (cf. Heb. 1:1,2).[42] In hermeneutics the discussion continues over the locus of revelation, i.e., whether God's revelation is to be identified with Scripture, church tradition, contemporary human experience, or some combination thereof (Osborne, 299).

Rhetoric (See RHETORICAL CRITICISM, ch. 4)

Sedes doctrinae (Lat., "seat of doctrine")

A portion of the biblical text that functions to provide guidance and set boundaries for the interpretation of other texts of Scripture which are textually or topically parallel. These "chair" or "seat" passages usually contain the largest single source of material on a respective doctrine. For example, in the NT, the seat of doctrine on the resurrection would be 1 Corinthians 15. In

[42] For an insightful theological presentation of these two categories of revelation, see "Revelation, General" by B. A. Demarest and "Revelation, Special" by C. F. H. Henry in the *Evangelical Dictionary of Theology,* ed. Walter A. Elwell (Grand Rapids: Baker Book House, 1984), 944–48.

the OT, Genesis 1 and 2 are the chair passages for the doctrine of creation (Kaiser and Silva, 201–2).

Semantic range

Refers to all the meanings assigned to a given word in a given literary context. For example, one discovers that the semantic range of the Greek word *nomos* ("law") in Romans includes references to OT scripture (8:7), the Mosaic law (7:7), and law as an operative principle, as in "the law of the Spirit of life" and "the law of sin and death" (8:2).

Semantics

Refers generally to the study of word meanings. It can include an investigation into a word's historical origin, usage, and change in meaning, as well as the theory of how words as "signs" come to signify, or denote, something. Its relevance to HERMENEUTICS is evident, as biblical word-studies must recognize that word meanings are fluid and that care must be taken to determine which meaning of a word is intended by the author in a given literary context.

Semiotics

Part of what is called structural linguistics and refers to the philosophical and linguistic theory of signs (usually associated with words) or sign systems and how they function in human language. A sign is both the word-sound "signifier" (e.g., "cat," "gato," "chat") and the object "signified" (i.e., the animal itself). The relationship between signifier and signified is determined by the shared perceptions of a community (Tate, 189; McKnight, 120–21).[43]

Semitism

Refers to a characteristic feature (usually a word or idiom) of a Semitic language occurring in another language. In biblical studies it commonly alludes

> Taking the child by the hand, He said to her, *"Talitha kum!"* (which translated means, "Little girl, I say to you, get up!"). –Mark 5:41, NASB

[43] When applied to literature, the text (e.g., a narrative) itself can be viewed as a sign. As such it has a DENOTATIVE MEANING that is identified with the author's intention. However, the text is said to also have connotative levels of meaning made up of a subconscious system of thought that precedes authorial intention. See W. Randolph Tate, *Biblical Hermeneutics: An Integrated Approach* (Peabody, Mass.: Hendrickson Publishers, 1991), 189. The problem with this understanding, however, lies in positing a textual meaning independent from the author who gave us the text. Texts do not think, people think, and driving a wedge between the author and the text seems odd, especially when it is the inspired author of Scripture whose message one wants to understand. See Stein, "Author-Oriented Approach," 453–54.

to the influence of Semitic language (Hebrew or Aramaic) on the Greek OT (i.e., Septuagint). In the NT, semitisms take the form of "Aramaisms" in Mark's Gospel when the author cites the Aramaic word(s) and then translates it, presumably for a non-Jewish audience.

Sensus literalis (Lat., "literal meaning")

Refers to the simple, ordinary, plain meaning of a word or text as acknowledged and understood in a particular cultural-historical and literary context. See *Usus loquendi*. It is opposed to a figurative, metaphorical, or allegorical meaning (Mickelsen, 33; Kaiser 1981, 88–89).

Sensus plenior (Lat., "fuller meaning")

Used of the view that there is a meaning to Scripture beyond the one originally intended by the biblical author. It is contended that this meaning emerges through the life experience of the reader (McKim 1996, 255). This fuller sense cannot be arrived at by a traditional Grammatical-historical method of interpretation (Klein, Blomberg, and Hubbard, 125). Debate continues over the legitimacy of assigning a fuller sense that cannot be located in the mind and thinking of the scriptural author, who allegedly "wrote better than he knew" (Kaiser 1981, 109–11). However, others contend that some fuller sense of meaning must be allowed with biblical prophecy and in light of the Progressive revelation within the biblical canon.[44]

Significance

Often paired with and distinguished from Meaning in the interpretation of a text. Meaning is said to refer to the sense represented by the text itself and the author's intent expressed by the choice of words, grammar, syntax, and literary techniques (Kaiser 1981, 32). "Significance," on the other hand, refers to the effect the meaning has on the reader-interpreter and his or her response to it.[45] It is sometimes related to the "implications" of a text (Stein 1994, 43; Silva 1996, 108) or its Application.[46]

---

[44] This issue is complex and debated differently depending on one's understanding of the fundamental nature and task of hermeneutics. For an excellent discussion of the issue at large and one evangelical's cautious adoption of *sensus plenior,* see Douglas J. Moo, "The Problem of *Sensus Plenior,*" in *Hermeneutics, Authority and Canon,* ed. D. A. Carson and J. D. Woodbridge (Grand Rapids: Zondervan, 1986), 175–212.

[45] Although not the first to make this distinction, E. D. Hirsch made it popular in his criticism of the subjectivity of Heidegger, Gadamer, and the proponents of the New Hermeneutic. See note 28.

[46] For a short but clear summary of the value of Hirsch's work (see note 45), its criticisms, and responses, see Kaiser, *Toward An Exegetical Theology,* 32–34. While agreeing with Hirsch's

Sitz im Leben (Ger., "setting/situation in life")

Refers to the occasion of a particular writing, more specifically to the set of historical circumstances that prompted its writing. It is a technical term most often used in New Testament CRITICISM and INTERPRETATION. See OCCASIONAL.

Spiritualize (or "spiritualization")

Literally "to make spiritual." When applied to hermeneutics it is often linked to ALLEGORICAL INTERPRETATION (Dockery, 81–89; Duvall and Hays, 179–86; McQuilken, 40–44), which also departs from the "grammatical-historical" meaning in search of a "spiritual" meaning. The goal is the same as the DEVOTIONAL APPROACH, i.e., to discover a spiritual sense to the text that is relevant and personally edifying. When spiritualizing, the interpreter will often take a text that has a clear literal and historical sense and find a hidden spiritual meaning, usually by verbal association. Thus, stories from the conquest of Canaan might be "spiritualized" to discover how Christians are to conduct spiritual warfare.

Some terminological distinctions are in order. If the spiritual meaning is presented as divinely intended, the earthly historical event being a foreshadow of a future spiritual reality, then spiritualization has become TYPOLOGICAL INTERPRETATION. If the historical setting is all but ignored and the spiritual truth discovered is regarded as the true meaning of the text, spiritually discerned, then spiritualization has become ALLEGORIZATION. The latter usually results in a meaning that has no logical, verbal, or conceptual relation to the text. Associations with the verbal content of the text are remote and alien to the literal and historical sense of the words.

Stichwort (Ger., "key word")

A term that appears frequently or conspicuously in a given text, the meaning of which the author seems to have adapted for a special purpose or to make a particular point. Often in the use of *Stichworten,* the author invests new meaning in the term, not normally associated with the term. For example, Paul uses the Greek *musterion* ("mystery," Col. 1:26,27) to refer to publicly declared knowledge of God's plan of universal salvation in Christ through the gospel.

---

identification of a text's meaning with that of the author, Kaiser sees validity in some criticisms, especially with his refusal to locate meaning in the text itself, and sets out to present a version of Hirsch's approach that responds to those criticisms. See Kaiser, "Legitimate Hermeneutics," in *A Guide to Contemporary Hermeneutics: Major Trends in Biblical Interpretation,* ed. Donald K. McKim (Grand Rapids: Wm. B. Eerdmans, 1986), 111–41.

Subjectivism

A philosophical position that the individual's experience, feeling, or private apprehension is the final determiner of truth. When used with regard to interpretation, it is often associated with existentialist approaches that emphasize the role of the interpreter in the determination (even "creation") of meaning.[47] Thus, interpretation is not *objective* (What does the text mean?), but *subjective* (What does the text mean to me as I existentially encounter or experience it?) (McQuilken, 49–56). (See also Eisegesis.)

Torah (Heb., "instruction" or "law")

The expression of God's will for the nation of Israel as revealed to Moses at Mount Sinai. Originally it designated the five books of Moses (the Pentateuch); over time it came to be applied to any expression of God's will (cf. John 10:34–36; 15:25) (McKim 1996, 284).

Totality transfer

A common but erroneous assumption when interpreting that a word's entire Semantic range of meanings and associations go with it wherever it is used (Fee and Stuart 1993, 227).

Tradition (Gk. *paradōsis*)

Refers to truth that has been preserved, passed on, and over time has come to occupy a place of authority in a given community as a *regula fidei* (i.e., "rule of faith"). Depending on the historical period, tradition can refer to various doctrines, writings of church fathers, creeds, and decisions of church councils. Traditional interpretation is Exegesis done with respect to an established doctrinal standard of Orthodoxy. Such interpretation is criticized because functionally the tradition has risen to collateral authority with Scripture and controls interpretation (Klein, Blomberg, and Hubbard, 33; Ramm 1970, 39–40).

Unity of meaning

The much-debated view that except for the literary device of Double entendre, there is only one meaning to a text—the one intended by the author (McQuilken, 88; Ramm 1970, 110–13; Terry, 383).[48]

---

[47] The meaning is knowingly not identified as the biblical author's in many existentialist approaches because each act of interpretation creates a new meaning. For popular examples of subjectivism in interpretation see Kaiser, *Toward an Exegetical Theology,* 198–99; D. A. Carson, *Exegetical Fallacies* (Grand Rapids: Baker Book House, 1984), 129f.

[48] Robert Stein argues that not only is the meaning singular, it can never change. The author's intended meaning when the text was written is fixed in time and cannot change any more

Unity of Scripture

The belief that the Bible presents a coherent unified perspective in its essential teachings (Ramm 1970, 174), stemming from the conviction that behind the diverse writings of Scripture there is a single divine Author (McQuilken, 21, 68–69; Terry, 383) who speaks a unified message in and throughout the biblical canon.[49] The interpreter who adopts this presupposition will see the entire Bible, in a sense, as the literary and theological context for interpretation.

Usus loquendi (Lat., "use in speech")

Refers to the ordinary, plain sense of a word used by an author in a given literary context. It designates the meaning the author would have assigned it at the time and setting in which he lived and how his intended audience would have understood it (Ramm 1970, 120; Terry, 181).

Verbal parallel

Occurs when two or more verses or passages contain the same words or expression. The interpreter must be careful to judge whether or not the author is addressing the same subject and whether the words in common have meaning in common. For example, the same phrase, "according to the flesh" (Gk. *kata sarka*), appears in Romans 1:3 and 8:13 but represents two very different meanings.

> . . . concerning His Son, who was born of a descendant of David *according to the flesh.*
> –Rom. 1:3 NASB
>
> . . . for if you are living *according to the flesh*, you must die; but if by the Spirit you are putting to death the deeds of the body, you will live.
> –Rom. 8:13, NASB

---

than a historical event of the past can change. See *Interpreting the Bible,* 38. Walter Kaiser provides a very helpful historical survey of advocates for both the "single meaning" and "multiple meaning" approaches. See *Toward An Exegetical Theology,* 26–40.

[49] Ramm sees no value in constructing a systematic theology that did not have a unified set of doctrines that faithfully represented the teaching of Scripture. See *Protestant Biblical Interpretation,* 173. D. A. Carson argues for the possibility of a systematic theology of the NT that recognizes both unity and diversity in its theological expression. He points out that all (but atheists) who hold a consistent set of beliefs about God have adopted a form of systematic theology. See "Unity and Diversity in the New Testament: The Possibility of Systematic Theology," in *Scripture and Truth,* ed. D. A. Carson and John D. Woodbridge (Grand Rapids: Zondervan, 1983), 65–100. Graeme Goldsworthy believes there is a Christological unity to the Bible that operates in a progressive salvation-history that finds its eschatological goal or fulfillment in Christ. See chapter 6, "What Kind of Unity Does the Bible Have?" in *Preaching the Whole Bible as Christian Scripture* (Grand Rapids: Wm. B. Eerdmans, 2000), 63–80.

Word loading

Refers to the practice of assigning to a word in a particular text many and even all possible meanings of that word (see SEMANTIC RANGE). For example, the Greek word *ekklēsia* can refer to the universal Church of Christ (see Matt. 16:18). However, it would be improper to read that meaning into its every use (cf. Heb. 2:12; Acts 7:38; 15:30).[50] (See TOTALITY TRANSFER.)

[50] This is also referred to as "illegitimate totality transfer." See Carson, *Exegetical Fallacies*, 62.

2

Historical Schools / Periods of Interpretation

Alexandrian school

Flourished in Alexandria, Egypt, from the third to fifth century AD.[1] It is most often associated with the ALLEGORICAL INTERPRETATION of Clement of Alexandria[2] (ca. 155–215) and ORIGEN (185–254), who were indebted to the Jewish philosopher PHILO OF ALEXANDRIA. Origen is credited with giving systematic development to the allegorical method in his work *De Principiis* (Book IV). The Alexandrian school had two key motivations behind allegorizing the OT: (1) to make it compatible to elements of Greek philosophy and (2) to show that NT teaching could be found in the OT, the Old being the preparation for the New (Ramm 1970, 31–33; Mickelsen, 32).

Allegorical interpretation

A method of interpretation where the interpreter looks beyond the historical (literal, plain) sense of the words to a hidden so-called spiritual meaning. Although the literal sense is not denied, the allegorical meaning is regarded as more important. One can readily see the influence of Platonic dualism here, where the physical is contrasted with the spiritual. Thus, Clement taught that Scripture had a twofold sense, corresponding to the body and soul of a human being. ORIGEN, his successor in the ALEXANDRIAN SCHOOL, using the words of Paul in 1 Thessalonians 5:23, posited three meanings of Scripture, corresponding to body, soul, and spirit. The literal sense is identified with the body, and is clearly inferior to the soul and spiritual meanings, which are only accessible

---

1 For a concise history of the Alexandrian school and a sympathetic discussion of its method as practiced by Clement and Origen, see Robert M. Grant and David Tracy, *A Short History of the Interpretation of the Bible* (Philadelphia: Fortress Press, 1984), 52–62.

2 For an excellent resource for investigating historical figures related to the field of biblical hermeneutics, see Donald K. McKim, ed., *Historical Handbook of Major Biblical Interpreters*, (Downer's Grove, Ill.: InterVarsity Press, 1998).

through allegorizing.[3] Origen would probably prefer to call his method "spiritualizing," and at times his exegesis is a mixture of Typological interpretation and Allegory. Nevertheless, there is no doubt that Origen saw Allegorical interpretation as true exegesis and the only way to uncover the deeper spiritual truths of Scripture (Mickelsen, 32; Ramm 1970, 33; Grant and Tracy, 55–56).

To be fair, Clement and Origen both developed rules and principles governing allegorical interpretation.[4] They did not see Scripture as capable of any meaning imaginable. However, because they saw the Bible as a spiritual book, symbolic and full of allegory,[5] the allegorical method gave rise to fanciful interpretations never imagined by the author or his intended audience.[6]

Antiochian school

A school of interpretation begun in Syrian Antioch and dating back to Theophilus of Antioch (ca. AD 115–188).[7] However, the founding of a later Antiochian School is credited to either Lucian of Samosata at the end of the third century AD or Diodorus of Tarsus (d. ca. AD 394). Adherents of this school rejected the Allegorization of the Alexandrian school in favor of an approach that is known today as the Grammatical-historical method of biblical interpretation, which seeks the literal and historical meaning of Scripture. However, they also rejected the hyperliteralism of

---

3 Origen saw these three senses as also relating to three levels of spiritual maturity. The simple Christian benefits from the "flesh," or literal, sense of Scripture; the "more advanced" profits from the "soul" sense of Scripture and the "perfect" is edified by the spiritual sense. See Origen *De Principiis* 4.2.4, cited by Walter C. Kaiser Jr. and Moisés Silva, *An Introduction to Biblical Hermeneutics: The Search for Meaning* (Grand Rapids: Zondervan, 1994), 219.

4 Bernard L. Ramm gives a concise summary of these principles in *Protestant Biblical Interpretation,* 3rd ed. (Grand Rapids: Baker Book House, 1970), 31–33. Grant and Tracy give several key quotes of Origen in justifying his abandoning the literal sense to pursue an allegorical one. See *Short History*, 57–59.

5 Ramm cites Jean Danielou's observation that for Origen "the Bible was one vast allegory, a tremendous sacrament in which every detail is symbolic." See *Protestant Biblical Interpretation*, 32.

6 A classic example often cited is Origen's interpretation of the story of Rebekah's drawing water for the camels of Abraham's servant Eliezer (Gen. 24). Origen maintained that this taught that we must come to the wells of Scripture if we would meet Christ. In the story of the triumphal entry where Jesus enters with the donkey *and* its colt, Origen sees the truth that the doctrine of Christ is supported by both the Old and New Testaments! See Mickelsen, *Interpreting*, 32.

7 For an insightful and informative introduction to this school, by discussing separately the views of its major proponents, see David S. Dockery, *Biblical Interpretation Then and Now: Contemporary Hermeneutics in the Light of the Early Church* (Grand Rapids: Baker Book House, 1992),103–28.

the Jewish community in Antioch. To avoid both extremes they proposed a middle ground based on the concept of *theoria* (Gk., "insight"),[8] which fused both the literal and spiritual, and the historical and typological, meanings of Scripture, the former being inseparably linked to the latter. A major concern of this school was to preserve the literal and historical senses of Scripture and make them foundational to spiritual or theological truth (Dockery, 103–7; Grant and Tracy, 63–72; Kaiser and Silva, 221).

Apostolic Fathers

Refers to a group of church fathers and their writings so named because of their alleged connection to the first-century apostles and authors of the NT. Their writings are actually postapostolic, having been written from the end of the first century to at least the middle of the second century. Nevertheless, it is the orthodox character of their teachings that earns them the title "apostolic."[9] Their extensive use and citation of NT Scripture sometimes makes them a valuable resource when interpreting a difficult text.[10]

Apostolic period

Refers essentially to the period when the NT was being written by the Apostles and their associates. It is generally regarded to end with the completion of the last book of the NT Canon (revelation) at the end of the first century AD. Note the difference in the use and meaning of the adjective "apostolic" in the previous entry.

---

8 *Theoria* is defined as the ability to perceive both the literal historical facts of a text and the spiritual reality they pointed to. See William W. Klein, Craig L. Blomberg, and Robert L. Hubbard, *Introduction to Biblical Interpretation* (Waco, Tex.: Word Publishing, 1993), 35. Thus, an OT prophet prophesying of the Lord's coming was able to see both the immediate historical reference to events in Israel's history and the final event of Christ's coming. See Dockery, *Biblical Interpretation,* 107.

9 John Lawson acknowledges the questionable historical connection between the NT apostles and the Apostolic Fathers but writes, "Nevertheless, there is a sufficiently distinctive body of orthodox Christian writings, not included in the authoritative Canon of the New Testament, yet answering to the life of the Church in the period immediately succeeding New Testament times, that it may conveniently and intelligently be designated 'the Apostolic Fathers.'" See his *Historical and Theological Introduction to the Apostolic Fathers* (New York: Macmillan, 1961), 1.

10 The author has searched the Apostolic Fathers and found well over three hundred quotations and verbal conceptual allusions to NT texts. James D. Hernando, "Irenaeus and the Apostolic Fathers: Inquiry in the Development of the New Testament Canon" (Ph.D. diss., Drew University, Madison, N.J., 1990), 359.

Christian existentialism

Uses the philosophical categories and insights of Existentialism within the basic Christian worldview. Christian existentialism affirms the freedom of the individual to make a personal decision and commitment to Jesus Christ. However, such is not viewed as a rational choice but as a "leap of faith," that is, a position based not on reason but on revelation. Its relevance for hermeneutics resides in the question of how one understands the Bible and its relationship to the revelation of the Word of God (McQuilken, 50–56). See Neoorthodoxy.

Jewish interpretation

Biblical interpretation begins with the ancient Israelites who possessed, studied, and interpreted the Scriptures. Discussion of the history of Jewish interpretation usually begins with Ezra in the postexilic period: Called a "skilled scribe" (Ezra 7:6, NKJV), he, along with other Levitical scribes, read (the Hebrew text) and then translated (into Aramaic) the law of God so as to give understanding to a large assembly of Jews (Neh. 8:7–8) recently released from Babylonian captivity. Jewish interpretation in the Talmud is founded on two unswerving convictions: (1) that all of Torah is inspired of God[11] and (2) that that Torah (whether oral or written) contained the all-sufficient truth to answer every need of life. Consequently, the goal of interpretation is to apply God's instruction (Torah) to all the issues and situations of life.[12]

Rabbinic exegesis is often discussed under five historical periods:[13] from Ezra (458 BC) to Simon the Just (ca. 320 BC); the 1st Talmudic Period (ca. 320 BC to the death of Hillel in AD 13); the Tannaitic Period (AD 13–200, from the death of Hillel to the completion of the Mishnah); 2nd Talmudic Period (AD 200–500, from the completion of the Mishnah to the completion of the Babylonian Talmud); and the Masoretic Period (ca. AD 500–950).[14]

---

[11] This is made clear from the following quote from the Babylonian Talmud, "He who says the Torah is not from God, or even [that] the whole Torah is from God with the exception of this or that verse, which not God but Moses spoke, from his own mouth that soul shall be rooted up" (Sanh. 99a Bab. Talmud).

[12] See Richard N. Longenecker's discussion of "Jewish Hermeneutics in the First Century," in *Biblical Exegesis in the Apostolic Period* (Grand Rapids: Wm. B. Eerdmans, 1975), 19–20.

[13] These periods are known for the contribution of successive schools of scribes: the Sopherim, the Chakhamim, the Tannaim, the Amoraim, the Seboraim, and the Gaonin. See Frederic W. Farrar, *History of Interpretation* (Grand Rapids: Baker Book House, 1961), 52–53.

[14] See Gleason L. Archer Jr., *A Survey of Old Testament Introduction*, rev. ed. (Chicago: Moody Press, 1974), 62–67.

Cabalists

Medieval (thirteenth century) Jewish mystics who practiced a Sod interpretation, finding symbolic and allegorical significance in the smallest details of the biblical text (Kaiser and Silva, 215).[15]

Gemara

A collection of Aramaic commentaries on the Mishnah, which together with the Mishnah make up the Talmud. Those who wrote these commentaries, and the commentaries themselves, are referred to as *Amoraim* (Heb., "interpreters") and cover the period from about AD 10–200 (Mickelsen, 27).

Mashal

A Hebrew term covering a wide range of linguistic forms, including parable, allegory, riddle, fable, taunt, dirge, and proverbial saying (Soulen 1981, 119, 137; Mickelsen, 204). In the Septuagint, it was translated by the Greek term *parabolē*. This served to raise the question of the literary form of Jesus' parables and whether they were to be treated as allegories (extended metaphors), a view strongly objected to by Adolf Jülicher (*Die Gleichnisreden Jesu* [*The Parables of Jesus*], 1899).[16] However, due to the fluidity of the term *mashal*, many scholars now believe that Jülicher's restriction is unwarranted and that the so-called allegorical elements were a part of the original parables of Jesus.[17]

---

[15] Ramm comments that with the Cabalists, letterism and allegorism find a grotesque alliance. He describes their arbitrary assignment of words for letters *(notarikon),* numerical values given to letters followed by comparisons and strange associations *(gemetria),* and the rearrangement of letters in words *(termura).* See *Protestant Biblical Interpretation,* 47–48.

[16] Jülicher based his objection partly on the bizarre and fanciful allegories that were produced by the early church fathers. Those who followed his lead object not to the basic parable but to the correspondence of the parabolic elements to spiritual or kingdom realities. For example, regarding the Parable of the Wicked Tenants (Matt. 21:33–44), the objection would not be to the basic parable (v. 33) but the application to the rejection and fate of the Jewish nation (vv. 34–44).

[17] Alluding to the conclusions of definitive works of P. Fiebig and M. Hermaniuk, Raymond Brown states that their efforts have shown "that there is no really sharp distinction between parable and allegory in the Semitic mind. In the Old Testament, the Apocrypha and the rabbinic writings, *mashal* covers parable and allegory and a host of other literary devices (riddle, fable, proverb, etc.) Therefore, there is no reason to believe that Jesus of Nazareth in his *meshalim* ever made a distinction between parable and allegory." Raymond E. Brown, "Parable and Allegory Reconsidered," *Novum Testamentum* 5 (January 1962): 36.

Middot

Refers to rabbinic rules of interpretation developed by different leading rabbis for their systems of exegesis.[18] The most relevant example for biblical interpretation are the seven Middot of Hillel (ca. 30 BC–AD 9), which can be illustrated from both OT and NT writings (Kaiser 1981, 53–54).

Midrashim

Rabbinic commentary on OT Scripture largely produced during the first two centuries of the Church (the Tannaitic Period; see Jewish Interpretation). The collection includes two types of material: *Haggadah* and *Halakah*.[19] The term "Midrash" (Heb., "exposition") also refers to the process (E. Ferguson, 462), i.e., the way rabbis interpreted OT Scripture in order to arrive at a relevant meaning and/or application to their contemporary situation[20] (Dockery, 29).

Haggadah (Heb., "declaration," "explanation")

Refers to commentary in the Midrashim that deals largely with edifying narrative material in the OT that is nonlegal (nonhalachic).

Halakah (Heb., "procedure")

Taken from the Hebrew word *halak*, "to walk," this term refers to that portion of the Midrashim that deals with legal material that teaches one how to conduct oneself ("walk") under the law.

Mishnah (Heb. *shanah*, "to repeat")

The collection of rabbinic oral traditions, allegedly dating back to the time of Moses. The collection of sixty-three tractates (essays) was pub-

---

[18] For a concise but informative survey of "Jewish Hermeneutics in the First Century," and especially the use of rabbinic rules of interpretation by NT authors, see Longenecker, *Biblical Exegesis*, 19–50.

[19] Debate exists whether these two midrashic terms are descriptive of subject matter or constitute hermeneutical methods. If the latter view is held, authors will attempt to characterize the method most often used by rabbis when interpreting that particular kind of material. See Longenecker, *Biblical Exegesis*, 23; Dockery, *Biblical Interpretation*, 29, Kaiser and Silva, *Introduction to Biblical Hermeneutics*, 212.

[20] Dockery cites the work of Renee Bloch in identifying five characteristics of Midrash: (1) It is grounded in Scripture; (2) it is homiletical in nature; (3) it seeks to clarify the meaning of texts; (4) it attempts to contemporize the Scripture under consideration; and (5) it seeks to draw out principles from the legal (law-related) material with the goal of solving problems not directly addressed in Scripture. See Dockery, *Biblical Interpretation*, 29.

lished ca. AD 200 by Rabbi Judah, who organized this collection of legal rulings into six topical divisions related to life in the Holy Land and how to maintain holiness (E. Ferguson, 463; Klein, Blomberg, and Hubbard, 23).

Peshat (Heb., "plain, clear, simple")

Refers to the plain meaning of a biblical text or the literal-historical method of interpretation that yields such a meaning. This approach was largely characteristic of rabbinic interpretation of *HALAKAH* (law-related) texts. It is often contrasted with the SOD meaning or method, which seeks a mystical or allegorical sense and is found more commonly in the *HAGGADAH* (Kaiser and Silva, 212; Kaiser 1981, 53).[21]

Pesher (Heb., "interpretation")

An approach to interpretation or commentary on the OT (esp. the Prophets) that was practiced by the Qumran community. The Qumranians believed that they were living in the last days and were themselves the generation that would witness the apocalyptic "Day of the Lord." Consequently, they saw OT prophecies as being fulfilled in their day and identified people, events, and situations mentioned in the biblical text with their own historical circumstances. They often introduced the text with the words "this is that." Through *pesher* exegesis the Teacher of Righteousness claimed to reveal the mysteries of OT prophecy and how the contemporary situation marked their fulfillment (Dockery, 190; Virkler, 51).

Vigorous debate continues over whether, or to what extent, NT authors used the pesher method of interpretation in citing OT prophecies and their fulfillments. The issue is controversial, since Qumran did not interpret OT prophecies in keeping with the historical intent of the author, raising questions regarding the UNITY OF MEANING and *SENSUS PLENIOR*.[22]

---

[21] Kaiser states that as the Christian era dawned Jewish rabbis distinguished between a *peshat* sense of Scripture and a *remaz*, or "hidden," sense. Under this latter term he seems to place the *derush* ("searched") meaning, which is the allegorical sense, and relates to *midrashic* exegesis. Finally, he lists the *sod* interpretation, which seeks a mystical and allegorical sense. See Kaiser and Silva, *Introduction to Biblical Hermeneutics*, 212.

[22] Walter C. Kaiser Jr. has argued consistently that NT authors did not use *pesher* exegesis in their citation of OT prophecy. See Kaiser and Silva, *Introduction to Biblical Hermeneutics*, 215–18; also Kaiser, *Toward An Exegetical Theology: Biblical Exegesis for Preaching and Teaching* (Grand Rapids: Baker Book House, 1981), 55–57. Kaiser has even devoted an entire book to

Rabbinic exegesis (See Jewish interpretation)

Sod (Heb., "secret")

Refers to a mystical or allegorical meaning given to Scripture often found by rabbis interpreting the *Haggadah*, which contained homilies and popular expositions of legendary material not found in the law-related *Halakah* material (Kaiser 1981, 53, 55–56).

Talmud (Heb., "instruction")

Refers to the body of authoritative Jewish tradition made up of a digest of topically arranged oral traditions: the Mishnah and its Aramaic commentary, the *Gemara*. Judaism produced two Talmuds, each containing tradition much earlier than its time of publication. The Palestinian Talmud was published in Palestine by Rabbi Judah (d. ca. 220) and his disciples. It was incomplete and made its appearance around AD 450. The Babylonian Talmud, nearly four times as large, was completed around AD 500. By and large, the latter has occupied a greater status of authority within Judaism (E. Ferguson, 466; Harris, 534).

Tannaim (Heb., "repeaters")

Refers either to the Jewish writings of the Tannaitic Period (see Jewish interpretation) or to the scribal teachers that produced them.

Targumim (Heb., "explanations"; Eng. "Targums")

A Targum is a free Aramaic translation or paraphrase of the Hebrew Scriptures. Such a practice dates back to the time of Ezra (Neh. 8:1–18) and was practiced in the postexilic period when such paraphrases followed the reading of the Hebrew Scriptures in the synagogues for Jews unfamiliar with biblical Hebrew. This practice, of course, includes an interpretive element (Neh. 8:8), and many *Targumim* included

---

the defense of his thesis. See *The Uses of the Old Testament in the New* (Chicago: Moody Press, 1985). However, other Evangelical scholars have argued that the NT authors were using current methods already in use. See E. E. Ellis, "How the New Testament Uses the Old," in *New Testament Interpretation: Essays on Principles and Methods*, ed. I. Howard Marshall (Grand Rapids: Wm. B. Eerdmans, 1977), 203–8. For a full description of *pesher* interpretation in the NT, see Longenecker, *Biblical Exegesis*, 19–132. One qualification seems appropriate: A similar format of literary citation and commentary, including introductory formulae, is not the equivalent of the *pesher* method of exegesis. One has to demonstrate that the NT author is interpreting the OT text by assigning a meaning different from the one intended by the OT author. See Kaiser, *Toward an Exegetical Theology*, 56–57.

explanatory comments. A widespread practice, it may explain why NT authors sometimes quote the OT with what appears to be a lack of precision (Harris, 534).[23]

Tosefta

Refers to supplemental interpretations of Jewish law and tradition that are contemporary with the MISHNAH but not included in it. This collection has the same topical arrangement and order as the Mishnah and addresses all but four of its sixty-three tractates (essays) (E. Ferguson, 465, 468–69).

Middle Ages

Generally refers to the interval between the Patristic Period and the Reformation (ca. AD 590–1500).[24] Interpretation in this period was "traditional." That is, scholars were more concerned with interpreting the Scripture by citing authoritative church tradition represented by the church fathers and councils of the Church than understanding the literal and historical sense of the text. The prevailing method of interpretation was allegorical. However, this was only one of four meanings assigned to Scripture: literal (or historical), allegorical, moral (tropological), and anagogical (eschatological).[25] This fourfold sense of Scripture was called the *QUADRIGA* and was routinely practiced from the fourth century until the time of the REFORMATION. The dominant figure in this period is THOMAS AQUINAS, whose *Summa Theologica* not only defined orthodoxy for the Catholic Church but systematized its theology. Aquinas, while holding to multiple meanings in Scripture, insisted on the

[23] For example, in Eph. 4:8 Paul seems imprecise in his citation of Ps. 68:18—but the form of the citation is found in the Targums on the Psalms. See David E. Garland, "Background Studies and New Testament Interpretation," in *New Testament Criticism and Interpretation*, ed. David Alan Black and David S. Dockery (Grand Rapids: Zondervan, 1991), 348–76.

[24] The date of AD 590 marks when Gregory I became pope. Sometimes the so-called conciliar period (ca. AD 400–600, when the church councils and their decisions became a "rule of faith" in determining correct doctrine and interpretation) is treated separately. See Klein, Blomberg, and Hubbard, *Biblical Interpretation*, 36. Some see the Renaissance (ca. AD 1350–1500) and the literary influence of the Christian humanists who emphasized the need for biblical study in the original biblical languages (J. Reuchlin, John Colet, Erasmus) as a prelude and bridge to the Reformation. See Grant and Tracy, *Short History*, 92; Kaiser, *Toward An Exegetical Theology*, 60.

[25] The fourfold sense of Scripture is illustrated by the oft-cited rhyme: "The *letter* shows us what God and our fathers did. / The *allegory* shows us where our faith is hid. / The *moral* meaning gives us rules of life. / The *anagogy* shows us where we end our strife." See Grant and Tracy, *Short History*, 85.

primacy of the literal sense as the foundation for the spiritual or allegorical meanings (Dockery, 159; Grant and Tracy, 88–91; McQuilken, 38–39).

Modern Period

From the theological and hermeneutical innovations of Friedrich Schleiermacher (1768–1834) to the present, encompassing a host of other developments. The nineteenth century saw the flowering of the historical-critical method (see Historical criticism). Undergirded by rationalistic and naturalistic presuppositions, it bred a radical skepticism toward biblical history and its witness to the supernatural (i.e., miracles). Darwin's evolutionary hypothesis, reflected in the philosophy of Friedrich Hegel, resulted in the view that all religions exhibit an evolutionary development in religious thought. Its application to the literary development of the OT gave rise to the Source criticism of Julius Wellhausen (1844–1918) and his "Documentary Hypothesis." With regard to the NT, it gave rise to the reconstruction of early church history and its theories about its theological developments by F. C. Baur (1826–1860) and Adolf Harnack (1851–1930). Schleiermacher and his successor, Wilhelm Dilthey (1833–1911), reacted to the detached and dispassionate approach of historical-critical exegesis and introduced a radical subjectivity into the interpretive process, one aimed at reexperiencing the author's creative impulse or moment of inspired thought.

The hermeneutical and theological innovations of the twentieth century are too numerous to mention.[26] It saw the rise of the history of religions school, which was a comparative religions approach to the Bible. Such an approach contended that the Bible is not unique in its origin or development of religious thought, that it is best understood and studied against the backdrop of its contemporary religious partners in the ancient world.[27] Other major developments in this century were the literary methods known as Form criticism and Redaction criticism and the rise of various theological expressions of Christian existentialism such as Neoorthodoxy

---

[26] The contributions of the major biblical interpreters in the twentieth century in Europe and North America are discussed in McKim, *Historical Handbook*, parts 5 and 6, 403–624.

[27] Major figures in this school were men like Wilhelm Boussett (1865–1920) and Richard Reitzenstein (1861–1931). Although this school did much to promote cultural-historical investigation into the religious world of the Bible, its presuppositions undermined the authority of the Bible by seeing the ideas of Scripture as mere products of human thought and religious experience and not the result of divine revelation.

and the New Hermeneutic (Klein, Blomberg, and Hubbard, 44–51, Kaiser and Silva, 229–48).

Neoorthodoxy

Christian existentialism applied to systematic theology. While Søren Kierkegaard is usually regarded as the father of Christian existentialism, Karl Barth[28] is credited with using the insights of Kierkegaard to start a theological revolution that broke rank with the Rationalism of modern liberalism. Also referred to as "Dialectical Theology," this movement held major implications for hermeneutics through its doctrine of the Word of God and its insistence that faith is not dependent on facts of history.[29] Although the revelation of the Word touches history, the historical writings of the Bible are not revelation itself, only a witness to it. Therefore, the propositional truths or doctrinal content of the Bible are not the Word of God; they are merely the instrument through which the revelatory Word is conveyed (D. Ferguson, 47f).

New Criticism

A movement in interpretation that was text-centered, its emphasis being on the form and literary character of the biblical text. The text was viewed as having an interpretive life all its own and a meaning independent of the author's intent. Its dominant influence was felt from about 1930–1960 (Osborne, 369). It paved the way for developments (e.g., the "New Hermeneutic"

---

[28] Barth's commentary on Romans *(Römerbrief)* has been described as a "theological bombshell." Of Barth's theology, Harvie M. Conn says that it brought about a "Copernican revolution" in Protestant theology that ultimately put an end to the dominance of liberal thought. See Conn, *Contemporary World Theology: A Layman's Guidebook* (Nutley, N.J.: Presbyterian and Reformed, 1973), 10. Barth, of course, was not alone in this movement. Other theologians of note were Friedrich Gogarten *(Religious Decision),* Emil Brunner *(Experience, Knowledge and Faith),* Barth's pastoral colleague, Eduard Thurneysen *(Dostoievsky),* and Rudolf Bultmann *(New Testament Theology).*

[29] Barth, like Kierkegaard, understood God as transcendent and "wholly other." Consequently, the truths that He reveals come to us as paradoxes (e.g., Jesus is both man and God) and create a dialectical tension of opposites. This tension cannot be resolved through reason, only by faith, which is brought into crisis at the proclamation of the Word (through the Scriptures). Any knowledge of God (including that mediated through Scripture) can take place only at God's initiative through a divine act of Self-disclosure. When an individual has a revelatory encounter with God through reading the Scriptures, the Bible has effectively "become the Word of God." Apart from that act of revelation the Bible is the historical *record of* and *witness to* God's revelation, but is not *revelation itself.*

and "Reader-response criticism") that would diminish the value of historical exegesis and increase the reader's subjective role in interpretation (Osborne, 369; Kaiser and Silva, 232, 239–40).[30]

New Hermeneutic (N-H)

An interpretative approach that arose in the mid-twentieth century, initially spearheaded by the followers of Rudolf Bultmann, whose existential approach to interpretation was indebted to the philosophical writings of Søren Kierkegaard and Martin Heidegger (Ramm 1952, 132).[31] Two notable proponents of the N-H were Ernst Fuchs and Gerhard Ebeling, who emphasized the active role of language to mediate a revelatory-existential encounter with God, calling for a decision of faith. They called this encounter a "speech-event" or "word-happening." The N-H was further developed by Hans-Georg Gadamer, who explored how language functions in the psychology of understanding and its capacity to express a person's understanding of him- or herself and the world around him or her (i.e., his or her existence).

When applied to hermeneutics, the N-H brought an entirely new understanding of the biblical text and its interpretation. The reader does not approach the text as an object to be interpreted but instead enters into a speech-event whereby the text interprets him or her, presenting the Word of God (Klein, Blomberg, and Hubbard, 50) in an existential moment calling for a decision of faith (Ramm 1970, 91). The meaning of the text is not the one intended by the author (which is impossible to retrieve), nor limited to what the reader can express (which is subjectively limited). In fact, the meaning of the text is open-ended and is "an unending process which is never exhausted or captured by an infinite line of interpreters!" (Kaiser 1981, 30).

Patristic Period

Extending from the end of the Apostolic period to the beginning of the Middle Ages (ca. AD 100–590). The church fathers were convinced that the OT was a Christian book and sought to interpret it Christologically. They

---

[30] New Criticism and its developments mark a revolt against the notion of "objective" textual meaning and shift to the creative capacity of the text to create meanings through a "subjective" interaction between reader and text. For a comprehensive summary of these developments, see Anthony C. Thiselton, *The Two Horizons: New Testament Hermeneutics and Philosophical Description with Special Reference to Heidegger, Bultmann, Gadamer and Wittgenstein* (Grand Rapids: Wm. B. Eerdmans, 1980), 327–56.

[31] For an insider's view of the historical development of the N-H, see James M. Robinson, "Hermeneutics Since Barth," in *The New Hermeneutic,* ed. James M. Robinson and John B. Cobb Jr. (New York: Harper and Row, 1964), 1–77.

attempted to show the unity and continuity between the OT and the NT revelation. To accomplish this they resorted to typological interpretation, which under their theological zeal often degenerated into ALLEGORY. Thus, the allegorical approach became the dominant method of interpretation.

This period includes two contrasting schools of interpretation: The ALEXANDRIAN SCHOOL, which was known for its allegorical approach, and the ANTIOCHIAN SCHOOL, which took a more literal and historical approach. During this period the NT canon was established, along with Christian orthodoxy relative to the doctrines of Christ, God, and the Spirit. EXEGESIS then became traditional, i.e., conducted within the framework of the "rule of faith" (Gk. *regula fidei*; see TRADITION) (Ramm 1970, 48–50; Grant and Tracy, 73–82).

Pietism

In the POST-REFORMATION PERIOD a reaction to Protestant SCHOLASTICISM and its sterile intellectual approach that tended to produce dry, lifeless orthodoxy. In its place Pietism advocated the reading and study of the Bible to foster spiritual devotion and growth in Christians. Although no less attentive to the grammatical and historical aspects of the text, Pietists saw the goal of Bible study not as doctrinal, but practical—to promote true spirituality in the believer. Among the notable figures in the German wing of this movement were Jakob Spener (1635–1705) and August Francke (1663–1727). English Pietism is represented by Richard Baxter (1616–1691) and John Wesley (1703–1791), the founder of Methodism (Ramm 1970, 60–62).

Post-Reformation period

A period (ca. 1650–1800) in which theologians sought to conserve the theological gains of the Reformation. It is well-known for two movements: Protestant SCHOLASTICISM and PIETISM. The former reinserted a DOGMATIC, authoritarian approach to hermeneutics, interpreting the Scriptures according to the orthodox confessions of faith.[32] The latter was in one sense a reaction to an approach that emphasized theological ORTHODOXY but produced no spiritual devotion and vitality in a Christian's life. The RATIONALISM of the Enlightenment made its mark on biblical interpretation during this period in two significant ways. Positively, it helped promote the historical investigation of the Bible, especially in the areas of linguistic and text-critical studies (see HISTORI-

[32] Ironically, while rejecting the authoritarian, dogmatic exegesis of the Catholic Church, Protestants developed their own authoritative creedal standards of orthodoxy, which influenced and controlled their exegesis.

cal criticism and Textual criticism).[33] Negatively, by setting up human reason as the final arbiter in determining truth, it challenged the authority of the Bible as divine revelation and the Church's authority to establish normative doctrine (Mickelsen, 41–44; Klein, Blomberg, and Hubbard, 42–43).

Reformation

A period of attempted ecclesiastical reform (ca. AD 1500–1650) that dramatically altered the theological and hermeneutical landscape of Christianity.[34] The two dominant figures of this period are Martin Luther (1483–1546), who led the revolt, and John Calvin (1509–1564), its premier exegete and theologian. Reformation hermeneutics can be characterized as independent and driven by biblical authority. It often broke rank with Roman Catholic tradition and dogma when they violated the teaching of Scripture. The principle of *sola scriptura* ("Scripture alone") established Scripture as the primary and final authority in determining matters of Christian faith and doctrine. Secondly, interpretation was marked by an emphatic rejection of Allegory[35] in favor of the literal sense of Scripture derived from a grammatical-historical study of the text in the original biblical languages. Thirdly, Reformation hermeneutics was Christological in its orientation. Luther and (to a lesser degree) Calvin both believed that the whole of Scripture gave witness to Christ (Mickelsen, 38–41; Klein, Blomberg, and Hubbard, 39–42; Berkhof, 25–28).

Scholasticism

A term used mainly in association with Christian theology during the Middle Ages. It is characterized by a theological method that made relatively little use of Scripture, instead relying heavily on reason and philosophical concepts borrowed from Plato and Aristotle.[36] The goal of scholasticism was to explain the revealed truth of the Christian faith by developing a coherent

---

[33] For a concise summary of the history of textual criticism, see Gordon D. Fee, "The Textual Criticism of the New Testament," in *The Expositor's Bible Commentary*, ed. F. E. Gaebelein (Grand Rapids: Zondervan, 1979), 1:419–33.

[34] A very helpful article for understanding how the Reformers viewed the Scriptures and the theological presuppositions that guided their interpretation is Paul Lehmann, "The Reformers' Use of the Bible," *Theology Today* 3 (1946): 328–48.

[35] Scholars sometimes note that Luther, for all his railing against allegory, engages in allegorization on occasion. However, this does not alter the fact that Luther rejected allegory in principle and together with Calvin ended the dominance of the allegorization in the Church. See Ramm, *Protestant Biblical Interpretation*, 54; Kaiser, *Toward an Exegetical Theology*, 61.

[36] See J. Kenneth Grider, "Scholasticism," in *Beacon Dictionary of Theology* (Kansas City: Beacon Hill Press, 1983), 473.

and logically consistent system of doctrine. Scholasticism has been described as a pre-Renaissance intellectual awakening within the monastic movement (see Victorines) that began with a rediscovery of Aristotelian philosophy for use in doing theology (Klein, Blomberg, and Hubbard, 39). The greatest scholastic of this movement was the philosopher-theologian Thomas Aquinas, who, in emphasizing the role of reason in interpretation and doctrinal development, reasserted the importance of the literal sense of Scripture for such formulation.

Victorines

A medieval school of interpretation named for its place of origin at St. Victor's Abbey in Paris. Among the names connected with this school are Hugh (Hugo), Richard, and Andrew. A second generation of Victorines include Peter (the Chanter), Stephen Langton, and Thomas of Chobham. The school is known for its emphasis on the study of the liberal arts (esp. language, history, and geography) as foundational to exegesis, an emphasis acquired by interaction with Jewish scholars of the medieval period. The result was to give primacy to the literal method of interpretation over the "spiritual" (i.e., allegorical) sense of Scripture. The latter was not completely abandoned, but was greatly limited and controlled.[37] The literal method was the goal of exegesis, exegesis was the basis of doctrine, and doctrine was the foundation for allegorization (Ramm 1970, 51; Bray, 150).

---

[37] See Gerald Bray, *Biblical Interpretation: Past and Present* (Downers Grove, Ill.: InterVarsity Press, 1996).

3

Prominent Figures in Hermeneutics

Aquinas, Thomas (ca. 1225–1274)

The premier theologian of the medieval period whose *Summa Theologica* gave rational systematic expression to the Christian faith and eventually defined orthodoxy for the Catholic Church. Although Aquinas argued that the Bible has symbolic meanings and was committed to the fourfold sense of Scripture (see *Quadriga*), he insisted on the primacy of the literal sense from which symbolic or spiritual meanings are derived. He identified the literal sense with the meaning intended by the author and the meaning upon which doctrine is to be founded. Thus, Aquinas is a transitional figure who marks the end of the total dominance of the allegorical method of interpretation and anticipates the literal emphasis of the Reformers (Dockery, 159; Grant and Tracy, 88–91; McQuilken, 38–39; Ramm 1970, 40; Klein, Blomberg, and Hubbard, 39). See Middle Ages.

Augustine (354–430)

A Church father and the most dominant figure in theology and biblical interpretation before Thomas Aquinas. His *De Doctrina Christiana* is a handbook of hermeneutics and homiletics. In it he develops a theory of signs that is an ancient precursor to semantics or philosophical linguistics (see Semiotics), an exploration of how language works in communication through signs, sounds, and speech that is foundational to hermeneutics. Augustine was driven to allegorical interpretation out of an apologetic concern for defending Christian orthodoxy (the rule of faith) against the heretical Manicheans, known for their extreme literalism (Grant and Tracy, 78–80; Ramm 1970, 35).

Quadriga

Denotes the fourfold method of interpretation of Scripture that was firmly established and widely practiced in Catholic exegesis from the fourth century (Augustine) to the Reformation in the sixteenth century. By this method a Scripture was seen to have four different meanings: literal, tropological (moral), allegorical (mystical, includes typological; see Typeology), and anagogical (prophetic or eschatological; see Eschatology).

Barth, Karl (1886–1968)

The Swiss pastor-theologian credited with giving birth to Neoorthodoxy with the publication of his commentary on Romans in 1919. Influenced by the existentialism of Søren Kierkegaard, he stressed a revelational encounter with the Word of God. In this he reemphasized the authority of the Scripture as the Word of God (Klein, Blomberg, and Hubbard, 47). However, he did not regard the Bible as revelation *itself*, only the *witness to* revelation and the medium through which God speaks His Word today. While his theological contribution was monumental to the movement, he did not significantly add to the development of hermeneutical theory. Nevertheless, his work provoked hermeneutical reflection and anticipated some of the interpretive features of Rudolf Bultmann and the New Hermeneutic, especially regarding the role given the interpreter's subjectivity in the interpretive process.[1]

Bultmann, Rudolf (1884–1976)

Professor of NT at Marburg (1921–51), Germany, best known as one of the pioneers of NT Form criticism (*History of the Synoptic Tradition*, 1921). However, Bultmann is equally famous as an existential theologian who advocated a program of interpretation known as Demythologization, which he believed was essential if the gospel proclamation *(kerygma)* was to be preached to moderns (Bray, 429).

Perhaps the most controversial aspect of Bultmann's approach was his historical skepticism. Because the *kerygma* is existential in nature, it cannot rest on facts of history.[2] According to this point of view, history can establish almost nothing of certainty about the historical Jesus. And even though historical-critical

---

1 Bernard L. Ramm describes the reader's response to the paradoxical truth of Scripture: "We do decide for them. We do embrace them. But we do not embrace them with a rational act, but with the inwardness of faith, with the passion of faith, with subjectivity." See *Varieties of Christian Apologetics* (Grand Rapids: Baker Book House, 1966), 56.

2 Duncan Ferguson describes Bultmann's method as an attempt to leap over history to an understanding mediated through existential identification and involvement with the text and its message. He writes, "The real issue for faith is not what happened *then* but what happens *now* in the moment of existential decision. . . . The meaning of the *kerygma* is not to be sought in uncovering the historical Jesus, which is impossible anyway, but in the awareness

studies are necessary, their results are irrelevant with respect to faith because *kerygma* calls one to make an existential choice about Christ.

Calvin, John (1509–1564)

French lawyer and humanist turned Reformer who was arguably the greatest exegete and theologian of the Reformation. He is responsible for giving systematic expression to Reformed theology through his work *The Institutes of the Christian Religion,* which he published in 1536 at the age of twenty-six! His humanist training caused him to insist that exegesis be done in the original biblical languages. Consequently, he came to reject allegory[3] with its multiplicity of meanings in favor of a literal-historical approach that emphasized the author's intended meaning as the goal of interpretation.[4] Calvin's interpretive method is essentially a grammatical-historical approach, which is careful to consider the literary and historical contexts of the passage (Mickelsen, 40). He was in total agreement with MARTIN LUTHER on *sola Scriptura,* which established the authority of Scripture over church tradition, and the interpretive principle of "Scripture interprets Scripture."[5] Like Luther he stressed not only the clarity (see PERSPICUITY) of Scripture but also the unity of both the OT and NT, especially in their witness to Christ.[6] These convictions flowed from his belief that the Holy Spirit is the divine author of all Scripture who continues to illuminate believers in the task of interpretation (McKim 1998, 171–79).

---

of one's responsibility before God. Brute facts, uncovered by disinterested and objective history, are unimportant for faith." See *Biblical Hermeneutics: An Introduction* (Atlanta, Ga.: John Knox Press, 1986), 171, 53 (Ferguson's emphasis).

3 Calvin regarded the allegorical method a contrivance of Satan, leading people away from the truth of the Scriptures. See Bernard L. Ramm, *Protestant Biblical Interpretation,* 3rd ed. (Grand Rapids: Baker Book House, 1970), 58.

4 In the preface to his commentary on Romans, Calvin writes, "The chief virtue of an interpreter lies in lucid brevity. Since it is almost his only task to unfold the mind of the writer whom he has undertaken to expound, he misses his mark, or at least strays outside his limits, by the extent to which he leads his readers away from the meaning of his author." Cited by D. L. Puckett, "Calvin, John," in *Historical Handbook of Major Biblical Interpreters,* ed. Donald K. McKim (Downers Grove, Ill.: InterVarsity Press, 1998), 172–73.

5 Calvin's prodigious command of Scripture is evident in his *Institutes of the Christian Religion,* which is literally peppered with scriptural references and quotes. If someone is tempted to dismiss this as an example of dogmatic proof-texting, they should note that Calvin was a prolific expositor of Scripture, producing commentaries on nearly every book (all but nine, one NT and eight OT) in the Bible. See Berkeley Mickelsen, *Interpreting the Bible* (Grand Rapids: Wm. B. Eerdmans, 1963), 39.

6 Nevertheless, Calvin gave priority to the NT as an exegetical guide for interpreting the OT. See Puckett, "Calvin, John," 178.

Chrysostom, John (ca. AD 354–407)

One of the best-known figures of the ANTIOCHIAN SCHOOL of interpretation. He was renowned for his preaching ability, which earned him the nickname *Chrysostomos* ("golden mouth"). His homilies, in addition to being known for their orthodoxy, are well-known for using Antiochian principles of exegesis, which stressed the literal and historical meaning of the text (Dockery, 113–20).

Clement of Alexandria (AD 155–215)

An early church father who adopted the allegorical method of PHILO OF ALEXANDRIA (see ALLEGORIZE) and became the first prominent figure of the ALEXANDRIAN SCHOOL of interpretation. Clement believed that the very nature of divine revelation in Scripture made ALLEGORICAL INTERPRETATION necessary. God reveals himself through multiple deeper meanings of Scripture to those who have differing levels of spiritual maturity and search for those meanings through allegorical interpretation (Dockery, 83). Acknowledging the literal sense as a necessary first step, he believed the allegorical method uncovered truth fit for faith, doctrine, and proclamation. Scholars identify at least five different senses that Clement gave to the Scriptures: (1) historical—as historical event; (2) doctrinal—includes moral, religious, theological truths; (3) prophetic—including TYPOLOGY; (4) philosophical—with Stoic cosmology and psychological meanings; and (5) mystical—deeper moral and spiritual truths (Grant and Tracy, 55–56; Ramm 1970, 31).[7]

Erasmus, Desiderius (1467–1536)

A Dutch humanist scholar whose writings contributed to the literary and theological innovations of the Reformation. As a Renaissance scholar, he emphasized the study of the Scriptures in the original languages, which led to his own brand of literal interpretation known as the philological method.[8] This in turn led to a growing dissatisfaction with allegorization, although unlike his humanist mentor, John Colet (1467–1519), or the Reformers,

---

7 David S. Dockery provides an illuminating description of Clement's hermeneutical approach including some of his guiding principles. See *Biblical Interpretation Then and Now: Contemporary Hermeneutics in the Light of the Early Church* (Grand Rapids: Baker Book House, 1992), 82–86.

8 Erasmus's philological method was an approach that combined textual, literary, and historical criticisms. It does not differ essentially from what is meant by the grammatical-historical approach to interpretation, although Erasmus would not limit the meaning of the text to a single or literal sense. See J. B. Payne, "Erasmus, Desiderius," in *Historical Handbook*, ed. McKim, 188–89.

Erasmus never rejected it as a valid method of interpretation[9] (Kaiser 1981, 60; Klein, Blomberg, and Hubbard, 40).

Erasmus also reflects the RATIONALISM of Christian humanists, which viewed human reason as autonomous and able to make independent judgments on the meaning of Scripture and to correct church tradition (D. Ferguson, 152).

Frei, Hans (1922–88)

One of the important hermeneutical figures in the twentieth century, a proponent of modern literary criticism who severely criticized the preoccupation of modern critical scholars with history. In his seminal work *Eclipse of the Biblical Narrative,*[10] he argued for a precritical reading of the Bible, that treats narratives (e.g., the Gospels) as literary creations that have their own meaning apart from and independent of the actual historical events they claim to record.[11] His work undergirds many modern literary approaches that dehistoricize the Scripture or deemphasize its historical value in pursuit of a so-called true hermeneutic that can appreciate the literary value of narrative independent of historical concerns (Osborne, 164, 368).

Gadamer, Hans-Georg

Along with MARTIN HEIDEGGER, Gadamer[12] is one of the main philosophical theorists behind the movement known as the NEW HERMENEUTIC. As an existentialist (see EXISTENTIALISM), Gadamer is not concerned with understanding

---

[9] Although his hermeneutical method placed an emphasis on the literal-historical sense of Scripture, he insisted on multiple meanings to Scripture. Erasmus acknowledged at least three senses: the literal, the allegorical, and the moral. The allegorical, after the example of Origen, was necessary to avoid absurdities with the literal method or when the literal sense conflicted with the moral teachings of Scripture or the doctrine of Christ. See Payne, "Erasmus, Desiderius," 189.

[10] See Hans Frei, *Eclipse of Biblical Narrative: A Study in Eighteenth and Nineteenth-Century Hermeneutics* (New Haven, Conn.: Yale University Press, 1974).

[11] Grant R. Osborne succinctly describes the problem for many evangelicals when he states that for Frei "the narrative is the meaning; there should be no search for the event behind the text but only a close reading of the text itself. Yet this fails to do justice to the texts themselves." Furthermore, one has to ask whether the biblical author or the intended audience would ever have envisioned such a dehistoricized reading of the text. Also the nature of biblical narrative suggests that literary purpose is tied to historical concerns. Again Osborne comments, "In reality the literary and historical exist side-by-side and are interdependent. As a literal representation of event and significance, both text and its background are essential components of meaning." See *The Hermeneutical Spiral: A Comprehensive Introduction to Biblical Interpretation* (Downers Grove, Ill.: InterVarsity Press, 1991), 164, 368.

[12] For a thorough survey and trenchant summary of Gadamer's understanding of the her-

the text in the grammatical-historical sense (see GRAMMATICAL-HISTORICAL METHOD). Rather, it is his goal to have a present existential encounter with the *subject matter* in the text. For Gadamer, the subject matter of the text is independent of author and reader, yet existentially shared by both (Kaiser 1981, 30), since both have language as an expression of "Being" in common. True understanding takes place when there is a "fusion of horizons,"[13] that of the text with that of interpreter. In interpretation our goal is not to understand the text in view of the author's historical situation, but to have a present involvement in what the text now speaks.[14] Neither is the goal to recapture the author's intended meaning, which for Gadamer is impossible. What was written in text has now detached itself from the author and his original thoughts are irretrievable. Thus we cannot study the apostle Paul, only his texts (Osborne, 370).[15]

One positive contribution of Gadamer is his analysis of and emphasis on the role of PRE-UNDERSTANDING in the interpretive process. In answer to the Enlightenment's emphasis on detached historical objectivity, Gadamer argues that such neutrality is impossible, nor is it desirable. The interpreter must be historically conscious of his or her pre-understanding with its biases, questions, and concerns if he or she is to enter into a conversation with the text and an authentic "fusion of horizons" (see HORIZONS, FUSION OF) is to occur (Grant and Tracy, 159–60).

---

meneutical process, see A. C. Thiselton, *The Two Horizons: New Testament Hermeneutics and Philosophical Description with Special Reference to Heidegger, Bultmann, Gadamer and Wittgenstein* (Grand Rapids: Wm. B. Eerdmans, 1980), 327–56.

[13] By "horizon" Gadamer refers to a perspective that belongs to a particular subject and historical situation. Thus, the "fusion of horizons" Gadamer refers to is that of the text and interpreter. Note that Gadamer does not equate or unite the horizon of the text with the author and his intent. It is simply the perspective reflected in the text.

[14] Robert M. Grant and David Tracy clarify that for Gadamer "the primary meaning of the text does not lie 'behind' it (in the mind of the author, in the original social setting, in the original audience) nor even 'in' the text itself. Rather, the meaning of the text lies *in front of* the text—in the now *common* question, the now common subject matter of both text and interpreter. Historically conscious interpreters do not seek to simply repeat, to reproduce the original meaning of the text, in order to understand its (and now their) questions. Rather, they employ all the tools of historical criticism *and then seek to mediate, translate, interpret the meaning into their present horizon.*" See *A Short History of the Interpretation of the Bible* (Philadelphia: Fortress Press, 1984), 160 (emphasis mine).

[15] One obvious problem with Gadamer's view is that it is self-defeating and unsustainable. Even as he writes, he assumes that his choice of words and syntax is adequate to convey his thoughts. It is most probable that Gadamer himself would be troubled if someone misconstrued his writings and interpreted them in such a way as to seriously misrepresent his ideas. Operating is the assumption that there is a fusion of text and the author's willed intent conveyed in the text. All public verbal communication is based on this assumption.

Horizons (fusion of)

A term made famous by Hans-Georg Gadamer and the New Hermeneutic. It refers to the perspective on reality that belongs to a particular historical context or situation. Gadamer pointed out that there is a historical conditioning that takes place on both sides of the hermeneutical equation—with the text and the interpreter. Whereas traditional hermeneutics stressed the need to explore the historical setting of the biblical text and remain neutral and detached so as to determine an objective historical meaning, Gadamer argued that interpretation occurs only when the interpreter engages the text to become aware of his or her own horizon over against that of the text.[16] This merging of horizons constitutes interpretation (Thiselton, 10–17).[17]

Heidegger, Martin (1889–1976)

The German philosopher whose brand of Existentialism greatly influenced the Hermeneutic of Rudolf Bultmann (colleagues at Marburg) (Kaiser and Silva, 230–31). This influence stemmed from his understanding of language and its capacity to both express human existence and interpret it. He argued that the mode of existence for human beings is radically different from other forms of life. Humans are not only aware of themselves (i.e., possess "self-understanding"), but uniquely have the capacity to reflect on their existence, or "being," and express it through language. It is this emphasis on the existential value of language that grabbed Bultmann's attention and caused him to apply it to interpretation.[18]

Hillel, Rabbi (ca. 30 BC–AD 9)

The Jewish rabbi who was contemporary with NT Christianity and developed a system of hermeneutics based on seven rules (see *Middot*) to interpret and expound the Torah. Many of these rules can be found and illustrated in the

---

[16] This represents a movement away from author-text hermeneutics, i.e., from the author and his intention expressed *in* the text to the reader's present experience and involvement *with* the text. For a fuller explanation, see the discussion of Gadamer's hermeneutic in Osborne, *Hermeneutical Spiral,* 369–71.

[17] The problem for many evangelical interpreters is not only that the author's willed meaning is forgotten (or dismissed as irretrievable), but that objective textual meaning becomes impossible, as no two interpreters share the same horizon and therefore the fusion will always produce different interpretations. Furthermore, this paradigm of the interpretive process clearly seems to confuse the Meaning and the Significance of the text, a distinction that E. D. Hirsch argues must be maintained if there is to be any validity to interpretation.

[18] Self-understanding for Bultmann was essential for establishing one's own relation to the subject matter of the text and a Pre-understanding which make interpretation possible.

sayings of Jesus and the writings of Paul (Kaiser 1981, 53–55; Kaiser and Silva, 213–14).

Hirsch, E. D.

An English professor who wrote a lucid critique of Hans-Georg Gadamer and the New Hermeneutic *(Validity in Interpretation).*[19] Hirsch claimed that German scholarship was blurring the distinction between *Erklarung* ("meaning") and *Verstehung* ("significance"), a distinction that must be maintained if there is to be any validity in interpretation and the possibility of deriving objective meaning and knowledge from written texts. He argued that the Meaning of the text is what the author intended to communicate through his words, grammar, and syntax at the time of composition. It is fixed and unchanging. Beyond this singular sense the numerous "meanings" assigned by readers to a text reflect its Significance, i.e., the relationship between the textual meaning and the changing circumstances of various interpreters (Kaiser 1981, 30–34, Kaiser and Silva, 30–31).

Jerome (ca. 347–420)

An early church father and biblical scholar who is best known for his Latin translation of the Bible, known as the Vulgate. Jerome was extremely well educated and had mastered both biblical languages (Hebrew and Greek) as well as Latin. His study of the Hebrew Bible led him to suggest that the Apocrypha was not on a par with Canonical Scripture. The school at Antioch influenced his approach to interpretation, which was historically grounded and literal, although he never completely abandoned Allegorical interpretation (Ramm 1970, 33–34).

Kierkegaard, Søren (1813–55)

Danish philosopher and theologian considered the ideological father of Christian existentialism through his influence on Karl Barth. A severe critic of rationalism and the Historical-critical method, his interests in the study of the Bible were pietistic (see Pietistic), desiring to understand and appropriate the message of Scripture for personal spiritual transformation. Kierkegaard's existentialism begins with an understanding of God as

See Rudolf Bultmann, *New Testament and Mythology and Other Basic Works,* ed and trans. Schubert M. Ogden (Philadelphia: Fortress Press, 1984), 70–73.

[19] Hirsch's thesis and rationale for writing this book can be found in his first chapter, "In Defense of the Author." See Edwin D. Hirsch, *Validity in Interpretation* (New Haven, Conn.: Yale University Press, 1967), 1–23.

transcendent, or "wholly other."[20] This being the case, humans cannot know anything of God unless He takes the initiative to encounter them in an act of self-disclosure (i.e., revelation). When God accordingly reveals himself, a so-called crisis encounter occurs calling for a "leap of faith"—a decision to embrace the paradoxical truth found in Scripture. That is to say, paradox is the way the transcendent God encounters us in Scripture. It is in this existential encounter and elicitation of faith through crisis that the Bible demonstrates its divine authority.[21]

Kierkegaard's existential approach anticipates and supports the plurality of meanings advocated by the READER-RESPONSE APPROACH. He held that Christianity is not a doctrine but a person, the God-man, the Lord Jesus Christ, and therefore must not be reduced to a set of propositional truths (Rosas, 334–35).[22]

Luther, Martin (1483–1546)

Credited with launching the Protestant Reformation by posting his ninety-five articles of dissent against Roman Catholic doctrine and practice on the chapel doors at Wittenberg. Luther became both a prominent leader and guiding theologian for the REFORMATION. His enduring hermeneutical legacy centers around his rejection of ALLEGORY and insistence on the literal sense of Scripture,[23] which coupled with the principle of *sola Scriptura* effectively replaced the Roman Catholic hierarchy with the authority of the Bible

---

[20] For a well-informed summary of Kierkegaard's hermeneutical presuppositions and an evaluation of his contribution to biblical interpretation, see L. J. Rosas III, "Kierkegaard, Søren Aabe," in *Historical Handbook,* ed. McKim, 330–36.

[21] Kierkegaard's perspective was adopted and expanded by Karl Barth in his doctrine of the Word of God. For Barth the Bible *becomes* the Word of God in this revelational encounter between God and humans through the medium of the Word. See Ramm, *Protestant Biblical Interpretation,* 70–72. One must ask and determine if the authority of Scripture is intrinsic due to the divine inspiration that produced it or due to its power to create an existential crisis of faith. It is certainly worth asking whether the Bible testifies to its own authoritative status, and if so on what basis. See Wayne Grudem, "Scripture's Self-Attestation and the Problem of Formulating a Doctrine of Scripture," in *Scripture and Truth,* ed. D. A. Carson and John D. Woodbridge (Grand Rapids: Zondervan, 1983), 19–64.

[22] It seems best to understand Kierkegaard's objection to dogmatic theology as a reaction to the skepticism engendered by the Enlightenment as well as the spiritual sterility of historical-critical exegesis. Certainly he invokes doctrine to make his objections and critique of Christendom. An Evangelical response to this objection is to affirm that Christianity is indeed a person and not doctrine per se, but that it is not less than the doctrine which the *incarnate Word* gave us in His teachings or that God grants us in the revelation of the Scriptures.

[23] In contrast to the use of the allegorical method, Luther stated that "every word should be allowed to stand in its natural meaning and not be abandoned unless faith forces us to it."

interpreted by a priesthood of all believers. His principles of interpretation[24] can be illustrated in the Augsburg Confession of 1530 (Grant and Tracy, 93–99; McKim 1996, 165; Dowley, 368–69).

Nicholas of Lyra (1270–1340)

One of the transitional figures helping to bring about the REFORMATION through his influence on MARTIN LUTHER. A Jewish convert to Christianity, Nicholas was ignorant of Greek but well-versed in Hebrew. While he acknowledged the four senses (see *QUADRIGA*) of Scripture (McKim 1998, 80–81), he objected to the abuses of mystical (i.e., allegorical) interpretation and insisted that doctrine be based on the literal sense of Scripture. His work seems to have made such an impression upon Luther that it was often said, "If Lyra had not piped, Luther would not have danced" (Bray, 142; Kaiser and Silva, 224; Virkler, 64).

Origen (185–254)

An early church father commonly associated with the ALEXANDRIAN SCHOOL and its use of ALLEGORICAL INTERPRETATION. Whereas CLEMENT OF ALEXANDRIA, his predecessor in the Alexandrian school, taught that Scripture has a twofold sense corresponding to the dual nature of humans, body (literal) and soul (spiritual), Origen found a threefold sense, corresponding to the tripartite nature of human beings that he saw in 1 Thessalonians 5:23 (Klein, Blomberg, and Hubbard, 34). Thus, Scripture when interpreted can have a literal meaning (body), a moral-ethical meaning (soul), and a doctrinal meaning (spirit). The literal meaning, identified with the body, is clearly inferior to the moral and spiritual meanings, which are accessible only through

---

Cited by Ramm, in *Protestant Biblical Interpretation,* 54. This approach, together with his emphasis on studying the Scriptures in the original biblical languages, constituted what is called today the GRAMMATICAL-HISTORICAL METHOD of interpretation.

[24] Bernard Ramm gives a trenchant summary of Luther's hermeneutical principles: (1) The *psychological* principle set faith and illumination as a prerequisite for correct interpretation; (2) the *authority* principle established Scripture as the final authority (above ecclesiastical authority) in determining theological matters; (3) the *literal* principle saw the rejection of allegory as a valid method of interpretation; (4) the *sufficiency* principle affirmed that Scripture was sufficiently clear to render its meaning to believers without the need for the teaching office of the Church acting as the official interpreter of Scripture; (5) the *Christological* principle set Christ at the theological center of the whole Bible, providing unity and coherence to the whole of Scripture; and (6) the *Law-Gospel* was more of an overarching theological perspective that separated and contrasted law and grace as characteristic of the old and new covenant respectively. Luther argued that any admixture of law and grace was a fundamental compromise of the gospel of Christ. See Ramm, *Protestant Biblical Interpretation,* 53–57.

allegorizing.[25] Origen would probably have preferred to call his method "spiritualizing." At times his exegesis is a mixture of Typological interpretation and Allegory. Nevertheless, there is no doubt that Origen saw allegorical interpretation as true exegesis and the only way to uncover the deeper spiritual truths of Scripture (Mickelsen, 32; Ramm 1970, 33; Grant and Tracy, 55–56).

Philo of Alexandria (ca. 20 BC–AD 50)

Philo was an aristocratic Alexandrian Jew. Although he had received a Hellenistic education, he defended the Jewish faith in his numerous works (e.g., *In Flaccum* and *Legatio ad Gaium*). He sought to reconcile Greek philosophy, which he loved, with the OT Scriptures and made much use of allegory in his commentaries (Grant and Tracy, 52–53).[26] Thus, he is thought to have influenced Alexandrian Christian writers, such as Clement of Alexandria and Origen in their allegorization of the OT (see Allegorical interpretation). Scholars of the NT often see a connection between thoughts expressed by John (in his Gospel), the writer of Hebrews, and Paul and the thought patterns expressed in Philo's writings (E. Ferguson, 450–54).

Hyponoia

The term used by Philo to designate the deeper, spiritual meaning of the Scripture that lay beneath the literal surface meaning of the words. This deeper sense could be uncovered only by Allegorical interpretation (Kaiser and Silva, 210, 215–16).

Schleiermacher, Friedrich (1768–1834)

The German Protestant theologian sometimes regarded as the father of modern theology and hermeneutics. Reared in the pietistic (see Pietism) tradition and educated under the influence of Romanticism, Schleiermacher believed that the fundamental ground of all religious experience was "feeling." Thus, he introduced a strongly subjective element into the interpretive process. Real understanding did not take place with literary or historical

[25] Origen saw these three senses as also relating to three levels of spiritual maturity. The simple Christian benefits from the "flesh," or literal, sense of Scripture; the "more advanced" profits from the "soul" sense of Scripture and the "perfect" is edified by the spiritual sense. See Origen *De Principiis* 4.2.4, cited by Walter C. Kaiser and Moisés Silva, *An Introduction to Biblical Hermeneutics: The Search for Meaning* (Grand Rapids: Zondervan, 1994), 219.

[26] Bernard Ramm points out that the tradition of Jewish allegorism dates back at least as far as Aristobulus (ca. 160 BC), who believed that Greek philosophy borrowed from the OT and that through the allegorical method teachings of Greek philosophy could be found in the Law and the Prophets. See *Protestant Biblical Interpretation*, 26–27.

analysis of the text but when the interpreter through intuition and imagination was able to arrive at an intense identification with the author. The goal of interpretation then was not to determine what the text said; it was to recapture the experience that produced the text and become one with it (Braaten, 132).[27]

In some ways Schleiermacher anticipates and parallels the Subjectivism of the New Hermeneutic and modern Reader-response approaches to interpretation. In both, there is no objective meaning, and certainly no single meaning or interpretation of a text.

Theodore of Mopsuestia (350–428)

One of the prominent theologians in the Antiochian school of interpretation. A contemporary and student colleague of John Chrysostom, Theodore is known for his consistent emphasis on historical exegesis and his orthodox Christology (Dockery, 109–13).

Zwingli, Huldrych (1484–1531)

A Swiss reformer and prolific expositor of the Bible. Although he held to the fourfold sense of Scripture, he nevertheless made the "natural" (or literal) sense his main concern.[28] He, along with Martin Luther and John Calvin, practiced a grammatical-historical approach to interpretation (see Grammatical-historical method). Nevertheless, he avoided a so-called wooden literalism that ignored the figurative and idiomatic use of language. Zwingli was known for his Dogmatic use of Scripture (Terry, 69), but his creed was the whole of Scripture and its teaching, which he regarded as clear compared to the often confusing and contradictory teachings of church tradition. As an ardent defender of *sola Scriptura* he sought to accept no doctrine unless it could be established from the clear teachings of Scripture. Furthermore, the Bible was uniquely the Word of God and Christ. Thus, understanding could come only via faith and the operation of the Holy Spirit on the human heart (McKim 1998, 250–53).

---

[27] For a brief but helpful summary of Schleiermacher's background, see James C. Livingston, *Modern Christian Thought from the Enlightenment to Vatican II* (New York: Macmillan, 1971), 98–112.

[28] For a clear descriptive summary of Zwingli's hermeneutical emphases and contributions, see McKim, ed., *Historical Handbook,* 249–55. Among the hermeneutical principles highlighted are (1) the necessity of faith and the illumination of the Holy Spirit for understanding Scripture; (2) the assertion of the "perspicuity of Scripture" and with it an appeal to let Scripture interpret Scripture, giving priority to the clear passage over the obscure; and (3) the emphasis and priority given to the natural, or literal, sense of Scripture.

4

Interpretive Approaches and Methods

Types of Biblical Criticism

Form criticism (F-C)

The attempt to get behind the written biblical text to a preliterary period when individual units of oral tradition first circulated before becoming part of a literary text. Form critics categorize these units by their literary form, which they believe reflect community needs and situations. They hypothesize that as these units of tradition circulated they were adapted and shaped by the needs of differing communities. Furthermore, they believe that by careful analysis of this shaping process, one can not only identify the original life setting (see *SITZ IM LEBEN*) that gave rise to a particular form, but also reconstruct the history of the early Christian movement.[1] The father of F-C is the OT scholar Hermann Gunkel. In the NT, a pioneering figure of F-C is RUDOLF BULTMANN.

Higher criticism / critics (See HISTORICAL CRITICISM)

Historical criticism (H-C)

The attempt to determine the historical and literary details behind a text that explain its composition (Erickson, 88). Sometimes called "higher criticism," it deals with a whole range of historical and literary considerations, including authorship, date of composition, intended audience, sources used, authenticity of content, historical purpose or occasion, literary unity, genre,

[1] One of the clearest explanations of F-C, its theory, goals, and method, is found in Millard Erickson's *Christian Theology,* 2nd ed. (Grand Rapids: Baker Book House, 1999), 89–98. See also Stephen H. Travis, "Form Criticism," in *New Testament Interpretation: Essays on Principles and Methods,* ed. I. H. Marshall (Grand Rapids: Wm. B. Eerdmans, 1977), 153–64.

and style (Ramm 1970, 9).[2] One goal of H-C is to write a chronological narrative reconstructing the pertinent events and revealing wherever possible the interconnection of the events themselves.[3]

Literary criticism

A flexible term applied to a wide range of concerns within biblical criticism. It is used to refer to "higher" criticism (see Historical criticism). More narrowly it has been applied to Source criticism and its concern to identify the literary sources used in the composition of a writing. It is commonly used to refer to the analysis of the Bible as literature in its formal literary characteristics: language, style, genre, form, and structure. Recent use has expanded its reference to various modern literary approaches, such as Rhetorical criticism, Narrative criticism, and Post-structuralism (Klein, Blomberg, and Hubbard, 428–40; Soulen 1981, 113; McKim 1996, 67).

Lower criticism / critics (see Textual criticism)

Narrative criticism

Traditionally the approach that seeks to explore the genre of narrative and its aesthetic literary quality in regard to characterization, plot development, thematic content, style, symbolism, figurative use of language, etc. (Klein, Blomberg, and Hubbard, 432–33). However, it resurfaces as a new development of modern literary criticism, which identifies the narrative story not with the narrative text itself but as the interaction between the text and the reader (Tate, 94–95).

Implied author

In modern Narrative criticism, the distinction is made between the "real author," who actually wrote the text, and the "implied author," who is a limited reflection of the author in the text. For example, the biblical author of more than one book reveals different portraits of

---

[2] I. Howard Marshall, "Historical Criticism," in *New Testament Interpretation,* ed. Marshall, 126–38.

[3] Note that implicit is a test of the historical accuracy (or authenticity) of the recorded events. Combined with naturalistic presuppositions, modern historical criticism rejects much of the supernatural accounts in Scripture and tends to be skeptical about the historical reliability of the Bible in general. See Robertson McQuilken, *Understanding and Applying the Bible,* rev. ed. (Chicago: Moody Press, 1992), 27–32.

himself from book to book, none of which fully represents the actual historical author (Tate, 195).[4]

Implied reader

Narrative criticism contends that not only is the real historical author lost to the reader (see above) but so also are the original readers. The theory holds that a narrative text is written with a group of readers in mind who are no longer present and therefore no longer accessible to the actual (or modern) reader. Instead the text and its intended message are directed at "implied readers" who represent the readership that the text suggests as the original audience. The actual reader today is called to identify with these "implied readers" and to read the text from their vantage point (Osborne, 162–63).

A controversial question arises as to whether identification with the implied reader is even necessary since, as some suggest, once written a text has an interpretive life all its own. Its meaning is not tied to or dependent on how the original audience understood it. Every reader and audience creates meaning in light of their own historical circumstances.[5]

New criticism

A movement in interpretation that tended to emphasize the form and literary character of the text apart from the historical circumstances that produced it. Furthermore, it held that a text had meaning independent of the author's intent. This not only reopened the fundamental question of where

---

[4] Narrative critics are forgetting that no author is exhaustively known through his/her writing, as writing is only one of many ways people reveal who they are. The writer's limited or incomplete self-disclosure does not mean that the reader has somehow lost contact with the historical author. Such a notion would render even autobiographies meaningless, not to mention all attempts to understand the world's great literary figures through their writings.

[5] Such a view is representative of the interpretation theory of Paul Ricoeur. See Walter C. Kaiser and Moisés Silva, *An Introduction to Biblical Hermeneutics: The Search for Meaning* (Grand Rapids: Zondervan, 1994), 29–30. This author again objects to creating an "implied reader" defined by the text, but then concluding that that reader is not a true reflection of the actual readers. It seems reasonable that exegesis that is diligent to understand the literary character of narrative, becoming informed as to its historical setting, and conducting a careful investigation into the cultural and historical particulars within the story itself can adequately (although not perfectly) recapture the hearing of the original readers. It also seems that this hearing is necessary if the exegete is to move to a contemporary and relevant understanding of the text that agrees with and is faithful to the biblical message.

one locates the meaning of a text,[6] but paved the way for later developments such as the New Hermeneutic and the Reader-response approach, which would emphasize the interpreter's subjective role in the interpretive process (Osborne, 369; Kaiser and Silva, 228, 232). It had its dominant influence from about 1930–60.

Redaction criticism (R-C)

Examines and charts the activity of biblical authors in shaping, modifying, or for some scholars, even *creating* material for the final written product.[7] This final product is seen as reflecting the theology and literary artistry of the author, who is much more than a compiler and passive recorder of tradition (Erickson, 88, 98–100).

Rhetorical criticism

The art of speaking or writing effectively; the study of principles and rules of composition governing writing or speaking as a means of communication or persuasion. Ancient Greeks and Romans stressed the need for rhetorical skill in public speaking, and in all forms of philosophical, political, and legal debate.

Biblical scholars see rhetorical criticism as a useful tool in analyzing biblical texts (especially speeches and epistles) that illustrate the development of thought and arguments used to persuade others of the truth of their beliefs (McKim 1996, 67; Kaiser and Silva, 285; Osborne, 122–23).

Deliberative

Refers to a rhetorical category of speeches or writings intended to persuade, convince, dissuade, or refute someone concerning a proposed action or view (Klein, Blomberg, and Hubbard, 357; Osborne, 419). In deliberative writings one would expect frequent use of exhortations and commands. See Paraenesis.

---

[6] Once again, the three loci of meaning in interpretation are the author, the text, and the reader. By separating the meaning of the text from the author's intended meaning, new criticism made it natural to emphasize the reader's interaction with the text as the place where meaning is to be found.

[7] Evangelicals, for the most part, reject the notion of "creative" redaction. See D. A. Carson, "Redaction Criticism: On the Legitimacy and Illegitimacy of a Literary Tool," in *Scripture and Truth,* ed. D. A. Carson and J. D. Woodbridge (Grand Rapids: Zondervan, 1983), 123–28. On the other hand, Evangelical scholars recognize the utility of R-C to clarify the meaning of the text by providing insight into the theological perspectives and emphases of the author. See Erickson, *Christian Theology,* 102–3.

Epideictic

Refers to a rhetorical category of speeches or writings that seeks to win consent to a particular position or point of view by using praise or blame (Klein, Blomberg, and Hubbard, 357).

Judicial

Refers to a rhetorical category of speeches or writings that addresses the correctness of an action and seeks to persuade an audience by way of accusation or defense (Klein, Blomberg, and Hubbard, 357; Osborne, 419).

Rhetorical Components

In Greco-Roman rhetoric a proper speech as discussed in the writings of Cicero and Quintilian would have the following six components:[8]

Exordium

The introduction of a speech that states the reason for the address and attempts to build rapport or create a climate of goodwill between the speaker and the audience.

Narratio

The part of the speech that would establish the facts of the case as agreed upon by both parties. It would also provide background information that provides a context for what is being proposed or argued.

Probatio / Confirmatio

The logical presentation of the proofs or arguments in support of the speaker's proposition. Often the speaker would appeal to his or her audience's feelings or sound judgment.

Propositio / Partitio

The enumeration of the contested points on both sides of the case, often delineating what is agreed upon and what is disputed.

---

[8] The descriptive definitions are a composite taken from Grant R. Osborne, *The Hermeneutical Spiral: A Comprehensive Introduction to Biblical Interpretation* (Downers Grove, Ill.: InterVarsity Press, 1991), 123–24; and Bernard Hungerford Brinsmead, *Galatians—Dialogical Response to Opponents* (Chico, Calif.: Scholars Press, 1982), 44–45. Two excellent works that explore the NT writings against the features of rhetorical criticism are G. A. Kennedy, *New Testament Interpretation through Rhetorical Criticism* (Chapel Hill: University of North Carolina Press, 1994); and Burton Mack, *Rhetoric and the New Testament,* Guides to Biblical Scholarship (Minneapolis: Fortress Press, 1990).

Refutatio

The negative counterpart to the Probatio and sometimes linked to it. This component contains the refutation of the opposing views. It could also include a digression (as with Paul) that provides additional information.

Peroratio / Conclusio

The conclusion where the main arguments are summarized and a final emotional appeal is made to the audience.

Sociological criticism (or "Social-scientific analysis")

An approach that attempts to understand the ideas and practices of the Bible as socioreligious phenomena. In other words, it views the religious ideas and practices in the Bible against the backdrop of various methods of sociological analysis. This approach can be very helpful in illuminating the cultural world behind the biblical text, thus aiding in interpretation. It can also be problematic as many social scientists come to the study of religion with humanistic and naturalistic assumptions that conflict with the biblical worldview.[9]

Source criticism

The effort to determine the various traditions and literary sources used in the composition of the books of the Bible. Its most notable proponent is Julius Wellhausen, who theorized that the Pentateuch was the compilation of various documents that reflect the evolutionary development of Israel's religion. His theory became known as the "Documentary Hypothesis."[10] That the biblical authors used written sources seems undeniable, not only because of their explicit statements (Num. 21:14; Luke 1:1) but also because of the ample evidence within the biblical documents themselves. For example, when parallel accounts in the Gospels are compared, there is both similarity and dissimilarity in words, order of events, content, ideas, and style. It is more than probable that in addition to knowledge of oral traditions, the authors of the Gospels had access to many written sources. Source critics look

---

[9] For a helpful introduction to sociological criticism, including an assessment of both strengths and weaknesses, see Robert Mulholland Jr., "Sociological Criticism," in *New Testament Criticism and Interpretation,* ed. D. A. Black and D. S. Dockery (Grand Rapids: Zondervan, 1991), 296–316.

[10] For a clear and concise survey of OT source criticism and the "Documentary Hypothesis," see Bill T. Arnold and Bryan E. Beyer, *Encountering the Old Testament: A Christian Survey* (Grand Rapids: Baker Books, 1999), 69–72. The authors point out that Wellhausen was

for internal evidence of the author's editorial work in combining a number of sources.[11] The emphasis shifts from interpretation to the literary development of the text and what it reveals about the theology of the author and/or the communities that produced it (Tate, 176–79; Wenham, 139–52). See also FORM CRITICISM.

Structural criticism (also "Structuralism")

A method of interpreting a text based on the presupposition that the human mind, irrespective of culture or time, processes data in a predictable way, reflecting universal patterns (DEEP STRUCTURES) of thought and worldview that are revealed through language. The assumption is that the text contains these embedded patterns whether the author was aware of them or not. Consequently, the meaning of the text does not lie in the words as they express the intentional thought of the author but in the text itself, in the words and its structure. How the text was understood historically is of little importance to the structural critic (Klein, Blomberg, and Hubbard, 429; Soulen 1981, 182–85).

Actantial analysis

Done by structuralists on narrative stories to analyze how a plot is developed in terms of six characters or objects (called "actants"). They are set in a predictable pattern that develops a conflict between actants and moves toward a proposed resolution of the conflict (Klein, Blomberg, and Hubbard, 429; Osborne, 371f).

Deep structures

Refers to modes of thinking or thought processes that are universal, constant, and transcultural, and which express themselves through language. They are constant despite the many ways they are expressed through the SURFACE STRUCTURES (see below) in a piece of literature.

Paradigmatic analysis

A second mode of analysis conducted by structuralists. It sees the Scriptures as religious myth, which they understand as written to address

---

one in a long line of source critics who, guided by Enlightenment rationalism, rejected the unique and supernatural character of divine revelation.

[11] David Wenham discusses the internal evidence that points to the author's editorial work in using his sources. See David Wenham, "Source Criticism," in *New Testament Interpretation*, ed. Marshall, 140–45.

some sort of opposition or conflict. Such myth attempts to alleviate or remedy that opposition. For example, the Book of Leviticus might be viewed as proposing sacrifice as a way to address the sense of alienation before a holy God (Klein, Blomberg, and Hubbard, 431f).

Surface structures

In structuralism, the overt or obvious literary components of a text. With narrative, for example, such components would include thematic content and development, plot, characterization, etc. Structuralism does not regard surface structures as overly important but secondary to the DEEP STRUCTURES, which reveal the deeper substructure of thought and thus the meaning of the text (Osborne, 372).

Textual criticism

Also called LOWER CRITICISM, refers to the science that seeks to restore or recover the original form of an ancient text.[12] To do this, it collects, analyzes, and compares all manuscript copies of a given text. Then, using established criteria and principles of evaluation, it seeks to determine the exact wording of the original manuscript.

Interpretive gloss

Refers to a marginal note that appears in a textual manuscript believed to be put there by a later editor (or "redactor") to provide information for an interpretive context. During the MIDDLE AGES scholars often penned quotations from various church fathers in the margins of the Bible and sometimes between the lines (Klein, Blomberg, and Hubbard, 38).

Variant

When two or more Greek or Hebrew manuscripts differ in wording from a critically prepared OT or NT text, the differing forms are called "variants." Textual critics compare all known variants of a particular reading to determine which represents the original form of the text.

---

[12] A short, concise, and clearly written article that contains a helpful description of the task and method of textual criticism is Michael Holmes, "Textual Criticism," in *New Testament Criticism*, ed. Black and Dockery, 101–34.

Methods, Movements, and Approaches

Allegorization (See ALEXANDRIAN SCHOOL and ALLEGORICAL INTERPRETATION, ch. 2)

Deconstruction (or "Deconstructionism")

A movement in hermeneutics, pioneered by Jacques Derrida, essentially calling into question whether language (or text) has the ability to communicate.[13] Basically Derrida's revolt is a philosophical one that denies the epistemological adequacy of language to convey truth about reality. This is so because language is metaphorical in nature. Derrida rejects the Western hermeneutical notion that there is metaphysical reality in the world that words refer to. Instead, writing as a human activity shapes culture and is shaped by culture, in effect creating its own perception of reality. The interpreter engages in a never-ending, ever-changing process of creating change in, and being changed by, culture. Therefore, writing has no intrinsic meaning or "presence." There is no fixed objective meaning to a text. There is no authorial intention to be determined, because in the act of writing the author's intention (presence) is immediately lost and there is no longer any connection between the original author and the text. Therefore, one cannot know the original meaning of a text (Osborne, 382–83; Tate, 202–4).[14]

Demythologization

A program of interpretation that rests on two philosophical presuppositions and commitments: existentialism and naturalism. For RUDOLF BULTMANN, the NT was written in a prescientific period. Consequently, the NT world is filled with mystery and miracle described through myth.[15] The enlightened

---

[13] For a clarifying description of this approach and an analysis of its relationship to structuralism and post-structuralism, see Osborne, *Hermeneutical Spiral,* 369–86. It is somewhat ironic that Derrida is forced to rely on language in order to deny its intrinsic or objective meaning. One wonders if Derrida did not secretly hope his readers would postpone the application of his theory long enough to understand the words used to convey it.

[14] The abstract and philosophical concepts behind Deconstruction make it difficult to define in a few words. A helpful article that deals with the philosophical roots of Deconstruction is Robert P. Scharlemann, "Deconstruction: What Is It?" *Dialog* 26, no. 3 (Fall 1978): 184–88.

[15] Myth is an attempt in a prescientific age to present unexplained phenomena according to a first-century worldview where angels, demons, and God's miraculous intervention abound.

modern knows that the universe is a closed continuum of immutable natural law. Anything in the NT that contradicts this paradigm can be discarded as the outmoded language of a mythological worldview. Since the true message/content (Ger. *Sache*) of the *kerygma* is existential by nature but was encrusted with mythological language, the interpreter must strip away the myth in order to uncover the existential truth embedded in the text.

Devotional approach

Is probably the most common approach to interpretation among Christians. It refers to reading and interpreting Scripture for the purpose of promoting spiritual growth and edification. As such it shares the same goals as the Pietists (see Pietism). However, this popular approach has two inherent weaknesses. First, it rarely takes note of what the words of Scripture meant to the biblical author, but seeks instead a private interpretation that is relevant and speaks to one's personal situation. Secondly, in pursuit of a blessing it frequently spiritualizes (see Spiritualize) and even allegorizes (see Allegorize) the text, often arriving at strange meanings totally unrelated to the meaning and message of the text (Duvall and Hays, 181–82).

Discourse analysis

The mapping of the propositional flow of thought in a passage of Scripture by showing the grammatical relationships of the words in a text and their syntactical structure within a larger literary unit, or Pericope. Of particular importance is identifying how subordinate clauses relate to their main clauses. Such analysis is often enlarged to include the literary connections between sections of a discourse or episodes in a narrative section (Klein, Blomberg, and Hubbard, 206–14; Duvall and Hays, 67–70).

Dispensational approach

Characterizes hermeneutics done within a dispensational framework of theology. Dispensationalism divides the history of salvation into a number of distinct periods, or dispensations.[16] Each is marked by a revelation of God concerning how humans are to respond to His will and the specific details of their obedience (Virkler, 122). As the Bible records, humans have consistently failed to comply with God's revealed will. This has elicited the mercy of God in giving a new set of responsibilities under a new discipline. Thus, each dispensation describes a different redemptive arrangement, or economy, with

[16] The exact number of these periods is disputed. Usually it ranges from four to nine. Very common among dispensationalists is the number seven.

specified terms of obedience whereby people are regarded righteous before God (Virkler, 121–28; Erickson, 1169).[17]

The problem this approach presents for hermeneutics is the same as that of any Dogmatic approach. Exegesis tends to be controlled by the theological system and cannot easily challenge or instruct the doctrines within that system (Kaiser and Silva, 264). Furthermore, dispensationalists tend to interpret the Scripture (especially prophecy) literally whenever possible. See Literal method.

Dogmatic approach

Refers to biblical interpretation done within the framework of a theological system or confession of faith to which the interpreter is committed. This surfaces the debate over what should have priority, exegesis or one's theological system and doctrinal commitments.[18]

Ethnohermeneutics

An approach to interpretation that seeks to bring the meaning of a text forward to a contemporary understanding and application in the modern world (Kaiser and Silva, 178).[19] For those desiring to communicate unchanging biblical truth in cross-cultural contexts, this approach obviously parallels the concerns of Contextualization. To do this there must be an examination and understanding of three "horizons": (1) the biblical culture, (2) the interpreter's culture, and (3) the receptor's culture. The challenge for

---

[17] Ryrie provides a list of seven dispensations: (1) of Innocence (Gen. 1:28–3:6) until the Fall; (2) of Conscience (Gen. 4:1–8:14); (3) of Civil Government (Gen. 8:15–11:9); (4) of Promise (to Abraham—Gen. 11:10–Ex. 18:27); (5) of Law (Mosaic—Ex. 19:1–Acts 1:26); (6) of Grace (Acts 2:1–Rev. 19:21); (7) of the Millennium (Rev. 20). See Charles C. Ryrie, *Dispensationalism Today* (Chicago: Moody Press, 1965), 57–64. It is important to add that the different dispensations do not represent different ways to salvation. The means of salvation remain constant—by grace through faith. Nevertheless, each dispensation does contain a revelation of how faith-obedience is to be expressed.

[18] Walter C. Kaiser, Jr. and Moisés Silva conduct a cordial debate in *Introduction to Biblical Hermeneutics*. Kaiser, in his chapter (11) on the theological use of the Bible, makes the point that to insure that doctrines do not go beyond the scriptural evidence, exegesis must be prior to any system of doctrine. Conversely, Silva, in chapter 14, makes a case for "Calvinistic hermeneutics." He states that one's doctrinal commitments inevitably affect exegesis and that is both essential and desirable. It is not a question of whether theological commitments have a say, but which ones—and do they aid in understanding Scripture as a whole.

[19] Kaiser credits Larry Caldwell with coining the term and developing the approach in Larry W. Caldwell, "Third Horizon Ethnohermeneutics: Reevaluating New Testament Hermeneutical Models for Intercultural Bible Interpreters Today," *Asian Journal of Theology*, no. 1 (1987): 314–33. See Kaiser, *Introduction to Biblical Hermeneutics*, 178.

practitioners of this approach is to keep one horizon from dominating or silencing the other two, such that the biblical message or truth is lost, distorted, or severely compromised.[20]

Ethnolinguistics

An outgrowth of ETHNOHERMENEUTICS whereby biblical statements are regarded as culturally conditioned and therefore binding only on the original receptor culture. They represent the cultural hull that can be discarded in order to reach the kernel or truth principle that has enduring validity (McQuilken, 34).[21]

Existential approach

An approach to biblical interpretation within the philosophical framework of existentialism and its worldview. In this approach a person's freedom to passionately choose the course or direction of life is the expression of true human existence. Interpretation that proceeds from this foundational perspective stresses a personal and subjective experience of truth rather than a rational and objective understanding of a text. See CHRISTIAN EXISTENTIALISM and NEOORTHODOXY.

---

[20] While not using the term "ethnohermeneutics," Rene Padilla insightfully describes this approach. See "The Interpreted Word: Reflections of Contextual Hermeneutics," in *A Guide to Contemporary Hermeneutics: Major Trends in Biblical Interpretation,* ed. Donald K. McKim (Grand Rapids: Wm. B. Eerdmans, 1986), 297–308.

[21] At first glance this looks very much like the process of CONTEXTUALIZATION. However, it is sometimes difficult to determine which statements are culturally conditioned and which transcend culture and have enduring validity. There is, of course, a marked difference between those statements that contain clear reference to a cultural form (e.g., Paul's command for women to wear a head covering [1 Cor. 11:2–16]) and those that do not (e.g., Paul's command to stop lying [Col. 3:9]). However, a problem arises when the modern receptor culture interjects dominant values which are at odds with the biblical culture. Then, it is not as easy to determine what is "hull" and what is "kernel." As modern culture becomes increasingly secular and postmodern, rejecting or challenging all moral and social norms tied to biblical revelation, Christians are pressured to broaden the scope of what they regard as "culturally determined" in the Bible and therefore no longer binding on modern Christians. There is a need to develop a method of interpretation that seeks enlightenment from the entire biblical canon and applies it to texts that bear on controversial social and cultural issues. While I do not endorse all of his conclusions, William J. Webb has admirably attempted the construction of such a method entitled a "redemptive movement hermeneutic." See William J. Webb, *Slaves, Women and Homosexuals: Exploring the Hermeneutics of Cultural Analysis* (Downers Grove, Ill.: InterVarsity Press, 2001).

Feminist hermeneutics

A movement within American biblical interpretation that emerged in the 1960s and rose quickly to prominence around 1970 (Soulen and Soulen 2001, 58–59).[22] Feminist biblical interpretation itself exists in a variety of forms, from the most liberal/radical to the nonevangelical to the evangelical. Distinctions can be drawn depending on how the Scriptures are viewed, used, and interpreted. The first category of feminists would have little use for the Christian Church or the Scriptures, viewing both as hopelessly patriarchal and contributing to the oppression of women.[23] Feminists of the second category see the Scriptures as inherently patriarchal and seek to liberate the Bible from itself. They do this by reinterpreting it so as to mute what is offensive or by viewing portions of Scripture as nonauthoritative.[24] Evangelical feminists hold to the authoritative status of Scripture.[25] They generally seek not to overturn the testimony of Scripture, but to correct what they view as a biased patriarchal interpretation within the Church (Klein, Blomberg, and Hubbard, 96–98). Their goal is better exegesis that will allow us to see and appreciate the role of women in God's plan and purpose for humanity and the Church.[26]

Grammatical-historical method (or "Historical-cultural")

Refers to interpretation that pays close attention to both the language the text was written in and the cultural-historical setting or occasion that produced

---

[22] For our purposes, feminist biblical interpretation must be distinguished from the movement known as the "feminist movement" or "feminism" which has more of a social and political agenda directed at achieving gender equality in society at large. Nevertheless, some would argue that they are inseparably linked, the movement providing the inspiration for challenging all social structures and all societal institutions that contribute to the oppression and discrimination against women, including that done by the Church. Thus, feminists view the Bible and its traditional interpretation as instrumental to that oppression, and advocate new ways of interpreting the Scriptures. For a very helpful discussion and evaluation of both the positive contributions and the pitfalls of feminist interpretation, see William W. Klein, Craig L. Blomberg, and Robert L. Hubbard, *Introduction to Biblical Interpretation,* rev. ed. (Nashville, Tenn.: Thomas Nelson, 1993), 96–101.

[23] Mary Daly would be representative of a feminist in this category. See her *Quintessence: Realizing the Archaic Future—A Radical Elemental Feminist Manifesto* (Boston: Beacon, 1998).

[24] Any of the works of Elizabeth Schüssler Fiorenza would serve to illustrate this category. See especially her classic work, *In Memory of Her: A Feminist Theological Reconstruction of Christian Origins* (New York: Crossroad, 1983).

[25] C. C. Kroger and R. C. Kroger, *I Suffer Not a Woman: Rethinking 1 Timothy 2:11–15 in Light of Ancient Evidence* (Grand Rapids: Baker Book House, 1992).

[26] Not all evangelical feminist interpreters are of the same stripe. Basically they are divided between the "egalitarians," who reject the notion of male headship and abiding roles in the

it (Kaiser and Silva, 19). Its first goal is to arrive at the meaning intended by the author and understood by the original recipients. Its second goal is to express that meaning in contemporary language consistent with the ideas understood and expressed in the biblical culture and context (Klein, Blomberg, and Hubbard, 174–79).

Hermeneutical circle

Refers to the interpretive process whereby the interpreter understands the words of text in relationship to their larger verbal and literary contexts: phrases, clauses, sentences, paragraphs, chapters/sections, and even the whole literary work. In turn, understanding the individual words helps to understand the text as a whole. This process of understanding the part by the whole and the whole by the part is circular and continues until the meaning of a text is achieved (Stein 1994, 33).

Proponents of the New Hermeneutic have developed what some have called the "vertical" dimension of the hermeneutical circle (Soulen 1981, 85).[27] Here the subjectivity of the interpreter comes into play. Both the interpreter and the text (i.e., the human mind expressed in it) share some common ground of human experience within their respective "horizons." Questions are put to the text from the interpreter's experiential framework, but the questions are shaped by the subject matter in the text that interprets human existence. The reader interprets the text by the questions he or she asks, but the text is also interpreting the reader by providing answers that shape and determine what questions are asked.

Since the above process is never ending, nor the outcome the same for any two interpreters, this version of the hermeneutical circle can never produce an objective, final meaning.[28]

---

family and/or Church based on gender; and "complementarians," who hold that men and women are equal in essential worth and dignity, but possess different roles in God's plan for both the family and Church that allows for the headship role of men. See A. J. Köstenberger, T. R. Schreiner, and H. S. Baldwin, *Women in the Church: A Fresh Analysis of 1 Timothy 2:9–15* (Grand Rapids: Baker Book House, 1995).

[27] This dimension was actually introduced much earlier by Friedrich Schleiermacher (1768–1834) and his successor Wilhelm Dilthey (1833–1911); however, it is the New Hermeneutic under the influence of Heidegger (1889–1976) and Gadamer that exerts the greatest influence on hermeneutical theory. See Richard N. Soulen, *Handbook of Biblical Criticism,* 2nd ed. (Atlanta: John Knox Press, 1981), 85.

[28] Evangelicals have developed their own version of this vertical dimension of the hermeneutical circle without surrendering the possibility of objective textual meaning. See Graham N. Stanton, "Presuppositions in New Testament Interpretation," in *New Testament Interpretation,* ed. Marshall, 68–70.

Hermeneutical spiral

A spin-off of the HERMENEUTICAL CIRCLE and a proposed solution to the problem of maintaining the distinction between objective textual MEANING and its SIGNIFICANCE for the interpreter, yet at the same time uniting both aspects in the interpretive process. The interpreter approaches the text with his or her own PRE-UNDERSTANDING and questions for the purpose of determining its meaning. There is a fusion of horizons (see HORIZONS, FUSION OF), and the interpreter's pre-understanding is adjusted by the answers given in this exchange. When the interpreter next approaches the text, his or her pre-understanding is different and so the questions put to the text will be modified. The process is continuous and spirals toward a more and more complete and accurate interpretation of the text.

An evangelical version of the hermeneutical spiral sees the goal of determining the author's intended meaning as legitimate. This is accomplished through grammatical-historical exegesis (see GRAMMATICAL-HISTORICAL METHOD). It is this meaning that informs the interpreter and shapes the questions he or she then asks of the text, resulting in a fusion of horizons. However, the text is given an authoritative role to challenge and reshape the interpreter's pre-understanding and proposed questions when they are at odds with what the Scriptures teach (Osborne, 324).[29]

The Pentecostal interpreter should recognize that the Holy Spirit plays a dynamic role in the hermeneutical spiral. As the "Spirit of truth," He has been given to guide and lead into all truth (John 16:13). As the interpreter seeks to understand not only the author's intended meaning but also its SIGNIFICANCE and APPLICATION to the Christian life, there must be a conscious dependence on and sensitivity to the work of the Spirit.[30]

Literal method (See *SENSUS LITERALIS*)

Taking the words of Scripture in their plain, simple, ordinary sense as intended by the biblical author in his own literary and cultural-historical setting. One does not depart from the literal meaning of words unless warranted by

[29] For example, the reader comes to the text of Acts 4:12 ("Salvation is found in no one else, for there is no other name under heaven given to men by which we must be saved") with a postmodern PRE-UNDERSTANDING of the nature of religious truth. His pluralism will be sorely challenged by the meaning of the text as it reflects that of the original author. If the reader is a Christian who regards the Scriptures as God's inspired, inerrant Word, he or she is not free to look for a meaning that circumvents the authorial intent of this text.

[30] This is not to suggest some mystical, irrational method of intuition detached from exegesis of the biblical text. The tradition of the Protestant REFORMATION by its insistence on both the clarity of Scripture and the need for the Spirit-illumination has long and wisely maintained the unity of both Word and Spirit (Bernard L. Ramm, *Protestant Biblical Interpretation,* 3rd

faith or the nature of the literature itself (McQuilken, 170–73).[31] Thus, this approach is not a "wooden literalism" that ignores idioms, figures of speech, or symbolic language (Ramm 1970, 119–27).

Naturalistic approach(es)

Approaches that deny that there is a supernatural origin or causation for anything.[32] Naturalism is a branch of philosophy that interprets all phenomena in the universe according to the belief that scientific laws of cause and effect are adequate to account for all events and objects. Consequently naturalistic approaches to interpretation tend to either reject the Bible's witness to the supernatural or minimize it by seeking naturalistic explanations for miraculous events. Such approaches also tend to be overly rationalistic and set human reason as a competing authority to the authority of Scripture. When there is a clash of worldviews or interpretations of reality, the naturalist usually defers to the judgment of reason over scriptural revelation.

Post-structuralism (P-S)

Sometimes referred to as the "new literary criticism" (see Literary criticism), encompasses hermeneutical developments that extend and surpass the work of structuralism. If the latter argues that the text (its structure) is the meaning, P-S reinserts the reader/interpreter into the interpretive process such that the "ultimate significance" (see Significance) of a text cannot be stated unless there is a creative engagement or interplay between the reader and text whereby the reader *completes* the meaning of the text. As such the mind, beliefs, and perspectives of the reader determine the meaning of the text, not the text itself.[33]

---

ed. [Grand Rapids: Baker Book House, 1970], 54–58). Luther, in his defense of literal interpretation, writes, "For the Holy Spirit is the all-simplest writer that is in heaven or earth." Cited by Walter C. Kaiser Jr. in *Toward an Exegetical Theology: Biblical Exegesis for Preaching and Teaching* (Grand Rapids: Baker Book House, 1981), 61.

[31] McQuilken provides some very helpful guidelines. The words of Scripture should be interpreted literally unless (1) to do so would result in a statement that is irrational, unreasonable, or absurd; (2) the context or literary character of the text indicates that a nonliteral sense is intended by the author; (3) to do so would result in a contradiction of a clear teaching taught elsewhere in Scripture. See McQuilken, *Understanding and Applying the Bible,* 170–71.

[32] For a helpful description of "naturalistic approaches" to interpretation, see McQuilken, *Understanding and Applying the Bible,* 27–35.

[33] Osborne gives two reasons for this: (1) In this approach the author is dead, and his historical intentionality died with him; he is no longer accessible. (2) The text takes on an autonomous life of its own independent of the author as soon is it is written. Therefore the meaning of a text cannot be limited to what the biblical author intended or what the original readers understood. See Osborne, *Hermeneutical Spiral,* 376.

Readers from differing perspectives interpret a text in dialogue with various faith communities. This generates plural meanings (see POLYSEMY), each containing valid truth within the perspective of the individual community.

P-S is grounded in the complex philosophy of language called SEMIOTICS and thus stresses how meaning is created through language (linguistic sign systems). It views language as metaphor, devoid of meaning until the meaning is supplied by the reader. The result is that no interpretation is final, complete, or correct, since each reader provides his or her own content and meaning (Osborne, 374–76; Klein, Blomberg, and Hubbard, 438–40).[34]

Proof-text method

The citation of a single biblical text or passage as support or justification for a doctrinal position or argument (also called "proof-texting") (McKim 1996, 223). In principle this practice is not objectionable, provided the verses cited are carefully exegeted or interpreted. However, the term usually refers to the arbitrary use of isolated verses that are detached from their immediate literary context (Virkler, 84; Kaiser and Silva, 31–32, 285).

Reader-response approach / criticism

An approach to textual interpretation that views the reader as the determining agent in the discovery and construction of meaning. The author's intent is often minimized and sometimes dismissed as irrelevant or irretrievable. The emphasis is not on determining what a text meant, but what it now means to the reader-interpreter. Meaning is derived from an interaction between text

[34] Osborne demonstrates the problem with this approach by pointing out that all verbal communication assumes the adequacy of language to convey the speaker/writer's thoughts and the importance of doing so for meaningful communication. He writes, "You, the reader, do not know me, the author. The text of this book does not truly reflect my personality. That is, of course, obvious; the question, however, is whether it adequately reflects my thoughts on the possibility of meaning. Can you as reader understand my opposition to polyvalence, or is this text autonomous from my views?" After he acknowledges that not all who read will agree with him he writes, "The question is not whether they will agree but whether they can understand my arguments? The issue has two aspects: can we know what another person meant in a written account, and is it important to know the original intended meaning?" See Osborne, *Hermeneutical Spiral,* 376–77. A personal experience illustrates the problematic nature of post-structuralism on a popular level. Recently, a friend of the author, after a lengthy visit, sent a thank-you card with a personal note attached. Whereas my wife and I read the note and sighed at her thoughtfulness, another family member read the same words as a slight and was offended. At that moment, the textual meaning which reflected the intent of the author became very important.

and reader, and the response of a reader constitutes its meaning. This approach assumes the plurality of meanings (see Polysemy), since no two readers will read the text in the same way or have exactly the same response to it (Kaiser and Silva, 285; Klein, Blomberg, and Hubbard, 439).[35]

Supernaturalistic approach(es)

Interpretive approaches that have as a foundational presupposition the belief that the Bible is supernatural in its origin and nature. Such an approach acknowledges God as the divine author behind the human authors of Scripture. Consequently the Bible is, in a literal sense, the Word of God. Nevertheless, the Bible is a literary product produced by human authors who received God's revelation through a unique process of divine inspiration (2 Peter 1:21). It accepts the accounts of God's miraculous activity recorded in the Bible as factual and historical and generally does not confine such activity to the biblical past (McQuilken, 37–47).

Syntactical-theological exegesis

Advocated by Walter C. Kaiser, Jr. as a necessary supplement to Exegesis by the Grammatical-historical method. The term "syntactical" refers to the search for the literal meaning of the words according to their grammatical function within a sentence and in relation to the immediate literary context. In addition, the words are understood according to the historical setting in which the text was written. However, the latter term, "theological," acknowledges that the historical sense of a text must be expanded to explore how that meaning can find theological relevance, both with respect to the larger theological enterprise and to its application to the contemporary life of the Church (Kaiser 1981, 88–89; Kaiser and Silva, 33–34).

Traditional interpretation

Exegesis done with reference to an established doctrinal norm or standard of Orthodoxy. Such interpretation is often criticized because functionally the

---

[35] Needless to say the reader-response approach produces a wide range of diverse interpretations without apology because in principle every reading can be a valid reading. There is no objective meaning in the text itself nor any "correct" interpretation, only the potential for limitless competing interpretations. One obvious problem for those who hold to the Bible as the authoritative Word of God is that the meaning intended by the inspired author is lost. Reader-response criticism offers no way to establish a normative interpretation, let alone the canonical one. See Klein, Blomberg, and Hubbard, *Biblical Interpretation,* rev. ed., 73–75. For a sympathetic literary analysis of this approach, see Edgar V. McKnight, *Postmodern Use of the Bible: The Emergence of Reader-Oriented Criticism* (Nashville, Tenn.: Abingdon Press, 1988), 217–63.

tradition is equated with what Scripture teaches and therefore controls interpretation (Klein, Blomberg, and Hubbard, 33; Ramm 1970, 39–40).

Typological interpretation (also "Typology")

Finding in OT events, persons, institutions, offices, actions, and objects a divinely inspired foreshadowing of God's later (usually in the NT) activity or revealed truth. This approach is best represented by the early church fathers of the Apostolic Period and the NT authors themselves. It flows out of the conviction that the OT is a Christian book, i.e., that both OT and NT bear witness to God's plan of redemption in Jesus Christ. As such it falls within the promise-fulfillment motif of prophecy (Duvall and Hays, 186) but lacks literal verbal prediction. To be sure, the symbolic nature of typology, where something represents something else, carries with it the danger of devolving into allegory. However, one cardinal distinction must be seen. Typology is rooted in the actual history of redemption and is present in Scripture by divine design and intention. Allegory is seldom, if ever, grounded in history and is a product of human imagination[36] (Kaiser 1981, 106–110; McQuilken, 259–66; Ramm 1970, 227–32).

Due to the expansive nature of prophetic symbols, identification of specific TYPES and their corresponding ANTITYPES can be quite subjective. It seems best to limit typology to those types and antitypes that the NT authors clearly identify (Duvall and Hays, 188; McQuilken, 265).[37]

Antitype

The anticipated truth or reality prefigured or foreshadowed by the OT TYPE.

[36] The oft-cited exception of Gal. 4:24 where Paul uses the verb *allēgoreo* to describe the old and new covenants under the figures of Hagar and Sarah is inconclusive. As Ramm and others have pointed out, the term is capable of a number of meanings, including reference to an expanded typological sense which includes the use of OT material for illustrational purposes. See Ramm, *Protestant Biblical Interpretation,* 226–27, 258–69; McQuilken, *Understanding and Applying the Bible,* 262–65.

[37] There is debate over whether typology should be limited to scriptural material that is specifically identified by typological language used by NT authors or expanded to include types that can be inferred from the identification of typological subjects (e.g., the tabernacle, priesthood, and sacrifices, as pictured in the Book of Hebrews). See Ramm, *Protestant Biblical Interpretation,* 218–21. A full-length treatment of typology is conducted by Patrick Fairbair in *The Typology of Scripture* (Grand Rapids: Zondervan, 1952).

Type

A prophetic symbol that uses some OT event, person, institution, office, action, or object to foreshadow some truth or divine action later revealed or accomplished by God in the course of redemptive history.

5

Literary Genres

Apocalypse (Gk., "uncovering, revelation")

A kind of ancient prophetic literature, Jewish and Christian, that claims to be God's revelation of his coming judgment and deliverance at the end of history (this "present age").[1] Most of the apocalyptic writings that exist today were written from about 200 BC to AD 200. However, biblical apocalypses have their roots in OT prophetic literature and can be found in portions of Daniel (7–12), Ezekiel (38–39), Isaiah (24–27), and Zechariah (9–14). The most notable NT apocalypse is the Book of Revelation, which has epistolary elements as well (Duvall and Hays, 273–76).

Apocalyptic literature is marked by a number of distinctive characteristics,[2] the most challenging of which is its use of symbolic language and imagery. In an apocalypse the "seer" is given a revelation through an angelic messenger in a dream or vision. What he sees through prophetic vision belongs to

---

1 Some distinctions in terminology are helpful: "apocalypse" refers to the genre of literature; "apocalyptic" (as a noun and adjective) refers to the eschatological framework and perspective within a select group of writings; "apocalypticism" refers to the sociological ideology (and historical movement) that marks the literature as distinct. Graeme Goldsworthy, *Preaching the Whole Bible as Christian Scripture* (Grand Rapids: Wm. B. Eerdmans, 2000), 219. An extremely helpful discussion of apocalyptic literature, its thematic content, and literary characteristics can be found in George E. Ladd, "Apocalyptic Literature," in *The International Standard Bible Encyclopedia*, Vol. 1, 1979, 151–61. Ladd not only discusses universal characteristics of apocalyptic literature, but shows how OT and NT apocalypse diverge from noncanonical apocalypses. Apocalyptic literature has been examined from both a literary and social perspective. As literature, it is described in terms of its internal thematic content and stylistic elements. As a social phenomena, it is regarded as a historical movement that reflects a distinct way of looking at the world from the particular socioreligious setting that produced or shaped that perspective. For an introduction to these two complementary approaches to apocalyptic literature, see J. J. Collins, *Daniel: With an Introduction to Apocalyptic Literature*, FOTL 20 (Grand Rapids: Wm. B. Eerdmans, 1984), 2–24.

2 Among those most commonly listed are (1) visionary motif, the source of revelation; (2) use of symbolic language; (3) pseudonymity, false claim of authorship (certainly not true of Revelation [1:4] and OT biblical apocalypses, unless traditional authorship is rejected); (4)

another world, a heavenly sphere of existence.[3] The symbolic images have hidden meaning and must be decoded before the message can be understood. Extensive historical and cultural investigation will serve to uncover much of the meaning behind apocalyptic imagery, which on the surface can seem strange, even bizarre and unintelligible (Fee and Stuart, 208; Goldsworthy, 218–21).

Futurist

The interpretive approach to Revelation that views most of the events recorded in the Apocalypse (esp. 6–21) as awaiting a future fulfillment.

Historicist

The interpretive approach to Revelation that views the events recorded in the Apocalypse as depicting events occurring throughout the entire Church Age.

Idealist

The interpretive approach to Revelation that does not view the events recorded in the Apocalypse as literal or historical (whether past, present or future), but as symbolic pictures of the perennial struggle between good and evil.

Preterist

The interpretive approach to Revelation that views the events recorded in the Apocalypse as past, depicting historical events in the first century of the Church.

Comedy

Not a funny or amusing story but one with a happy ending. That is, a biblical comedy has a characteristic plot in which problems or crises develop

---

pessimistic tone, the present and future paints a bleak picture; (5) eschatological, emphasis on God bringing about an end to history (this age); (6) deterministic, God is in control of history, which is moving toward a divinely appointed end; (7) dualism, contrasting opposites are seen in two distinct ages, the present age and the age to come, and two rival supernatural powers, God and Satan (note that in biblical apocalypses, Satan is not an adversary equal to God, although his moral and spiritual antagonist. He remains a creature and ultimately under God's dominion and control).

3 J. J. Collins sees the revelation of otherworldly reality via angelic mediation as essential to the genre of an apocalypse. His definition reads, "Apocalypse is a genre of revelatory literature with a narrative framework, in which a revelation is mediated by an otherworldly being to a human recipient disclosing a transcendent reality." See "Towards the Morphology of a Genre," *Semeia* 14 (1979): 9, cited by Goldsworthy, *Preaching the Whole Bible*, 219.

and must be resolved or overcome. Characteristic features in comedies are disguises or mistaken identities, escapes from danger, dramatic reversals, or an unexpected turn of events. The most recognized comedies in the Bible are the stories of Joseph (Gen 37–50) and the Book of Esther[4] (Ryken, 81–82; Klein, Blomberg, and Hubbard, 268–70).

Dominical saying (Lat. *Dominus,* "lord")

Refers to any saying attributed to the Lord, usually in the Gospels, e.g., "For even the Son of Man did not come to be served, but to serve, and to give his life as a ransom for many" (Mark 10:45).

Doxology (Gk., "a word of glory")

A formal expression of praise, often in poetic form. In religion it refers to a formal liturgical prayer of praise or adoration to God or Christ.

> Now to the King eternal, immortal, invisible, the only God, *be* honor and glory forever and ever. Amen.
> —1 Tim. 1:17, NASB

Epistles

NT letters[5] written to churches and individuals by various apostles and other apostolic associates[6] (see APOSTOLIC FATHERS). In a sense NT letters were authoritative substitutes for the personal presence of the author (usually an apostle). They were written not as literary works but to address real-life problems and situations in the church (see OCCASIONAL). Thus, the primary purpose behind their composition was practical, and the theology that we find is harnessed in the service of a particular need (Fee and Stuart, 49). This being the case, the interpreter of epistles must work to reconstruct the occasion of the letter, i.e., the original situational context that brought forth a particular NT letter (see SITZ IM LEBEN). In doing so, it is helpful to determine not only

---

4 A concise description of the literary features of biblical comedies is found in Ryken, *Bible as Literature*, 81–82. A helpful discussion of how to interpret biblical comedy is found in Klein, Blomberg, and Hubbard, *An Introduction to Biblical Interpretation*, 269–70.

5 While Adolf Diessmannt argued for the distinction between true letters, which were not formal literary compositions, and epistles, which were formal literary works, most scholars do not adhere to that distinction and use the terms interchangeably. See Aune, *The New Testament in Its Literary Environment*, 161.

6 Foremost among the criteria used by the first century church in determining the scriptural status of an early Christian document was apostolicity. A document was considered "apostolic" not only if it came from an apostle (or someone close enough to insure access to the apostolic well-spring of tradition), but whether the character of its content conformed to the teachings (oral and written) of the Apostles. See F. F. Bruce, *The Canon of Scripture* (Downers Grove, Ill.: InterVarsity Press, 1988), 256–59.

its structure[7] but the type of letter represented, as each type is tied to a specific literary purpose (Aune 1987, 158–62; Duvall and Hays, 217–29). Keep in mind also that a letter can incorporate the elements of more than one type.

Ambassadorial letter

One kind of official letter that would be sent in the Greco-Roman world. Its purpose was to establish goodwill in preparation for the visit of a dignitary, thus securing a favorable reception. Paul sent such a communication to Rome,[8] which he hoped to visit (Rom. 15:22–33) on his way to Spain. He no doubt intended to seek their support for his missionary travels (Klein, Blomberg, and Hubbard, 358).

Apologetic letter (Gk. *apologia,* "defense")

An apology is a type of Judicial rhetoric, which conducts an oral or literary defense of a particular position. Thus, an "apologetic" letter seeks to persuade or convince by arguing in defense of someone or something. In 2 Corinthians Paul seeks to defend the legitimacy of his apostleship over the criticisms and false accusations of his opponents who seek to replace him (see esp. 10–13).[9]

Deliberative

> I am amazed that you are so quickly deserting Him who called you by the grace of Christ, for a different gospel; which is *really* not another; only there are some who are disturbing you and want to distort the gospel of Christ. –Gal. 1:6-7, NASB

A rhetorical category of speech employed in epistles that have as their literary purpose to convince or dissuade someone concerning the advantages or disadvantages of a future course of action (Klein, Blomberg, and Hubbard, 357). Galatians is a deliberative letter in that it seeks to convince the Galatians of their foolishness in

---

[7] Ancient Greco-Roman letters had three components, much like our letters today: an introduction, a body, and a conclusion. Each of the main parts have different elements depending on the letter type. Scholars differ over the number of epistolary types but most agree that the types reflect function and thus serve to illuminate the literary purpose of the letter. Aune lists six widely acknowledged types: (1) friendship letters, (2) family letters, (3) epideictic letters of praise and blame, (4) letters of exhortation, (5) letters of recommendation, and (6) juridical letters that accuse, defend, or give an accounting. For a comprehensive survey of the proposed types of letters, see Aune, *New Testament*, 158–82.

[8] Jewett explains the long salutation at the end of the letter (ch. 16) as the evidence that Paul is using commendation (Epideictic rhetoric) to secure a favorable response to his visit and message. See Robert Jewett, "Romans as an Ambassadorial Letter," *Interpretation*, 36 (1982): 5–20.

[9] For a concise summary of the criticisms and accusations Paul faced from his Corinthian

abandoning the grace of Christ by insisting on circumcision and the keeping of the law.

Epideictic

A rhetorical category of speech employed in epistles that uses praise or blame to urge people to adopt a position or continue to practice a set of values. In this regard, the letter to the Hebrews is epideictic in that the author both commends and censures[10] his readers in exhorting them not to abandon their Christian faith (Aune 1987, 212–13; Klein, Blomberg, and Hubbard, 357).

Haustafeln (Ger., "household rule")

A technical term within LITERARY CRITICISM that refers to a series of rules that define the reciprocal roles of various relationships, e.g., husbands and wives, parents and children, masters and slaves. These rules reflect the social culture of the first century and the Early Church's accommodation to it. The interpreter seeking relevance and application for today must look for the abiding truth principle behind the culture-laden "household rules" (Soulen 1981, 91; Fee and Stuart, 65–69).

> Wives, submit to your husbands...
> Husbands, love your wives...
> Children, obey your parents...
> Fathers, do not exasperate your children...
> Slaves, obey your earthly masters...
> Masters, treat your slaves...
> –Eph. 5:22,25; 6:1,5,9

Judicial

A rhetorical category of speech originally used in Greco-Roman courts to convince an audience (usually the judge) of the merits of a case. As used in NT epistles, it attempts to convince the readers of the rightness or wrongness of a past action (Aune 1987, 198).

Paraenesis (Gk., "exhortation, advice")

A technical term of FORM CRITICISM that refers to moral or ethical exhortation, counsel, and instruction. In Paul's writings, it comes

opponents, see James D. Hernando, "2 Corinthians," in *The Full Life New Testament Commentary* (Grand Rapids: Zondervan Pub. Co., 1998), 920–22.

[10] See Heb. 2:1–3; 5:11–12; 6:1–12; 10:25–27,32–36; 12:4,5; 13:7. Richard Soulen makes the following insightful comment: "Paul admonishes believers to become what faith declares him to already be in Christ." See *Handbook of Biblical Criticism*, 140.

> *I urge you*, brethren, by the mercies of God, *to present your bodies a living and holy sacrifice*, acceptable to God, which is your spiritual service of worship.
> –Rom. 12:1, NASB

characteristically at the end of his epistles, after he has laid down a foundation of theological truth.[11] These sections are marked by a concentration of commands (imperatives) and exhortations (Soulen 1981, 140–41).

Fable

A short fictitious story given to teach and emphasize an important truth or message. Often the story is legendary, where unreal supernatural happenings occur. In Jud. 9:8–15 Jotham, the sole surviving son of Gideon, tells the people of Shechem a fable about trees (the Shechemites) searching about for a king among different kinds of trees only to find a thorn bush (Abimilech) to rule over them. The symbolic character of the fable in some ways resembles a Parable, but the surreal nature of the story sets it apart (see also Allegory) (Klein, Blomberg, and Hubbard, 272).[12]

Genre (see Genre, ch. 1)

A specific type of literary composition characterized by a particular form (literary style and characteristics), function (purpose), and content (subject matter). The Bible is composed of a wide range of literary genres and no book is made up of only one genre. Each genre is tied to the preunderstanding of its author and his purpose in writing. Therefore, understanding the literary genre of a work leads us toward the author's purpose. Moreover, insight into the literary nature of a genre helps us frame appropriate questions of the text that are in line with that purpose (Aune 1987, 17–43).

Gospels

Faith-portraits of the life, teachings, ministry, death and resurrection of Jesus Christ. Although predominantly narrative, the gospels are not historical biographies in the strict sense of the term. They combine historical memory and theological reflection.[13] That is to say, while there is considerable debate

---

[11] For example, 1 Thess. 4–5; 2 Thess. 2:15ff; Gal. 5–6; Rom. 12–13; Col. 3–4; Eph. 5–6.

[12] Both parables and fables are fictitious; however, parables have an earthly quality in that the story is grounded in real-life situations.

[13] This combination does not warrant the conclusion that because the gospels are theologically motivated they are for that reason historically suspect or unreliable. For an excellent discussion of this issue, see Craig L. Blomberg, *The Historical Reliability of the Gospels* (Downers Grove, Ill.: InterVarsity Press, 1987). For a brief but illuminating introduction to this issue, see Lee Strobel's interview with Blomberg in *The Case for Christ* (Grand Rapids: Zondervan, 1998).

over the influence of ancient literary types on the Gospels, it is generally conceded that Christianity created a new literary genre.[14]

Because there are four gospels about Jesus (rather than by him), each of them represents a complementary presentation of the story. Each author, or "evangelist," has a story to tell from his own perspective, informed no doubt by experience as well as by his oral and written sources (see Luke 1:1–4).[15] Thus, the interpreter should read and interpret a gospel both "horizontally," in comparison with parallel passages in other gospels, and "vertically," within itself according to the structure and thematic content given by the individual evangelist (Fee and Stuart, 109–16; Klein, Blomberg, and Hubbard, 327–30). See Redaction criticism.

Aretalogy (Gk. *aretē*, "virtue")

In Hellenistic literature a praise-filled work recounting the miraculous deeds and exploits of a particular deity. It was used as propaganda to promote the worship of that deity. In relation to Source criticism, aretalogies are seen as collections of miracle stories that were used to extol the virtues and powers of a heroic "divine-man" (Gk. *theios aner*) figure. Modern critics think the Gospels were an adaptation of this genre of ancient literature in form and content. However, it seems apparent that the Gospels possess a balanced reality that is absent from aretalogies[16] and a main character whose deeds far surpass the heroes of the Greco-Roman aretalogies (D. Ferguson, 258; Soulen 1981, 25–26).

---

[14] David Aune conducts a thorough comparative analysis of the Gospels with a wide range of Jewish and Hellenistic literature, after which he concludes that the Gospels should be regarded as a subtype of Hellenistic biography (37). However, even before his analysis he has to admit that "The gospels are also 'unique' in the sense that no other ancient composition, Greco-Roman or Jewish, is exactly like them." See David E. Aune, "The Gospels: Biography or Theology?" *Bible Review* 6, no. 1 (February 1990): 15–37. A fuller analysis is made in his earlier book with the same conclusion, but one quickly becomes aware that when the form, function, and content (genre elements) of the Gospels are compared to a wide range of Greco-Roman historical and biographical writings, Aune is pointing out as many differences as parallels. See Aune, *New Testament*, 17–76.

[15] The Gospels reflect at least three historical contexts that must be considered in their interpretation: (1) that of first century Judaism, (2) the immediate historical setting in the time and life of Jesus, and (3) the historical context of the Gospel author. This author acknowledges that the third context is embedded in the Gospel text but offers a word of caution: Exegesis is compromised when interpretation becomes so fixated on the evangelist and his community and what he was experiencing and teaching through the text that the historical Jesus and his circumstances are all but ignored.

[16] While a collection of miracle stories has a significant parallel in the Gospels, the exaggerated accounts of hero worship in aretalogies does not compare well with the sober reality of the Gospels. In the latter the passion accounts of Christ's rejection, suffering, and death occupy an

Law (Heb. *torah*, "instruction"; Gk. *nomos*, "law")

Usually refers to the more than six hundred commandments found in the OT.[17] It also refers to the first five books of the OT known as the "Book of the Law" (Josh. 1:8) (written by Moses), which defined the terms of God's covenant with Israel. Inasmuch as the whole OT contains instruction on how Israel may live faithfully in covenant with God, it is not surprising that the NT used the term to refer to the OT in its entirety.[18]

The question that immediately comes to the surface is, How should a NT Christian interpret and apply OT laws originally intended for historical Israel? Paul certainly understood the Law to be a part of "all Scripture" that is "inspired" and "profitable for teaching, for reproof, for correction, for training in righteousness" (2 Tim. 3:16, NASB). The challenge, then, for the NT believer is to discover the meaning and relevancy of OT law for Christian life and faith.[19]

Apodictic laws

> When you reap the harvest of your land, *do not reap to the very edges of your field or gather the gleanings of your harvest.*
> –Lev. 19:9

Refers to laws that are stated in an absolute, unconditional, or unqualified manner, either as commands or prohibitions (e.g., "you shall" or "shall not" do something). Behind apodictic law lies some moral, spiritual, or theological principle that has relevance and instructional value for NT Christians. However, because these laws

---

even more central focus than his miracles. The one notable exception may be Philostratus' *Life of Apollonius of Tyana*, which has numerous parallels with the life of Jesus in the Gospels. See D. Ferguson, *Backgrounds of Early Christianity*, 361–63. However, as H. C. Kee has demonstrated in his careful inductive search of Philostratus' work, the so-called miracles of Apollonius are hardly the kind that point to his divinity. Moreover, neither in Philostratus' account of Apollonius nor in any extant aretalogy is there a clear example of the hero *being martyred*. See Kee, "Aretalogy and Gospel," *Journal of Biblical Literature* 92 (1973): 405–8.

[17] OT form critics identify four collections of law codes: Covenant (Ex. 20:22 through 23:33), Holiness (Lev. 17–26), Deuteronomic (Deut. 12–26), and Priestly (Ex. 25–31; 34:29; Lev. 16; parts of Numbers). See Klein, Blomberg, and Hubbard, *Introduction to Biblical Interpretation*, 275.

[18] The Hebrew OT Scriptures in Jesus' day comprised three sections: the Torah, or Law (the Pentateuch); the *Nebim*, or Prophets; and the *Kethubim*, or the Writings. What is interesting is that in the NT the term "law" is used to summarize the "Law or the Prophets" (Matt. 5:17–18) or refer to material in the Psalms (part of the so-called Writings) (John 10:34). Thus, the "law" was capable of referring to the whole of the OT. See Luke 16:17 and Titus 3:9.

[19] For very helpful guidelines and principles for interpreting OT law, see Fee and Stuart, *How to Read the Bible*, 150–56, and Klein, Blomberg, and Hubbard, *Introduction to Biblical Interpretation*, 278–84. Duvall and Hays provide illustrative examples of such interpretation in *Grasping God's Word*, 321–31. For a survey of scholarly views regarding the relevance of the Law for the Christian and an attempt to present Paul's understanding of the subject, see Stephen Westerholm, *Israel's Law and the Church's Faith* (Grand Rapids: Wm. B. Eerdmans, 1988).

are usually culturally specific, careful historical and cultural study is needed to uncover the relevant principle to be applied. Moreover, the commandments or prohibitions, although stated categorically (without exceptions), are not exhaustive but offer a principle by way of a representative example. The interpreter who tries to replicate the literal obedience of the original recipients will more often than not miss the truth principle these laws were intended to convey[20] (Klein, Blomberg, and Hubbard, 276–77; Fee and Stuart, 139–40).

Casuistic laws

> If a man uncovers a pit or digs one and fails to cover it and an ox or a donkey falls into it, the owner of the pit must pay for the loss.
> –Ex. 21:33,34

Case-by-case laws related to the religious, civil, and ethical life of Israel, describing a situation and then the prescribed action to be taken. As a consequence, they are culturally specific and conditional. As such they belong to the old covenant and are limited in their applicability to the Christian. However, they do reveal the character of God and his will regarding various culturally specific situations, and so provide teaching that can instruct us today as we seek God's guidance and will for our lives (Fee and Stuart, 141–42; Klein, Blomberg, and Hubbard, 275–76).[21]

Narrative (also "historical narrative")

The literary form that tells a story. The most common and extensive genre in the Bible,[22] it recounts specific time-space events within the larger context of redemptive history (i.e., God's dealings with humanity for the ultimate purpose of salvation) in Scripture (Kaiser and Silva, 69). Consequently, narratives are not merely stories about Bible characters and events but stories

[20] The example given in the text box from Lev. 19:9 has to do with God's concern for the poor, which is a reflection of his mercy and compassion. God's people, Israel, who were themselves the recipients of that merciful compassion, were to reflect this aspect of God's nature in their treatment of the poor and aliens among them.

[21] Ex. 21 is filled with casuistic laws that deal with situations that demand a respect for human life and property. Here, as elsewhere, the need to compensate the victim is clear. The principle of just compensation/restitution can guide a Christian's personal and business dealings whether or not we ever dig a pit, leave it uncovered, and have an animal fall into it.

[22] Scholars differ on the amount of biblical material identified as narrative, depending no doubt on the characteristics they deem essential to this genre. The figures range from well over a third to nearly half. See Kaiser and Silva, *Introduction to Hermeneutics*, 69, and Duvall and Hays, *Grasping God's Word*, 249.

with a theological purpose. Simply put, they tell us something about what God did, what God is like, and something about his redemptive purpose for humanity. However, the genre of narrative is also complex. Interpretation requires insight into the author's use and development of setting, plot, dialogue, characters, rhetorical devices, and narrative structure.[23] Thus the narrative's teaching is more implicit than explicit, the story illustrating a truth that is often directly taught elsewhere (Fee and Stuart, 75–78).[24]

One important and multifaceted issue often raised among literary critics deserves mention. It involves the question of whether the stories of the Bible are historical, since a story can yield a message whether or not the events recorded in the story actually happened. The assertion is made that the narrative story has meaning in and of itself and is not dependent on the historicity of what it records, or the author's intended meaning (see Hans Frei). Keep in mind, however, that the theological truth-message of the biblical narrative often rests on the historical reality of the events recorded. Furthermore, not only do the biblical authors assume this reality, but it is their interpretation of those events that we seek as God's inspired message.[25]

Epic

A kind of Heroic narrative (see below) that consists of an expansive narrative recounting the exploits of a virtuous hero whose life is identified with the destiny of a nation. Epics often contain a series of heroic narratives surrounding the life of a prominent biblical figure. The story of Joseph (Gen 37–50) and the Book of Joshua are examples of biblical epics (Ryken, 79–80).

Heroic Narrative

A hero story that focuses on the life and exploits of a prominent biblical figure. The hero's life not only shares the struggles common to people, but also embodies and exemplifies values and virtues esteemed by the

[23] Two very helpful introductions to narrative as a literary genre and a discussion of its key literary features are Kaiser and Silva, *Introduction to Hermeneutics*, 69–79, and Duvall and Hays, *Grasping God's Word*, 296–305.

[24] The reader of OT narrative comes across some very negative behavior without it being said that what the person did was evil or wrong. For example, Jephthah's vow does not have to be labeled "foolish" or "sinful." The story judges it so by the outcome. However, beyond that, the story is written to people who already knew the law and its condemnation of human sacrifice (Lev. 18:21; Deut. 12:31; 18:10).

[25] Robert Stein summarizes various attempts to salvage meaning while denying the historicity of biblical narrative. See *Interpreting the Bible*, 153–57. A fuller treatment of narrative as history is provided by Walter Kaiser in *Exegetical Theology*, 79–84. The importance of history to theology is

people of God. Biblical examples would be the lives of Moses, Abraham, Joseph, Ruth, and David. The Book of Judges is a collection of heroic narratives (Ryken, 75–78; Klein, Blomberg, and Hubbard, 264–65).

Report

Refers to biblical narration that contains short accounts of a past situation or event written about in the third person. Reports contain the plain record of the facts without literary enhancement or development. They are the building blocks of more elaborate narrative stories, such as the HEROIC NARRATIVE and EPIC. There are different kinds of reports, which are categorized by the kind of subject matter reported (Klein, Blomberg, and Hubbard, 262–64).[26]

Parable (Gk. *parabolē,* "something placed alongside")

Simple stories that illustrate a moral or spiritual truth, most commonly about the kingdom of God. The literary definition of a parable[27] is a SIMILE extended into a story. However, the term is used of a number of related figures of speech,[28] including SIMILITUDES, PARABOLIC SAYINGS, and even ALLEGORY (Ryken, 145–53).[29] So-called true parables contain a story with a beginning, ending, and plot: e.g., the parables of the Good Samaritan, the Lost Sheep, the Prodigal Son, the Great Supper, the Laborers in the Vineyard, and in the OT, Nathan's parable told to David (2 Sam. 12:1–4).

For a functional definition, it is hard to improve on that of C. H. Dodd: "A parable at its simplest . . . is a metaphor or simile drawn from nature or com-

---

evident throughout Scripture. What possible theological value could the passion narratives in the Gospels have if the events surrounding Jesus' sufferings, death, and resurrection never happened?

[26] Klein, Blomberg, and Hubbard list six kinds of reports: anecdote (an individual's personal experience), battle report, construction report, dream report, epiphany report, and memoir (written in the first person). See *Introduction to Biblical Interpretation*, 262–64.

[27] A most helpful work for introducing students to the interpretation of parables is McQuilken's chapter (13) on "Parables" in *Understanding and Applying the Bible*, 185–97. Mickelsen's chapter on "Extended Figures of Speech" in *Interpreting the Bible*, 212–30, is helpful for understanding the structure and thematic emphases of NT parables. Two more recent and comprehensive works on NT parables are Craig L. Blomberg, *Interpreting the Parables* (Downers Grove, Ill.: InterVarsity Press, 1989), and David Wenham, *The Parables of Jesus* (Downers Grove, Ill.: InterVarsity Press, 1989).

[28] This is so because *parabolē* is related to the Hebrew poetic device *mashal*, which can refer to a wide range of figurative speech. See MASHAL.

[29] Ryken does not think parables and allegories are identical in nature, but that they certainly share common characteristics and that parables are allegorical and can be interpreted as such. See *How to Read the Bible as Literature* (Grand Rapids: Zondervan, 1984), 145–53. For an opposing view see Berkeley Mickelsen, *Interpreting the Bible*, 212–35.

mon life, arresting the hearer by its vividness or strangeness, and leaving the mind in sufficient doubt about its precise application to rouse it into active thought."[30] See also Mashal.

Parabolic saying

Pithy sayings that employ metaphors or similes, e.g. "You are the salt of the earth," or "The kingdom of heaven is like a mustard seed" (Matt. 5:13) (then followed by a Similitude).

Similitude

A running metaphor which compares things that share common traits or characteristics. E.g., the Parable of the Leaven, the Sower and the Seed, the Mustard Seed. These are similar to modern day sermon illustrations that are used to make a point.[31]

Poetry

A literary genre characterized by figurative language and imagery, the use of parallelism, terseness of form, and Rhetorical devices.[32] Next to narrative, poetry is the most common biblical genre, composing a significant portion of the Bible, especially the OT. Poetry is further characterized by its frequent use of Commissive language that is aimed at either creating vivid mental images or evoking a strong emotional response (Kaiser and Silva, 87–91; Klein, Blomberg, and Hubbard, 241–50; Stein 1994, 123).

Stich (Gk. *stichos,* "row or verse")

The technical term for a line of poetry, commonly used to describe Hebrew Parallelism. Two parallel lines are called a "distich," and three lines are called a "tristich" (Klein, Blomberg, and Hubbard, 227).

Prophecy

Refers to the proclamation of the revealed will of God to his people by an inspired prophet who is acting as his mouthpiece or spokesperson. Prophecy is a complex genre posing far too many challenges to enumerate here. For ex-

---

[30] C. H. Dodd, *The Parables of the Kingdom*, rev. ed. (London: Nisbet, 1955), 16.

[31] Mickelsen sees parables and similitudes as "almost identical" and therefore includes both under his discussion of "parables." See Berkeley Mickelsen, *Interpreting the Bible* (Grand Rapids: Wm B. Eerdmans, 1963), 212–30.

[32] A descriptive summary of "The Poetry of the Bible" and "Types of Biblical Poetry" can be found in chapters 4 and 5 of Leland Ryken, *Bible as Literature*, 87–129.

ample, people often associate biblical prophecy with the foretelling of future events, yet for as many prophetic books as there are in the Bible,[33] by comparison there is far more proclamation than prediction, more "forthtelling" than "foretelling."[34]

The prophetic books are collections of prophetic Oracles spoken on specific historical occasions to Israel, Judah, and sometimes other nations. In them God often reminded his people of their responsibilities under his covenant, its blessings and its curses (e.g., Deut. 27–28). When that message touches the future, the prophecy often becomes predictive.

Predictive prophecy presents a multitude of interpretive challenges. One important task for the interpreter is to deal with the Occasional nature of a prophetic oracle and determine what it meant to the original recipients.[35] Other challenges are determining whether the prophetic language is literal or figurative, whether the predictive prophecies are conditional or unconditional, were fulfilled in whole or in part (i.e., in the past or if some part awaits future fulfillment), whether the audience is individual or corporate, and whether they apply only to Israel or embrace the NT church (Ramm, *Protestant Biblical Interpretation*, 245–57).[36]

---

[33] Isaiah, Jeremiah, Ezekiel, and Daniel are called the major prophets. The last twelve books of the OT are referred to as the minor prophets. The designations "major" and "minor" make no judgment as to importance but are a recognition of the length of the books in those collections.

[34] Fee and Stuart make this point, but to the extreme, pointing to the meager percentages of predictive prophecy dealing with the coming of the Messiah (2%), the new covenant (5%), and events yet to come (1%). (See *How to Read the Bible*, 150.) But such a narrow focus distorts the picture. In J. Barton Payne's comprehensive encyclopedia on biblical prophecy, he presents a more accurate picture in that he deals with all topics treated in predictive prophecy. He calculates that there are 8,352 out of a total 31,124 verses in the Bible or 26.83% that can be categorized as predictive (*Encyclopedia of Biblical Prophecy* [New York: Harper and Row, 1973], 631–82). Walter Kaiser endorses the latter picture, which includes all prophecy dealing with future events. See Kaiser and Silva, *Introduction to Hermeneutics*, 139–40. However, even if we accept Payne's analysis, both scholars agree that prophecy is predominantly "forthtelling."

[35] The historical gap between the modern reader and the original setting of the oracle is a considerable obstacle to interpretation. The prophet is responding to a situation many details of which he does not rehearse or explain. Moreover, the cultural and language gaps create additional obstacles. Interpretation of prophecy demands an understanding of Israel's history in general and a careful reconstruction of the historical setting of the oracle. See *Sitz im leben*.

[36] For a discussion of the nature of prophetic literature, see Osborne, *The Hermeneutical Spiral*, 211–14; Fee and Stuart, *How to Read the Bible*, 149–55; Kaiser and Silva, *Introduction to Hermeneutics*, 139–47; and Ramm, *Protestant Biblical Interpretation*, 244–50. Concerning the basic types of prophecy, see Klein, Blomberg, and Hubbard, *Introduction to Biblical Interpretation*, 292–302; and Osborne, 214–16. For principles of interpreting prophecy and extracting teaching relevant for the NT church, see Duvall and Hays, *Grasping God's Word*,

Hortatory/Paraenetic prophecy

The type of prophecy that exhorts God's people to a specific course of action (e.g., repentance from sin, true worship). The prophets were God's spokesmen who had the primary responsibility of declaring the will of God to his people and to encourage them to remain faithful to His covenant with them.

Oracle

A self-contained unit of inspired prophetic speech recorded in the Bible. Prophetic books are a collection of oracles given at different times and under a specific set of historical circumstances. It is best to interpret passages within the context of the oracle that contains them. Oracles include a variety of literary genres and forms. Interpreters of prophecy are wise to become familiar with the character and content of these forms. Three of the more common forms are legal (or lawsuit) oracles, woe oracles, and salvation (or promise) oracles (Fee and Stuart, 160;[37] Klein, Blomberg, and Hubbard, 292–302).

Prophetic perspective

> As for me, I baptize you with water for repentance, but He who is coming after me is mightier than I . . . *He will baptize you with the Holy Spirit and fire.* –Matt. 3:11, NASB

One of the problematic aspects of prophetic interpretation: Often the prophet brings together separate events in his prediction of the future so that events that are distinct and distant in respect to time are presented as one event. It can be likened to looking through a telescope, which flattens the landscape so that objects both near and far appear on the same horizon and the same distance away. Similarly, the prophets received prophetic visions of the future but did not see the time gaps between future events (Duvall and Hays, 370–71; Kaiser and Silva, 143–44; Fee and Stuart, 164–65). See text box.[38]

365–73, Fee and Stuart, 151–67; and Kaiser and Silva, 148–56; Kaiser, *Toward an Exegetical Theology*, 185–96; Osborne, 216–20; and Ramm, 251–72.

[37] Legal/lawsuit oracles recount God calling Israel to trial on charges of violating the terms of his covenant. Thus it is sometimes called a covenant lawsuit speech. The woe oracle is a type of disaster prophecy introduced by a declaration of "woe" upon evil doers and an announcement of impending judgment. Salvation/promise oracles look forward in hope to a day of restoration and blessing for people or nations after judgment has been served. For a fuller discussion and literary analysis of these and other types of oracles, see Klein, Blomberg, and Hubbard, *Introduction to Biblical Interpretation*, 292–99.

[38] Rather than interpret John's words in such a way that Jesus' baptism in the "Holy Spirit and fire" refer to one event, it seems more likely that John, due to "prophetic perspective," is collapsing two

Psalm(s) (Gk. *psalmos*)

> O daughters of Israel, weep for Saul, who clothed you in scarlet and finery, who adorned your garments with ornaments of gold.
> –2 Sam. 1:24

The Greek term *psalmoi* in the Septuagint translates the Hebrew word *tehillim*, which means "praises."[39] This indicates that the Psalms were a collection of inspired prayers and hymns used in Israel's temple worship,[40] and often sung to musical accompaniment. The title or superscriptions attribute seventy-three of the psalms to David,[41] suggesting the collection may have begun during Israel's united monarchy, although the final collection probably was completed in the postexilic period for worship in the rebuilt temple.

Psalms as Hebrew poetry are a distinct genre, having a number of categories, all functioning to give inspired expression of prayer, praise, lament, and other forms of reflection on God.[42] The purposes vary according to the circumstances and perspectives of the psalmist, whose passion, candor, and vulnerability make for easy identification with the modern reader. The most distinguishing literary feature of the Psalms is PARALLELISM.

---

events into one: the Baptism in the Holy Spirit, fulfilled on the Day of Pentecost, and the eschatological judgment symbolized by "fire" at his second coming. This seems more likely when you observe that the surrounding metaphors—"the axe being laid to the root" (v. 10), the "winnowing fork," the "threshing floor," and burning chaff with unquenchable fire (v. 12)—are all clearly symbolic of judgment. See C. Keener, *IVP Bible Background Commentary*, 52–53.

[39] For a very helpful nontechnical introduction to the interpretation of the Psalms, see Tremper Longman III, *How to Read the Psalms* (Downers Grove, Ill.: InterVarsity Press, 1988). A more comprehensive treatment, guiding the reader toward independent interpretation and theological understanding, is provided by C. Hassell Bullock, *Encountering the Book of Psalms: A Literary and Theological Introduction* (Grand Rapids: Baker Academic, 2001).

[40] This is suggested also by the structure of the collection in the Bible. The 150 psalms are divided into five books (I—1–41; II—42–72; III—73–89; IV—90–106; V—107–150) with Ps. 1 acting as an introduction and Ps. 150 providing a closing doxology. See Stephen L. Harris, *Understanding the Bible*, 4th ed. (Mountain View, Calif.: Mayfield Publishing Co, 1997), 213.

[41] In addition, Moses is credited with authorship of one (Ps. 90), Solomon two (Ps. 72, 127), twelve to the sons of Korah, twelve to Asaph, and one each to Ethan and Heman. It should be noted that the superscriptions were not added until the final editing of the collection and are not regarded as the inspired text. Consequently, the historical value of these titles must remain an open question.

[42] This is evident from the functional/thematic categories the Psalms can be divided into: (1) of lament, (2) of thanksgiving, (3) of praise, (4) of salvation history (review of), (5) of celebration and affirmation (includes covenant renewal, enthronement, and royal psalms, plus the so-called Songs of Zion), (6) wisdom psalms, and (7) of trust. The categorization of the Psalms differs from scholar to scholar, depending on whether his/her categories stress theme or function. Fee and Stuart (above) have combined both and given a helpful description of these categories. See *How to Read the Bible*, 175–77.

Two cautions are needed for interpreters of the Psalms. First, while the Psalms contain doctrine, their primary purpose is liturgical not doctrinal.[43] Therefore, we need to exercise caution in assuming that what is stated or described translates immediately into doctrine. Secondly, as Hebrew poetry, the Psalms are full of metaphors, symbols, i.e., nonliteral language. Moreover, the language of the Psalms is often highly emotive (see COMMISSIVE LANGUAGE) and expresses the raw emotion of the psalmist's reaction to trial, tragedy, and triumph. The interpreter must distinguish between what is expressed in the psalm and what is taught by the psalmist (Fee and Stuart, 169–85; Harris, 212–15; Duvall and Hays, 351–52).[44]

Dirge

A funeral lament that was part of ancient mourning rites. It included expressions of lament, description of some disaster (the cause of lament), and a call to people to join in mourning. Although the Psalms contain no pure examples of dirges, their literary influence can be seen in several psalms (35, 44, 74, 137), in the Book of Lamentations, and in the private laments of David (2 Sam. 1:19–27; 3:33–34), as well as being embedded in the prophetic material (Klein, Blomberg, and Hubbard, 272–73, 285–86).

Imprecatory (psalms)

Psalms of lament (or complaint) that vividly call for God's judgment and wrath to fall on the author's enemies. The problem for many critics lies in the fact that both what the psalmist asks for and the disposition he petitions in seem anything but "Christian." The interpreter must remember that imprecatory language is intentionally exaggerated (see

[43] That is, they were given by God to help us to express ourselves to him and to reflect on his person and ways in the course of life's joys, sorrows, and changing circumstances. See Fee and Stuart, *How to Read the Bible*, 169. This author needs to make a qualifying comment in view of 2 Tim. 3:16 and the fact that an OT professor and friend is in the process of writing a book on the theology of the Psalms. In a Sunday School course he admirably demonstrated that collectively the Psalms has a lot to teach about God and that when a content analysis is conducted, the doctrine in Psalms is substantive, coherent, and consistent. Another point he makes questions why we conclude that inspired worship and religious reflection cannot have a theological or didactic purpose. Simply put, why do we not consider the possibility that the Psalms represent just another (albeit different) way God teaches His people?

[44] A clear and illustrated way of interpreting two different kinds of psalms is given by Fee and Stuart in *How to Read the Bible*, 178–81. For a list and discussion of the principles of interpretation for Hebrew poetry, see Klein, Blomberg, and Hubbard, *Introduction to Biblical Interpretation*, 290–91.

HYPERBOLE) to convey the intensity of the psalmist's feelings of outrage over evil, injustice, etc. Moreover, in the majority of cases the psalmist is speaking as a representative of God's people who under his covenant had promised to avenge Israel on her enemies (Ps. 94:1–1; Deut. 32:35). Therefore, imprecatory psalms are not requests for personal vengeance but a passionate appeal to God for national justice.[45]

Wisdom literature

A collection of biblical writings[46] that contains a description of how to live in a "wise" manner before God.[47] Wisdom in the Bible is the life application of knowledge or truth learned from experience (Fee and Stuart, 187, 189). That is to say, wisdom is very practical and does not expound truth that is merely theoretical. Wisdom literature does not designate a single genre but is made up of a combination of various subgenres (see below).[48] Consequently, interpreters must acquaint themselves with the various literary features and characteristics of each subgenre they encounter (Kaiser and Silva, 99–103).

Admonition

A subgenre of wisdom literature that teaches what wisdom is not by issuing a warning against a particular course of action. Often there is some

> *Do not say*, "I'll pay you back for this wrong!" Wait for the LORD, and he will deliver you.—Prov. 20:22

[45] For an excellent presentation of the imprecatory psalms, the moral problem raised, proposed solutions, and an exploration of their theological context, see Bullock, *Encountering the Book of Psalms*, 227–38.

[46] The three universally recognized wisdom books in the Scriptures are Proverbs, Ecclesiastes, and Job. Some scholars include the Song of Songs in the wisdom category. See Kaiser and Silva, *Introduction to Hermeneutics*, 87, and Duvall and Hays, *Grasping God's Word*, 376, 379. In addition, a number of Psalms are regarded as wisdom psalms, depending on what characteristic features are used to qualify them as such. Fee and Stuart list eight: 36, 37, 49, 73, 112, 127, 128, 133. See *How to Read the Bible*, 177. Kaiser and Silva drop two from the above list and add six of their own: 1, 19b, 32, 34, 37, 49, 78, 111, 112, 119, 127, 128, 133. See *Introduction to Biblical Hermeneutics*, 199.

[47] Wisdom literature for the most part assumes its readers are members of God's covenantal people. Therefore, if the "fear of God" is the beginning of wisdom (see Ps. 111:10), then a wise person lives and demonstrates such wisdom by keeping the commandments of the Lord (i.e., the Torah). As the "Preacher" of Ecclesiastes writes, "Fear God and keep his commandments, for this is the whole [duty] of man" (Ecc. 12:13).

[48] An extremely helpful introduction to the nature of wisdom literature, its various forms and their interpretation can be found in Gordon D. Fee and Douglas Stuart, *How to Read the Bible For All Its Worth* (Grand Rapids: Zondervan, 1982), 187–204. See also Duvall and Hays, *Grasping God's Word*, 376–95.

indication of the negative consequences that will follow if the counsel is left unheeded (Kaiser and Silva, 102).

Dialogue

A literary device wherein some aspect of wisdom or a perplexing question is discussed between two or more parties. Job is the clearest example of a wisdom dialogue that tackles the question and meaning of human suffering. The dialogue between Job and his so-called comforters explores the question in view of their understanding of the nature of God, His righteousness, and sovereignty in particular.

Proverb

> Misfortune pursues the sinner, but prosperity is the reward of the righteous.
> –Prov. 13:21

A pithy wisdom saying,[49] which often uses figurative language to express a general truth about life. They are found throughout the Bible, but concentrated in the OT book of Proverbs. Proverbs give God's perspective on a wide range of topics. They describe what is generally true as observed in life and nature. They should not be treated as statements of universal law, promises, or absolute truth without exception (Stein 1994, 83–87; Kaiser and Silva, 99–100).[50]

Riddle

> He replied, "Out of the eater, something to eat; out of the strong, something sweet."
> –Jud. 14:14

A literary device designed to perplex and befuddle the reader or hearer by obscuring or hiding some elements so that the meaning is not easily understood. This obscurity is by design, intended to test the mental skills of those attempting to solve it (Kaiser and Silva, 100).

[49] Terms used interchangeably with "proverb" are "maxim," "adage," "aphorism."

[50] In Matt. 26:52 Jesus utters this wisdom, saying to Peter, "For all who draw the sword will die by the sword." Obviously this does not mean that every murderer who ever lived suffered a violent death. Reason and history tell us this is not the case. However, the presence of exceptions does not make the proverb untrue. Through the proverb Jesus is attempting to say that violence breeds violence and that to resort to violence to protect him from death is not the Father's will for the Son (vv. 53–56).

6

Literary Devices

Parallelism

A structure of two or more poetic lines or verses that are conceptually related to each other. The poetic lines cohere and work together to develop a shared thought, sometimes by repetition, contrast, or addition (Klein, Blomberg, and Hubbard, 225–36). Because of the structure of thought, it is helpful to read line by line rather than sentence by sentence (Duvall and Hays, 337–38).

The most characteristic feature of Hebrew poetry, parallelism falls into three basic types: antithetic, synonymous, and synthetic (Fee and Stuart 1982, 162). However, scholars sometimes break down one or more of these types into additional types in order to more precisely describe the development of thought.

Antithetic parallelism

A type of parallelism wherein the thought of the second or subsequent line contrasts with that of the previous line (Fee and Stuart 1982, 180; Kaiser and Silva, 89).

A wise son brings joy to his father,
but a foolish son grief to his mother. –Prov. 10:1

Chiasm

A literary technique that uses a form of parallelism wherein the words, phrases, or concepts given in successive lines are inverted in the following lines (Kaiser 1981, 225f). This technique was considered a

But when the time had fully come, God sent his *Son,* A
born of a woman, born under *law,* B
to redeem those under *law,* B′
that we might receive the full rights of *sons.* A′
–Gal. 4:4,5

most dignified and stately form of presentation and therefore was reserved for solemn and important portions of Scripture (Bullinger, 374).[1]

Climactic parallelism

> Sing to the Lord a new song;
> Sing to the Lord, all the earth.
> Sing to the Lord, *praise his name.*
> –Ps. 96:1–2a

A repetition of two or more words over two to four lines. The lines develop a thought or action in ascending fashion (lending this literary feature the alternate name of "staircase parallelism"), sometimes ending with a culminating thought (Kaiser and Silva, 92).

Emblematic symbolism

> As water reflects a face,
> so a man's heart reflects the man.
> –Prov. 27:19

A common rhetorical feature of Hebrew poetry involving parallelism: one line gives a literal or factual statement and the other line a simile or metaphor (Kaiser 1981, 223).

Synonymous parallelism

> I have swept away your offenses like a cloud,
> your sins like the morning mist. –Isa. 44:22

A strengthening or reinforcing of a line by a line that follows it, usually restating the first line's thought in some fashion but without significant addition or subtraction of thought (Kaiser and Silva, 88–89).[2]

Synthetic parallelism

> He will not let your foot slip–
> he who watches over you will not slumber.
> –Ps. 121:3
> Praise be to the Lord,
> for he showed his wonderful love to me.
> –Ps. 31:21

A second line further developing the thought of the first (consequently, also called "developmental" parallelism) (Duvall and Hays, 338). However, sometimes there is a series of parallel lines with similar structure but no real development of thought (see Ps. 148:7–12).

---

[1] It no doubt also served as a memory aid when reciting something orally.

[2] A related parallelism is that of "continuation," where what initially appears to be a simple repetition of the original thought actually advances it. For example, see Isa. 40:9: "You who bring good tidings to Zion, *go up on a high mountain.* You who bring good tidings to

Rhetorical / Literary Devices

Alliteration

The repetition of the same or a similar sound, usually the initial consonantal sound, in two or more neighboring words or syllables. The purpose of alliteration is to create a notable sequence of sounds. Native speakers of English will likely remember the alliteration in the children's tongue twister: "Sister Susie sells seashells by the seashore." However, alliteration in the Bible is discernible only to those who read the Scriptures in the original biblical languages.

> And this is <u>the victory that has overcome</u> the world—our faith. –1 John 5:4, NASB
> *Kai hautē estin <u>hē nikē hē nikēsasa</u> ton kosmon—hē pistis hēmōn.*

Assonance

The repetition of the same or similar vowel sound in a sequence of words. As with Alliteration, the purpose of assonance is to create a notable sequence of sounds that gives emphasis to the words (Klein, Blomberg, and Hubbard, 221). For example, in English you can express the thought of being unwilling to compromise your wishes by saying, "It's my way or the highway."[3] As with alliteration, assonance is lost in translation and so is discernible only by taking note of the original biblical languages.

Asyndeton (Gk., "without conjunctions")

Refers to the omission of conjunctions that ordinarily join coordinate words or clauses in a list or sequence of thoughts. The terseness of expression usually adds effect to the words. Often the elements in the asyndeton lead up to a climactic thought, which the asyndeton serves to emphasize (Bullinger, 37); e.g., "I came, I saw, I conquered."

> Saul said to the Kenites,
> *"Go,*
> *depart,*
> *go down* from among the Amalekites,
> so that I do not destroy you with them."
> –1 Sam. 15:6, NASB

Jerusalem, *lift up your voice with a shout*" (cited and discussed in William W. Klein, Craig L. Blomberg, and Robert L. Hubbard, *Introduction to Biblical Interpretation* [Waco, Tex.: Word Publishing, 1993], 232).

[3] An informal expression by which the speaker insists on having his or her own way and those who do not like it can leave in the most direct fashion (the highway being one such route).

Diatribe

> Therefore, I was not vacillating when I intended to do this, was I? Or what I purpose, do I purpose according to the flesh, so that with me there will be yes, yes and no, no *at the same time?* –2 Cor. 1:17, NASB

A lengthy speech that has a harsh and bitter tone, filled with sarcasm, criticism, or denunciation. However, as a subgenre, it refers to a method of instruction in which the instructor enters into dialogue with opponents (real or imagined) who raise hypothetical questions or objections. These are then addressed and answered (Klein, Blomberg, and Hubbard, 356). In his letters Paul often anticipates his opponents' criticism of him in the form of a question which he then responds to.

Double entendre (Fr., "double meaning")

> In Him was life, and the life was the Light of men. The Light shines in the darkness, and the darkness did not *comprehend* it.
> –John 1:4,5, NASB

A word or expression capable of two interpretations or meanings, both of which would fit the immediate literary context. The two senses would also produce true statements (Bullinger, 805). This device is relatively rare in Scripture and assumes that the audience is well aware of the dual sense of the text. However, which sense the author intended, if he had both meanings in mind or if he purposely intended to be ambiguous, is impossible to know with certainty. The text box illustrates this device in John 1:5 where "comprehend" translates *katalambanō,* which can mean to "lay hold of" or "overtake" in the sense of subdue or overpower (Mark 9:18; John 12:35; 1 Thess. 5:4), or metaphorically to "seize" or "grasp" something, i.e., to understand it (Acts 4:13; 10:34; Eph. 3:18).

Epizeuxis (Gk., "duplication")

> "Behold, *I, even I* am bringing the flood of water upon the earth." –Gen. 6:17, NASB
> They . . . woke Him up, saying, "*Master, Master,* we are perishing!" –Luke 8:24, NASB

A very common literary device whereby a word is repeated for strong emphasis. The repeated word must be used in the same sense (Bullinger, 189).

Inclusio (or "inclusion")

A rhetorical device that utilizes the repetition of words, phrases, or expressions to mark off the beginning and ending of a section (Kaiser and Silva, 75). The repetition serves to bracket the passage and emphasize and draw attention to the repeated term(s). Note that the *inclusio* illustrated in the text box is unusual in that Luke creates it by attaching the words "and they shall prophesy" to the quotation from Joel 2:28,29, indicating his emphasis that on the Day of Pentecost God was creating a prophetic people.[4]

"And it shall be in the last days," God says, "That I will pour forth of My Spirit on all mankind; *And your sons and your daughters shall prophesy,* And your young men shall see visions, And your old men shall dream dreams; Even on My bondslaves, both men and women, I will in those days pour forth of My Spirit *And they shall prophesy."* –Acts 2:17,18, NASB

Onomatopoeia

A form of wordplay in which pronunciation reproduces the sounds of the actions they describe. For example, in English, bees are said to "buzz," cats to "purr," and bells to "ring." Onomatopoeia is a feature of Hebrew poetry and serves to highlight the words the authors wished to emphasize (Klein, Blomberg, and Hubbard, 224–25).

Paronomasia

An alignment or sequence of words with similar sounds (but not meaning) to catch the attention and interest of the reader/hearer because of the peculiar sound effect. This figure of speech is similar to the rhyming of words in English but goes undetected in translations of the biblical languages (Kaiser and Silva, 95).

The earth was *formless and void* [Heb. *tōhû wābōhû*]. –Gen. 1:2, NASB

Parenthesis

A pause in writing where the author inserts an amplifying or explanatory word, phrase, or sentence. The insertion may appear as a digression of thought but usually clarifies something the author thinks is important for the reader to know. If such a device is used in discourse the parenthetical remark is not part of the original discourse. This is indicated by the editors of the biblical text by placing the words in parentheses.

Therefore the Samaritan woman said to Him, "How is it that You, being a Jew, ask me for a drink since I am a Samaritan woman?" *(For Jews have no dealings with Samaritans.)* –John 4:9, NASB

[4] For a book-length development of this thesis, see Roger Stronstad, *The Prophethood of All Believers: A Study in Luke's Charismatic Theology* (Sheffield, England: Sheffield Academic Press, 2003).

Sarcasm

Fill up, then, the measure *of the guilt* of your fathers. –Matt. 23:32, NASB

Sharp and often satirical or ironic utterances designed to cut or give pain. It is often scornful or contemptuous in tone and is used in contexts where the speaker is taunting or seeking to provoke someone. Sarcasm relates to IRONY but is broader in its purpose, often using irony to accomplish its ends.

Figures of Speech

There are hundreds of literary devices and figures of speech. The most comprehensive guide to their identification and description is E. W. Bullinger's *Figures of Speech in the Bible: Explained and Illustrated* (repr., Grand Rapids: Baker Book House, 1968). The terms selected represent a sampling from entry-level textbooks on biblical interpretation.

Figures of Comparison

Anthropomorphism

Behold, the LORD's hand is not so short That it cannot save; Nor is His ear so dull That it cannot hear. –Isa. 59:1, NASB

A description or depiction of God as if He were a human being, sharing some human characteristic or function. As a result, anthropomorphic language helps the author convey truth about God in human terms, ascribing to God some attribute or action that belongs to humans.

When interpreting texts with such figurative language, it is important not to accept it as literal, but to look first for the meaning behind the metaphorical language (Kaiser 1981, 125).[5]

Anthropopathism

"I will forgive their iniquity, and their *sin I will remember no more.*" –Jer. 31:34, NASB

Related to ANTHROPOMORPHISM but depicting God as sharing some emotional or psychological aspect of human personality rather than physical characteristics or functions.[6]

---

[5] The problem is illustrated in the text box. Isaiah is not attempting to describe God physically or imply that God literally has a body with "hands" and "ears." His words convey to Israel that God's lack of action on their behalf (see context) is not to be interpreted as a lack of His power or an unawareness of their need for deliverance.

[6] Due to the personal nature of God, anthropopathisms are more difficult to interpret. It is

Apostrophe (Gk., "a turning away from")

> Where, *O death,* is your victory? Where, *O death,* is your sting? –1 Cor. 15:55; see Hosea 13:14

A rhetorical device by which the author abruptly "turns away" from the audience and addresses someone or something (e.g., an abstract quality) that is absent as though they were present. It is a dramatic expression of strong emotional sentiment by the writer/speaker, suddenly redirecting his or her focus (and that of the audience). In that the object of address is sometimes impersonal or inanimate, the address takes on the form of PERSONIFICATION (Bullinger, 901; Duvall and Hays, 346–47; Ryken, 98).

Metaphor

> The LORD is my *shepherd.* –Ps. 23:1
>
> He replied, "Go tell that *fox* [Herod Antipas]." –Luke 13:32

A figure of speech wherein an implicit comparison is made, one thing being spoken of in terms of another (McKim, 1996, 173). The subtlety of this literary device differs from a simile, where the comparison is explicitly identified by the use of the words "as" or "like." Evoking a strong symbolic image, metaphors communicate not so much what is true to *fact* as to *feeling* (Bullinger, 737).

Personification

> Lift up your heads, O gates, And be lifted up, O ancient doors. –Ps. 24:7, NASB
>
> Listen, O heavens, and hear, O earth. –Isa. 1:2, NASB

Occurs when personal qualities or activities are attributed to something that is impersonal, from animals to ideas. This literary technique is used to create vivid and colorful images and is sometimes referred to as "figures of humanization." When God is described as having human form or characteristics, it is called an ANTHROPOMORPHISM, e.g., "The LORD's hand is not so short that it cannot save; nor is His ear so dull that it cannot hear" (Isa. 59:1, NASB).

---

common to assume that statements with anthropopathic language are to be understood literally. The wise interpreter will not do so if such an interpretation results in God being described in such a way that His divine nature is compromised, i.e., that He is depicted as being less than God in His divine nature. For an illuminating discussion on how anthropopathisms affect the theology of God's nature, see Erickson, *Christian Theology,* 304–8.

Simile

> All of us *like sheep* have gone astray.
> –Isa. 53:6, NASB
> *As the deer* pants for the water brooks, So my soul pants for You, O God. –Ps. 42:1, NASB

A figure of speech that explicitly compares one thing to another by using the words "like" or "as." What is being compared may be either objects or actions, but the nature of the comparison is formally expressed and easily identified.

Symbol (cf. Emblematic symbolism)

> Behold, the *Lion* that is from the tribe *of Judah*, the Root of David [i.e., the Davidic Messiah-King], has overcome so as to open the book and its seven seals. –Rev. 5:5, NASB

Something used to represent something else, usually something material representing something immaterial (McQuilken, 260). Like a metaphor, a symbol carries an implied comparison but a comparison that is more universal in association than that of metaphor. The symbol is considered to express the reality it represents, but is not literally equivalent to it (McKim, 1996, 274). For example, today a tiger is often used as a symbol of ferocity or predation; a dove as a symbol of gentleness or peace. However, culture, history, and context create symbols and their associations so that the same symbol is capable of multiple meanings.[7] Consequently, interpreters of the Bible must make themselves aware of symbolism in the text through careful attention to its language and cultural-historical background.

Figures of Addition or Fullness of Expression

Euphemism

> None of you shall approach any blood relative of his *to uncover nakedness* [to have sexual relations]; I am the Lord. –Lev. 18:6, NASB

A figure of speech that stands as a substitute for a term that is harsh, unpleasant, or offensive, the euphemism being a word or expression that is more acceptable or less offensive (Bullinger, 684). Euphemisms are best understood against the backdrop of cultural values and sensitivities.

[7] Language within culture and history is dynamic. It constantly changes symbols and their associations. Consider Peter's use of "lion" as a symbol of the rapacious activity of the devil toward believers (1 Peter 5:8). Contrast this with John's use of the same word to create the imagery of royal kingship when referring to the "Lion of the tribe of Judah" (Rev. 5:5).

Hendiadys

> Then the Lord rained on Sodom and Gomorrah *brimstone and fire* [i.e., burning brimstone/sulfur]. –Gen. 19:24, NASB

The expression of an idea or description of an object by the use of two words connected by "and." For example, people say the water is "nice and warm" instead of the usual combination of an independent word and its modifier—such as "nicely (or pleasantly) warm." The two words of a hendiadys are the same part of speech, e.g., adjective, noun, or verb (Bullinger, 647).

Hendiatris

> For Yours is the *kingdom* and the *power* and the *glory* forever [i.e., a powerful and glorious kingdom]. –Matt. 6:13, NASB

A figure of speech where three words are employed to express a single concept. The three words are conceptually related so that together they express a complex idea. In the case of three nouns, the second and third often expand or emphasize the first as adjectival modifiers (Bullinger, 671).

Hyperbole

> You blind guides, who *strain out a gnat and swallow a camel!* –Matt. 23:24, NASB

A deliberate and usually extreme exaggeration in order to emphasize a point or to produce an effect without being taken literally.[8] The parent who says "If I've told you once, I've told you a thousand times" is attempting to communicate something like "I'm tired of telling you the same thing and being ignored."

Merismus / Merism (Gk. *merismos,* "distribution")

> In the beginning God created the *heavens and the earth* [i.e., the whole universe].–Gen. 1:1

Reference to the totality of something by naming its extremes or opposite parts. For example, geographically "from Dan to Beersheba" (Jud. 20:1) represents all the land of Israel and its inhabitants (Klein, Blomberg, and Hubbard, 239–40; Kaiser 1981, 198, 225–26). Another type of this

---

8 Robert H. Stein has an illuminating chapter on hyperbolic language in the Bible. He illustrates its extensive use and gives ten rules that help one recognize it. See *A Basic Guide to Interpreting the Bible: Playing by the Rules* (Grand Rapids: Baker Book House, 1994), 123–35.

device names the totality of something followed by the parts that make up the whole. In Galatians 5:22,23 we read, "The fruit of the Spirit is love, joy, peace, patience, kindness, goodness, faithfulness, gentleness and self-control" (Bullinger, 435).

Pleonasm (Gk. *pleonasmos,* "something in excess")

> I am torn between the two: I desire to depart and be with Christ, which is *better by far* [lit. "much more better"]. –Phil. 1:23

A redundancy for the sake of emphasis,[9] the author hoping to produce some effect on the mind of the reader or hearer (Kaiser and Silva, 94). The redundancy usually consists of repeated words or synonymous terms that occur directly after the words to be emphasized.[10]

Figures of Association and Relation

Antonomasia (Gk., "a different name")

> And the Lord said to him, "Name her *Lo-ruhamah* [Heb., "no compassion"], for I will no longer have compassion on the house of Israel." –Hosea 1:6, NASB

Substituting a proper noun or title for a common noun. The purpose is to assign some quality or attribute to the noun by association. In the United States we commonly refer to a traitor as a "Benedict Arnold" because of Arnold's well-known treachery during the American Revolution (Bullinger, 682).

Metonymy

> Abraham said, "They have *Moses and the Prophets* [i.e., the books written by Moses and the Prophets or the entire OT]; let them hear them." –Luke 16:29, NASB; cf. 24:27.

A substitution for the name of a thing itself the name of one of its attributes or of something closely associated with it (Klein, Blomberg, and Hubbard, 249). Using such a figure of speech assumes the audience is well-acquainted with the association. A newspaper might write "Today, the *White House* issued

---

[9] E. W. Bullinger astutely comments that the "redundancy is only apparent" and the words "are not really superfluous when used by the Holy Spirit, nor are they idle or useless." See *Figures of Speech in the Bible: Explained and Illustrated* (repr., Grand Rapids: Baker Book House), 405.

[10] This device might be associated with the term "tautology," a needless repetition of a statement, word, or idea. However, a pleonasm is not a careless repetition of unnecessary words but rather an intentional overstatement for literary effect.

the following statement . . .," knowing that the reader will understand that the *President of the United States* (or one of his official spokespersons) is meant.

Synecdoche

A part representing the whole or the whole representing the part. This figure of speech is used to draw attention to something of greater significance than the part; e.g., "He doesn't even have a roof over his head" points to the homelessness of a person. It may also narrow one's focus to something specific within (or in association with) the whole; e.g., "Will this ethnic dispute be resolved only by *bloodshed?*" images the violence of war (Duvall and Hays, 346; Ryken, 101).

> Some trust in *chariots* and some in *horses* [i.e., in military might and resources], but we trust in the name of the LORD our God. –Ps. 20:7

Figures of Contrast

Irony

Words meant to convey the *opposite* of their meaning. This literary device is often used in sarcasm or ridicule.

> Then Job responded,
> *"Truly then you are the people, And with you wisdom will die!"* –Job 12:1,2, NASB

Litotes ("plain"; also meiosis, "a belittling")

A figure of speech in which a thing is affirmed or emphasized by understatement and/or negation, in a manner opposite that of hyperbole (Bullinger, 154; Kaiser 1981, 124). For example, Paul identifies himself as "a citizen of *no ordinary* city" (Acts 21:39), and asserts that God's "grace to [him] was *not without* effect" (1 Cor. 15:10).

> For I am *the least of the apostles.*
> –1 Cor. 15:9, NASB
> (Paul uses this device to magnify the grace of God in choosing him; see v. 10.)

Figures of Omission

Ellipsis

An intentional omission of words so that the sentence is grammatically incomplete. However, the meaning of the sentence is not in doubt, as the author expects the reader to supply the missing word(s) to complete its sense. The author of ellipsis uses it not out of error, but by design. It serves to focus

He blessed, and brake, and gave the loaves to *his* disciples, and the disciples [gave] to the multitude. –Matt. 14:19, KJV

the reader's attention on the words that are present which are emphasized by the omission.[11]

Zeugma (Gk., "yoke")

"I gave you milk to drink, not solid food" (1 Cor. 3:2, NASB), is better translated, "I did not feed you solid food" or "not solid food to eat."

A special kind of Ellipsis where two subjects or objects are linked by a verb or participle that is appropriate only with the first, but not the second. The literal rendering often makes no sense. The omission seems to have been caused by the author's economy of words, expecting the reader to supply the appropriate verb. Translations will often indicate by italics which words were inserted out of necessity (Kaiser and Silva, 97–98; Bullinger, 131).

[11] Bullinger points out that by omitting the verb "gave" (see the text box), the author does not stress the instrumentality of the disciples in the giving (although that is there) but instead draws our thoughts to Jesus as the Giver of bread. See *Figures of Speech,* 1–2.

7

Related Terms from Other Disciplines

Biblical Studies—Introduction / Background

Abyss (Gk. *abyssos*, "deep / bottomless pit")

A transliteration of the Greek, appearing nine times in the NT.[1] When translated it appears most often as "the bottomless pit" and carries the sense of some place very deep beneath the surface of the earth.[2] In the NT it designates a place assigned to demons, but to which they were unwilling to be sent (Luke 8:31). It is also the place of the dead (Rom. 10:7). The Book of Revelation describes it as the place from which the "beast" ascends to earth, bringing war and destruction (Rev. 11:7; 17:8), governed by the "angel of the Abyss," called Abaddon (in Hebrew) and Apollyon (in Greek). It is also the place where Satan will be bound for a thousand years (Rev. 20:1–3) before the occurrence of the Great White Throne Judgment described in Rev. 20:11–15.

Amanuensis

Designates a scribe who writes from dictation or copies a manuscript. Tertius was Paul's amanuensis for the letter to the Romans (Rom. 16:22). In all probability Paul used an amanuensis to write his epistles but often penned the closing greeting himself (1 Cor. 16:21; Gal. 6:11; Col. 4:18; 2 Thess. 3:17; Phile. 19).

Aramaic (language)

A Semitic language related to Hebrew but not derived from it. It was the language of state diplomacy used by the Assyrian, Babylon, and Persian empires. Portions of

---

1 See Luke 8:31; Rom. 10:7; Rev. 9:1,2,11; 11:7; 17:8; 20:1,3.

2 Interestingly, the Septuagint translates the Heb. *tehôm* ("deep place") with the Gk. *abyssos*, which is parallel to the "face of the waters." The oceans are viewed as the fathomless deep on which the earth rested. Ironically, the demons within the Gersene demoniac of Luke 8 entreat Christ to send them into a herd of pigs rather than into the "Abyss," but wind up in the sea. One wonders if Luke's choice of detail is his way of using tragic irony—pointing to the sea as the entrance to the Abyss.

the OT are in Aramaic (e.g., Dan. 2:4–7:28; Ezra 4:8–6:18; 7:12–26; and Jer. 10:11). It was used by the Jews in the time of Jesus, who probably spoke in Aramaic.[3]

Archaeology

The scientific study of the material remains of human society, culture, and activity, especially as it applies to antiquity. It is most often associated with the excavation of ancient sites of human occupation to uncover fossils, relics, artifacts, tools, monuments, buildings, etc., i.e., all physical evidence that reveals how people lived.

Armageddon (Gk. *Harmagedōn*)

A geographical location mentioned only in Rev. 16:16. Its exact location is disputed and uncertain. A popular identification is with the "hill of Megiddo" (Heb. *har Megeddon*), some 50 miles northeast of Jerusalem, which was the site of significant OT battles (e.g., Jud. 4, 7). In the Book of Revelation it marks the final battle in the "war of the great day of God" (16:14) between Christ and the Antichrist. This has led some scholars to see it not as a literal place but a symbol of God's final triumph over evil. The term is broadly used in secular literature of a final catastrophic battle between the forces of good and evil that marks the end of the world (G. E. Ladd, *BDT*, 50).

Artemis

A goddess in Greek mythology and patroness-protector of the city of Ephesus (Acts 19). Known as Diana to the Romans, Artemis was a fertility goddess who presided over childbirth. The Ephesian idol depicts a many-breasted woman, a symbol of sexual fruitfulness. She is depicted in Greek literature as a hunter and lover of nature (Ferguson, 18, 162–63).

Asceticism

The practice of strict (and often extreme) self-denial in order to advance one's spiritual development. Such practice usually includes the denial or delay of certain physical needs or desires in order to devote oneself to spiritual matters. Asceticism, as sometimes practiced by Gnostic groups in the Early Church, proceeded from a Greek notion that the body, being material, is inherently evil and the root of sin. Humans also possess a spirit which is good. Therefore, ascetic practices served to promote spirituality by destroy-

---

[3] See Neh. 8, where after Ezra read the Book of the Law, it had to be translated, presumably into Aramaic. Moreover, certain Aramaic words appear in the Gospels along with their translations. E.g., *Talitha koum* ("Little girl, I say to you, get up!"—Mark 5:41); Golgotha ("Place of the Skull"—Matt. 27:33); *Eloi, Eloi, lama sabachthani?* ("My God, my God, why have you forsaken me?"—Mark 15:34).

ing sin and bodily desires. Such a belief is foreign to biblical teaching which presents human personhood as a unity and integration of body, soul, and spirit (1 Thess. 5:23). In principle the NT teaches spiritual discipline that includes self-denial.[4] However, it does not teach asceticism as a means of overcoming sin or the desires of the flesh (Col. 2:20–23) (Mattke, *BDT*, 52–53).

Asherah

The Canaanite mother-goddess closely associated in the OT with idolatrous worship of Baal (Jud. 3:7; 6:25),[5] but not to be confused with Ashtoreth, another Canaanite goddess of fertility, love, and war (Jud. 2:13; 10:6; 1 Kings 11:5). The name is also used of the carved images (*Asherim*) used to worship Asherah. Israel was repeatedly called to tear down, destroy, or burn these images (Ex. 34:13; Deut. 12:3;1 Kings 15:13).

Assyria

The powerful nation situated northeast of Israel, whose capital was Nineveh. Assyria took the ten northern tribes of Israel into captivity ca. 722 B.C. and was itself conquered by Babylon in 612 B.C. Assyria plays prominently in the history of Israel recorded in 2 Kings and 2 Chronicles, as well as the prophetic books of Jonah and Nahum.

Autographa (Gk. *autographos,* "written by one's own hand")

The original manuscript of a biblical text as written by its inspired author. While the Church possesses no autographs of a biblical text, the work of textual criticism compares and analyzes all manuscript copies of a text in an attempt to determine what was written in the autograph.[6] The tremendous quality and volume of manuscripts available to the modern textual critic has resulted in the reproduction of a text that scholars regard as extremely close to the autographa.[7]

---

[4] Jesus endorsed the practice of fasting (Matt. 9:15) and even celibacy "for the sake of the kingdom" (Matt. 19:12, NASB). Paul acknowledged that celibacy was a noble and beneficial "gifting" for some, but not for all (1 Cor. 7:7–9). Couples might even temporarily postpone sexual relations to concentrate on prayer but are warned against prolonged abstinence that would lead to temptation (7:5).

[5] It may be that Asherah was viewed as the consort (wife) of Baal. However, in the Ras Shamra texts, Asherah is a goddess of the sea and consort of El, the chief Canaanite god. See T. C. Mitchell, "Asherah" in *NBD*, 95.

[6] It is important to note that the text of Scripture is incredibly reliable and unparalleled in its authenticity compared to any other piece of ancient literature. See F. F. Bruce, *The New Testament Documents: Are They Reliable?* (Leicester, England: InterVarsity Press, 1988), and Walter Kaiser, Jr., *The Old Testament Documents: Are They Reliable and Relevant?* (Downers Grove, Ill.: InterVarsity Press, 2001). For an extremely informative description of the work of

Baal (Heb., "lord" or "master")

The name given to the god of the Canaanites, thought to control the fertility of humans, livestock, and the land. Since the Canaanites held to territorial gods, there were numerous Baals (Heb. *Baalim;* 1 Kings 18:18) in the land of Canaan when Israel entered.[8] The worship of Baal was seduction to the Israelites that threatened their worship of the Lord throughout their history.[9] In addition to the sexual immorality associated with fertility cults, one form involved the human sacrifice of infants (Jer. 19:5).

Babylon

The city on the Euphrates River that became the capital of the Babylonian Empire, which ruled the world from 612–539 B. C. The name is used in Scripture of both the city and the empire. Under Nebuchadnezzer Babylon destroyed the temple in Jerusalem and took Judah (the Southern Kingdom of Israel) into captivity ca. 586 B.C. Babylon was depicted in Daniel's visions as the head of gold (Dan. 2) and the lion (Dan. 7). In Revelation John appears to use the name Babylon to refer to Rome (Rev. 18:2, 10, 21; Cf. 1 Peter 5:13) and symbolically of the world system in alienation and opposition to God and his saints.

Circumcision

A Jewish rite performed on male infants where the foreskin of the male sex organ is cut away. It served as the sign of the covenant relationship God established with his people through Abraham (Gen. 17). It also was a rite of initiation signifying entrance into the covenant community of Israel. It came to symbolize the consecration and moral-spiritual transformation that God sought among his people (Deut. 10:12–20; 30:6; Jer. 4:4; Cf. Isa. 52:1; Jer. 9:25–26). In the NT Paul recognizes that circumcision was the seal of Abraham's faith (Rom. 4:11) but quickly points out that Abraham was declared righteous while uncircumcised. God through Christ has brought about a new inward circumcision of the heart by the Spirit (Rom. 2:28–29; Cf. Col. 2:11).

NT textual criticism, see Lee Strobel's interview with Bruce Metzger in *The Case for Christ* (Grand Rapids: Zondervan, 1998), 57–72.

7 For example, after considering all possible variations in the Greek texts of the New Testament, it is possible to restore a text that is 99.5 percent pure! See Norman Geisler and William E. Nix, *A General Introduction to the Bible* (Chicago: Moody Press, 1980), 367.

8 For example, Baal of Peor (Num. 25:3), Baal-Berith (Jud. 8:33), and Baal-Zebub (2 Kings 1:2,3,6).

9 This may have been because Baal was the name given to the chief god of the Canaanite pantheon. This would have placed it as a natural rival to Yahweh, whom the Israelites regarded

Codex

An ancient manuscript made of papyrus (reed paper) or vellum (animal skins) that was compiled in book form as opposed to a scroll. The Early Church often used the codex when they collected and bound manuscripts of the NT.

Colossian heresy

Applies to the false teachings that Paul addressed in his letter to the church of Colossae. Although many scholars have identified the so-called Colossian heresy as Gnostic, this conclusion is unlikely because Gnosticism is a later religious system of the 2nd century. Furthermore, the errant teachings emphasizing rules, ascetic practices, and secret knowledge that promotes spirituality can be found in first century Jewish sects (Elwell and Yarbrough, ENT, 320).

Day of Pentecost

The Jewish feast celebrated on the 50th day after the Sabbath wave offering of barley sheaves at the beginning of the Passover (Lev 23:15–16). It was also called the Feast of the Harvest (Ex. 23:16), the Feast of Weeks (Deut. 16:10), and the "day of the first fruits" (Num. 28:26).[10] In the OT this feast recognized God's gracious and bountiful provision in the land. In the NT the phrase refers to the specific Day of Pentecost when the Holy Spirit was poured out upon believers in Jerusalem (Acts 2), establishing the NT church as an end-time, Spirit-empowered, prophetic community (Acts 2:17–18).[11]

Dead Sea Scrolls (see ESSENES)

Demon possession

A widely used term that refers to the condition of being controlled by a demon. It is variously described in the NT, such as to have a spirit or demon (Mark 9:17; Luke 8:27), to have an "unclean spirit" (Mark 3:30), or the "spirit of an unclean demon" (Luke 4:33). The most common verb that describes this condition is the Greek *daimonizōmai*, most often translated "to be demon-possessed." When it is used, the effects on the victims are severe (Matt. 15:23), even bizarre (Mark 5:2–5; Luke 4:33) and life threatening (Matt. 17:15), accompanied by a wide range of sicknesses or physical maladies. Examples

---

as the one God and Lord of creation. See Bill T. Arnold and Bryan E. Beyer, *Encountering the Old Testament: A Christian Survey* (Grand Rapids: Baker Books, 1999), 285.

[10] In 1 Cor. 15:23 Paul uses "firstfruits" as a figure, or type, of Christ's resurrection.

[11] For a development of this perspective from a classical Pentecostal, see Roger Stronstad, *The Prophethood of All Believers: A Study in Luke's Charismatic Theology* (Sheffield, England: Sheffield Academic Press, 2003).

include muteness (Matt. 9:32), blindness and muteness (Matt. 12:22), insanity (Mark 5:15; Cf. John 10:20), and seizures (Matt. 17:15; Luke 9:42).[12]

Drink offering

One of the supplementary offerings in the OT that accompanied the burnt offering or fellowship offerings (Num. 15:1–12; 28:7, 24) along with a grain offering of flour and oil. The drink offering consisted of about a liter (1¼ quarts) of wine. Paul viewed his eventual martyrdom as a life "poured out like a drink offering" in sacrifice to God in the service of the gospel (2 Tim. 4:6; Phil. 2:17).

Dynasty

Refers to a succession of kings or rulers from the same family or line of descent. For example, the Seleucid dynasty denotes the kings descended from Seleucus I, who ruled Syria from 301 to 168 B.C. The most infamous member of the Seleucid dynasty was Antiochus IV (175–163 BC), whose harsh persecution of the Jews led to the Maccabean Revolt.

Ephesus

The leading city in the Roman province of Asia in Paul's day. It was famous for its wealth, beauty, and temple to the Greek goddess Artemis. Paul ministered there for about three years and conducted an evangelistic outreach that spread the gospel to all of Asia (Acts 19:1–20). The Ephesians were also the recipients of one of Paul's Prison Epistles.[13]

Epicureans

The followers of the philosophical teachings of Epicurus (341–270 BC). Paul encountered members of this school in Athens (Acts 17:18). Epicurus held a

---

[12] A concise article defining demon-possession and exorcism is provided by L. G. McClung, Jr., in *DPCM*, 290–94. Controversy and debate exists over the question of whether a Christian can be "demon-possessed," "have a demon," or the extent someone can be influenced by one. Some have made the distinction between demon *possession* and demonic *oppression*. Others have drawn an unsupportable distinction between *demon-possessed* and *demonized*. McClung has surveyed various aspects of the debate and repeatedly points to what can be validated from Scripture. The NT provides no clear example of a true Christian being demon-possessed, or having a demon or demonic spirit that requires exorcism as practiced by Jesus, his disciples, apostles, or the NT church.

[13] Whether Ephesus was the original recipient of Paul's epistle or one of several cities to receive a circular letter is disputed. The absence of personal greetings and the fact that several good manuscripts omit "at Ephesus" at 1:1 argue for the latter. If the letter was intended to be circular, it was probably sent first to Ephesus by Tychicus (Eph. 6:21–22).

form of materialism that saw everything in the world as made up of atomic particles. Consequently, nothing survives death. The chief goal of Epicureans was to pursue happiness by meeting life with serene detachment. By Paul's day, however, Epicureanism had degenerated and come to view happiness in terms of sensual pleasure (Cressey, *NBD*, 383).

Essenes (fr. Aramaic *hasayya,* "the pious ones")

A Jewish sect known through the writings of Josephus, Philo, Pliny the Elder, and others. Their origins are commonly dated to some time shortly after the Maccabean Revolt (ca.168 BC), during the Hasmonean dynasty (E. Ferguson, 488).[14] Essenes lived together in monastic-type communities during the time of Jesus. Although differing somewhat, these communities had common characteristics: a withdrawal from the world, a strict observance of the Mosaic law, a strong eschatological expectation, material possessions in common, and generous hospitality to other Essenes. Since the discovery of the Dead Sea Scrolls, it is commonly thought that the Qumran community was Essene in nature.

Euphrates River

The largest river in western Asia, a region known in the Bible as Mesopotamia. It once marked the northern boundary of Israel (Gen. 15:18; Deut. 11:24; Josh. 1:4). Along its banks the ancient city of Babylon was built.

Firstborn (Gk. *prōtotokos,* "first born")

Can refer to the first child born to a set of parents (Luke 2:7, 23), but more often, when applied to Christ, it takes on the meaning of special privilege, rank, or status as the "firstborn" within a given relational context.[15] For example, Jesus is the "firstborn of / from the dead" in that he was the first to be raised permanently from the dead (Rev. 1:5; Col. 1:18). He is the "firstborn" in the world and "of creation" because of his unique status as Creator of that world (Heb. 1:1–6; Col. 1:15–16).

---

[14] If the identity of the Qumran Community with the Essenes is maintained, then the founding date of the sect hinges on the identity of the "Wicked High" priest (mentioned in the Dead Sea Scrolls) among the Hasmonean rulers: Jonathan, Simon, or Alexander Jannaeus. See Everett Ferguson, *Backgrounds of Early Christianity*, 2nd ed. (Grand Rapids: Wm. B. Eerdmans, 1993), 488.

[15] Note that God speaks of an exalted status in his covenant with David when he writes, "I also shall make him My firstborn, The highest of the kings of the earth" (Ps. 89:27, NASB). While the passage is speaking specifically of David and his enthronement, it is not hard to see in its grandiose language (see vv. 20–37) an ultimate fulfillment in the exaltation of the Messiah, the seed of David.

Galatia

Refers to both an ethnic district in north central Asia Minor and a Roman province that included cites such as Antioch of Pisidia, Iconium, Lystra, and Derbe, where Paul founded churches during his first missionary journey. A long-standing debate exists over whether Paul in his Galatian epistle wrote to churches in ethnic (north) Galatia, or to those in the Roman province of (south) Galatia.[16]

Glossalalia (Gk., "tongues" or "languages")

A technical term for speaking in tongues. It occurs in Acts as a sign-evidence of Spirit-baptism (Acts 2:4; 10:46; 19:6) and in Paul's writings as one of the "gifts of the Spirit" (1 Cor. 12–14). See also Baptism in the Holy Spirit.

Gnosis (Gk., "knowledge")

The Greek term for knowledge, which was greatly esteemed in the Greek culture as reflected in Paul's letters (e.g., 1 and 2 Corinthians, Ephesians, Colossians). Some scholars interpret NT references to *gnosis* as evidence of an early form of Gnosticism, which saw special knowledge as the means of salvation or deliverance from sin. However, Gnosticism as pictured in the writings of the Church Fathers is a second-century religion, too late to have influenced the first-century Christian church. Nevertheless, the elevated status of *gnosis* is very early extending back to the Persian period.[17]

Gnosticism

A complex religious belief system of the second and third centuries. A syncretistic blend of Christian, Jewish, and Greek ideas (Elwell and Yarbrough, 398), it held that individuals could attain salvation through knowledge

---

[16] The debate is complex and multifaceted and good scholars support both views. Generally, conservative scholars favor the "south Galatia" position as being able to explain the chronology of Paul in his journeys and correlate with the data of the Galatian epistle and Acts. See Donald Guthrie, *New Testament Introduction*, 3d ed. (Downers Grove, Ill.: InterVarsity Press, 1970), 450–65.

[17] Elsewhere this author has pointed out the error of labeling Paul's opponents as Gnostics (see Colossian heresy). As for the label "Gnostics," we must recognize that Gnosticism was a second-century religion of the larger Greek world. It was highly syncretistic and borrowed its concepts from a variety of sources. Scholars now recognize that the religious ideas and terminology of "Gnosis" long preceded the religion of Gnosticism. For example, Paul does not need to have Gnostics in mind simply because his writing contains what appears to be a dualism of body and spirit. Such a dichotomy was found in the Greek world from the time of Plato. In addition, a careful examination of 1 and 2 Corinthians uncovers none of the essential features of Gnosticism. Therefore, it is safe to conclude that among Paul's opponents were Gentiles who shared many of the religious and philosophical ideas of the Greek world. See James D. Hernando,

(*gnosis*). There were numerous expressions of Gnosticism, but one of the better-known varieties, Valentinian Gnosticism, was seen as a Christian heresy and condemned by the church father Irenaeus (Against Heresies) in the second century. It constructed an elaborate theory of the origin of the universe, which was viewed in terms of a cosmic dualism (spirit-good vs. material-evil). This of course led to a theological problem when interpreting the incarnation of Christ.

Gog and Magog

In Ezek. 38:2, "Gog, of the land of Magog, the chief prince of Meshech and Tubal," Gog is clearly an individual ruler "of the land of Magog." The Greek in the SEPTUAGINT suggests that Magog is a people group, not a country or nation.[18] The exact meaning and derivation of these names is uncertain, and the identification with a modern political state (e.g., Russia) is improvable speculation. Ezekiel uses the names in his prophesy of a ruler residing in territory north of Israel[19] who will invade Israel and be defeated by divine intervention in two great end-time battles (Ezek. 38–39). The apostle John seems to use the names to represent all wicked nations deceived and moved by Satan against Israel (Rev. 20:8)

Gospel (Gk. *euangelion,* "gospel / good news")

Refers to the message that God's salvation, promised and prophesied in the OT, has now accomplished through the life and ministry of Jesus Christ. It focuses especially upon his death, burial, and resurrection (1 Cor. 15:1–4). This message was proclaimed by Christ's apostles and the Early Church. Although the term is used in the modern Church to refer to any of the first four books of the NT, the NT itself refers only to a singular "gospel" and does not use the term to refer to literary "gospels." See EVANGELISM.

Hades (Gk. *hadēs,* "hell, grave, the depths")

In the NT, designates the state of the dead or the place where the human spirit resides after death (see Luke 16:22–23). When the transliterated

"2 Corinthians," in *Life in the Spirit New Testament Commentary*, ed. French L. Arrington and Roger Stronstad (Grand Rapids: Zondervan, 1999), 920–21. An excellent discussion of the nature and origins of Gnosticism can be found in Ronald H. Nash, *Christianity and the Hellenistic World* (Grand Rapids: Zondervan, 1984), 203–24.

[18] The Gk. syntax for the phrase "of the land of Magog" indicates that the land belongs to or is associated with Magog, not the land that is Magog.

[19] Attacks on Israel by nations (e.g., Assyria, Babylon) have historically and strategically come from the north.

English word is not used, the term is translated "hell," "the depths," "death," or "the grave" (1 Cor. 15:55). As such it appears synonymous with the Hebrew term *sheol* in the OT. It can allude to death (or the grave) in a neutral sense (Acts 2:27, 31) or as a symbol of punishment (Matt. 11:23; Luke 10:15) or God's final judgment (Rev. 20:14).

Hasmoneans

The name given to the priestly and royal descendents of Mattathias, the priest of Modein, who in 167 BC led what became a successful revolt against the Syrian (Seleucid) rulers of the region. They are more commonly known as the Maccabees, after Mattathias's eldest son, Judas, nicknamed Maccabeus ("the hammer"). The name Hasmonean is given by Josephus and seems to be an older ancestral name (Patzia and Petrotta, *PDBS*, 55), first given to Simon, the third leader who was able to consolidate his power and secure a lasting peace. The Hasmoneans ruled Judea from 142 until 63 BC, when the area was conquered by the Roman general Pompey. The family was allowed to retain its priestly role but was eventually replaced by the Herodian dynasty in 37 BC.

Hellenistic (fr. Gk. *hellene,* "a Greek [person]")

Adjective that describes something related to Greek history and culture from the time of Alexander the Great (353–323 BC) and his successors. In Alexander's quest for world domination he sought to spread the Greek language, culture, and philosophy as a way of life. His dream of "hellenizing" the world was cut short by an early death but pursued vigorously by his successors who began the Ptolemaic and Seleucid dynasties (Ferguson, 10–15).

Herod, the Great (37–4 BC)

A Jew of Idumean (Edomite) descent marking the beginning of the Herodian Dynasty. His father, Antipater, was appointed PROCURATOR of Judea by Julius Caesar in 47 B.C. For his service to Rome during their civil war, the Roman senate conferred upon Herod the title "King of the Jews." He reigned from 37 to 4 BC. However, because of his Idumean heritage, he did not gain favor with his Jewish subjects, despite his capable rule and magnificent reconstruction of the Temple at Jerusalem. Among his other notable building projects were Masada and the port city of Caesarea. Herod was a ruthless and paranoid tyrant. To secure his throne he wiped out the Hasmonean descendents (see HASMONEANS) and assassinated numerous rivals, even from among his own family, including wives and sons. Perhaps his most infamous deed is recorded in Matthew's gospel: the slaughter of all the male children in and around Bethlehem who were two years old and younger (2:16) in an attempt to keep the newly born "king of the Jews" from threatening his throne. After his death his kingdom was divided up and given to his sons Archelaus, Philip, and Antipas (F. F. Bruce, *NBD*, 521–23).

Hillel, Rabbi (see ch. 2)

Immersion (see BAPTISM)

Intertestamental Period

A period of about 400 years between Malachi (ca. 430 BC) and the birth of Christ (ca. 4–6 BC). Many historical and cultural developments take place in this interval. Politically Israel experienced the rule of the Persians (ca. 450–330 BC), the Greeks (ca. 330–168 BC), and the Romans (from 63 BC forward). The brutal persecution and oppression of Israel by the Seleucid king Antiochus IV (see SELEUCID) led to the Maccabean Revolt (see JUDAS MACCABEUS) and about a century of Jewish self-rule during the Hasmonean Dynasty (ca. 168–63. BC) (see HASMONEANS). While no canonical OT books were written, Jewish religious literature flourished. The APOCRYPHA, PSEUDEPIGRAPHA, and SEPTUAGINT were all produced in this period. The apocalypses (see APOCALYPSE) of the first two collections contain evidence of a growing expectation of a Messiah.

Josephus (ca. AD 37–110)

A Pharisee and priest of Hasmonean descent who lived in the first century AD. He fought as a general in the first Jewish War, was captured, and was sent to Rome in AD 67. He won the favor of the emperor Vespasian, who made him an interpreter to Titus. After the war, he was given Roman citizenship, a new name (Flavius), and support for his literary pursuits. His writings, which include *Jewish Antiquities*, *The Jewish Wars*, and *Life*, are the main sources for Jewish history in the first century (Bruce, *NBD*, 661).

Judaizers

Jewish Christians who opposed Paul's preaching and missionary work among the Gentiles. They argued that circumcision and obedience to the Law was necessary for salvation (Acts 15:1, 5). Paul understood this to be an abandonment of the "grace of Christ" by making salvation dependent on "works of law" rather than faith in Christ (Gal. 2:16). Seeing it as a perversion of the true gospel (Gal. 1:6–7), he would not bend to their pressure and compromise the truth of the gospel (Gal. 2:2–5). The Conference at Jerusalem (Acts 15) sided with Paul and embraced the Gentile mission.

Judas Maccabeus

A Jewish patriot and freedom fighter who led Israel in revolt against Syrian oppression and persecution of his people beginning in 168 BC. Nicknamed Maccabeus, "the hammer," for his fierce battle tactics, Judas and his brothers fought and won Jewish independence from the Seleucid king Antiochus Epiphanes (see SELEUCID). Israel's self-rule under the brothers and descendents of Judas are referred to as the Hasmonean Dynasty. See HASMONEANS.

Kingdom of heaven

The term "kingdom" (Gk. *basileia*) in this phrase speaks of the dynamic reign, or rule, rather than a place (*DBAG*, 168). Therefore the kingdom of God refers to the active reign of God, which Jesus came to inaugurate in his life, preaching, ministry, and self-sacrifice as the Messiah. Some have tried to draw a distinction between the kingdom of God and the kingdom of heaven, but the phrases are clearly parallel and synonymous in many verses in Matthew and Mark (e.g., Mark 1:15 and Matt. 4:17; cf. 3:2).[20]

Koinōnia (Gk., "fellowship")

Derived from the Greek verb *koinōneō,* meaning "to share, or jointly participate" in something, that something being defined by the context. Thus, koinonia refers to Christian fellowship, partnership, mutual participation, or sharing in something, most notably the life in Christ (1 Cor. 1:9; 1 John 1:3–7) through the Spirit (2 Cor. 13:14; Phil. 2:1).[21]

Kyrios (Gk., "Lord, master lord, sir")

Could serve as a title of polite address but was employed regularly in the SEPTUAGINT to translate the divine name (Heb. *Yahweh*). This is certainly the sense Peter gave it (after quoting Ps. 110:1) in Acts 2:36, as did Thomas in John 20:28. It was used as a title for Jesus ("The Lord," Mark 11:3), but more importantly to refer to the resurrected and exalted Lord of the Church: Lord Jesus (Acts 1:21) and the Lord Jesus Christ (Rom. 1:7).

Maccabee (see JUDAS MACCABEUS)

---

[20] The phrase "kingdom of heaven" appears thirty-three times in the NT but only in Matt. Probably Matthew, due to his Jewish reverence for and reluctance to use the divine name, chooses "heaven" as a verbal replacement for "God."

[21] Keep in mind other objects of sharing in the NT: the support of the work of the Gospel (Phil. 1:5; cf. 4:14,15), either light or darkness (2 Cor. 6:14), Christ's suffering (Phil. 3:10), and the Christian life (faith) in general (Phile. 1:6).

Magi (Gk. *magos*, "astrologer")

A word borrowed from the Persians referring to a sage or priest who skillfully practiced astrology, divination, and other occult arts (*DBAG*, 608). In Matt. 2 they came to Jerusalem from the east, having observed some stellar configuration in the heavens that indicated to them the birth of a great Jewish king. They later visited the Christ child in Bethlehem and worshipped him (2:11).

Messiah (Gk. *christos*, Heb. *meshiach*)

Both the Greek and Hebrew terms mean "Anointed one." The Greek word *messias* is an attempt to simply spell out the Hebrew word with Greek letters. The terms came to be used as a title for the Messiah, God's anointed servant (Isa. 42:1) who would deliver Israel and ultimately bring salvation to Israel and the world (Luke 2:30–32; John 4:25–26, 29, 42).

Midrash (See MIDRASHIM, ch. 2)

Millstone

A large, very heavy circular stone used in grinding grains into flour. Two such stones (upper and lower) were combined and the grains crushed between them. The upper stone was turned by either a person or an animal. The largest such stone was turned by a donkey, and it is this stone (Gk. *mulos onikos*) that Jesus referred to (Matt. 18:6) in his warning against causing the "little ones" to stumble (Millard, *NBD*, 823).

Myth (Gk. *muthos*)

A term that has a number of different meanings, depending on the field of scholarship using it.[22] In popular literature, myth is a purely fictional story that is imaginative, untrue, and unbelievable (Soulen, 124). However, it has been used by literary critics to classify a particular type of story. For example, BULTMANN saw myth as an attempt to present transcendent truth that is beyond earthly reality in terms that belong to an earthly framework.[23] Most who use the term in this way tend to treat the facts within the mythical story as unhistorical while affirming the truth behind the myth.[24]

---

[22] See the article by James Dunn, "Demythologizing: The Problem of Myth in the New Testament," in *NTI*, 285–88.

[23] For example, the virgin birth is a myth to Bultmann created to convey the truth that Jesus is "divine."

[24] See Dunn, "Demythologizing," in *NTI*, 288–92.

Nicolaitans

A group mentioned and condemned in Revelation for their "deeds" (2:6) and "teaching" (2:15). In John's day it was a heretical sect whose teaching, after "the error of Balaam" (Jude 1:11), encouraged immorality and idolatry. Comments by later Church fathers suggest that the sect became aligned with Gnosticism (Blaiklock, *NBD*, 886).

Northern Kingdom

The kingdom formed when the northern ten tribes of Israel broke away from Solomon's son, Rehoboam (1 Kings 12), resulting in two kingdoms. The Northern Kingdom is variously referred to as Israel (1 Kings 12:16); Ephraim, the largest tribe (Isa. 7:17); or Samaria, its capital city (1 Kings 13:32). The Southern Kingdom was referred to as Judah, its largest tribe (2 Kings 23:27–28). The Northern Kingdom is notorious for having had no righteous king. It fell to the Assyrians and was taken into captivity in 722 BC. See also Southern Kingdom.

Paradise (Gk. *paradeisos,* "garden, paradise")

In the OT the Hebrew word (*pardēs*) refers to a "garden" in several places (Neh. 3:15; Ecc. 2:5; S. of Sol. 4:12). Interestingly, the Septuagint uses *paradeisos* to translate the Hebrew for the "garden of Eden." However, in the NT we find the word only three times. From these verses we can learn that Paradise is (1) a place in the presence of Jesus (Luke 23:43; cf. Phil. 1:23). It is (2) a place of incomparable revelation associated with what Paul called the "third heaven" (2 Cor. 12:4). And it is (3) a place where believers eat of the "tree of life," in the New Jerusalem (Rev. 2:7; 22:2,14). If "paradise" is synonymous with "Abraham's bosom" in Luke 16:22, then it is also a place where the righteous go after death to await the resurrection.

Passover, Feast of

The Jewish feast established by God to commemorate his deliverance of Israel from Egypt (Ex. 12), especially by sparing it from the final plague which took the life of every firstborn in Egypt. The Israelites were to kill a lamb without defect (12:5) and place its blood on the top and sides of the door frames of their houses (12:7). This blood was a sign to the Lord to "pass over" that house and not destroy the people inside. This beautifully pictures what Jesus, God's Passover Lamb (John 1:29), did for us in his death on the cross. His blood (life) poured out for us saves us from eternal death (John 3:16) by providing an atonement that takes away our sins.

Pentecost, Feast of (see Day of Pentecost)

Pharisees (Heb. *parush,* "separated")

One of the more popular and influential Jewish sects in the NT period. The exact origin of this group is uncertain, but it is likely they are related to the *Hasidim*[25] during the time of the Maccabean revolt (Ferguson, 481). The Pharisees were religious conservatives who sought to strictly obey the Law and Jewish tradition (see Mark 7), both regarded as equally authoritative. In the Gospels they, along with the scribes, are the chief enemies of Jesus. From Acts we learn that unlike the Sadducees, they believed in angels, spirits (demons), and the resurrection (Acts 23:6–8).

Philo of Alexandria (see ch. 3)

Phylacteries (Heb. *totaphoth,* "bands, frontals")

Small leather containers worn strapped to the forehead and left arm of pious Jewish men of Jesus' day. In them were parchments containing handwritten verses from the OT (Ex. 13:1–10; 11–16; Deut. 6:4–6; 11:13–21) to remind them of their covenant relationship with the Lord. They believed this was commanded by him in Ex. 13:9, 16 and Deut. 6:8; 11:18. Jesus condemned the prideful display of them in Matt. 23:5.

Polygamy (Gk. *polu,* "many"; *gamos,* "wife")

The practice of having more than one wife, which existed in biblical times, especially in the OT. However, in dealing with the question of divorce, Jesus' quotation of Gen. 2:24 suggests that from the Creation of humanity "monogamy" (marriage to one wife) was the ideal God intended for marriage.

Postexilic / Post-exile ("after the Exile")

Can refer to something that took place in the period following Judah's captivity and seventy years of exile in Babylon or to the period of the Exile itself.[26]

Post-Resurrection

Used to describe something taking place after the resurrection of Jesus from the dead.[27]

---

[25] See Josephus *Antiquities* 13.5–9; 13.10.5,6

[26] There is debate over how the 70 years should be calculated. Where do you start counting, from what event to what event? It is interesting that whether you count from Judah's first deportation to Babylon (ca. 606–605 BC) to the return of the remnant under Zerubbabel (ca. 537–536 BC) or from the destruction of the temple (ca. 586 BC) to the completion of the postexilic temple (ca. 516), you have about seventy years.

[27] Some modern scholars will make a distinction between the faith of the disciples before and after the resurrection. They propose that the "post-Easter" faith of the first Church was read back into

Procurator

The name given to a Roman magistrate or administrator who served as the chief financial officer under a Roman governor, or prefect (Lat. *praefectus*). However, after the time of the emperor Claudius (AD 41–54), a governor of a smaller province, originally called a prefect, also became known as a procurator.

Pseudepigrapha (Gk. "falsely inscribed")

Various Jewish religious writings of the period 200 B.C. to A.D. 200 that are either anonymous or falsely ascribed to some well-known OT figure, such as Job, Solomon, Ezra, or Baruch (e.g., the Psalms of Solomon). These works are quite diverse, consisting of a number of literary types, including wisdom literature, apocalypses, testaments, prayers, psalms, et al. These works were never considered to be part of the inspired canon of Scripture by Jews or Christians (Elwell and Yarbrough, 62; E. Ferguson, 422–35).

Qumran community

An ancient community that lived on the northern shore of the Dead Sea and existed in the time of Jesus. In 1947 scrolls of Scripture were discovered in clay jars, hidden in nearby caves. These scrolls were extremely valuable in assessing the status of the Hebrew Bible in the first century as well as providing insight into a fascinating Jewish communal sect. Many scholars believe the community was a branch of the Essenes, a Jewish sect mentioned in the writings of the Jewish historian Josephus (Ferguson, 489–90).

Romans / Rome / Roman Empire

People who originally came from central Italy and formed a confederation of cities known as Latium, out of which evolved the Roman Empire, with Rome as its capital. It conquered Macedonia, Greece (Achaia), and the province of Asia before the end of the 2nd century BC. In 63 BC the Roman general Pompey settled a dispute within the Hasmonean dynasty (see HASMONEANS) and from that time exercised control of the land of Israel. In Jesus' day the Romans controlled territory from the western end of the Mediterranean Sea to the Euphrates River (Ferguson, 19–30).

Sadducees

A Jewish religious sect in the time of Jesus that claimed lineage from Zadok, high priest during the kingship of David. Their origin as a sect is unclear, but

---

the Gospels and onto the lips of Jesus and the apostles. See Lee Strobel's discussion with Ben Witherington III in *Case For Christ*, 144–54; see also Millard Erickson on the axioms of form criticism in *Christian Theology*, 2d ed. (Grand Rapids: Baker Book House, 1999), 90–93.

they seem to have come from the POST-EXILIC period of the time of Ezra. We know that they stood in opposition to the Pharisees during the Hasmonean Dynasty (see HASMONEANS). As a priestly aristocracy they exerted a powerful role in Jewish politics, especially through the Sanhedrin, in which they were the dominant party. In the Gospels they are often mentioned along with the PHARISEES in their opposition to Jesus (e.g., Matt. 16:1). Unlike the Pharisees, they rejected the doctrine of the resurrection (Matt. 22:23, cf. Acts 23:7–8) along with that of angels and spirits (demons).

Samaritans

An ethnic group in the time of Jesus. They were descendants of northern Israelites who had been left in the land after the Assyrian exile of 722 BC. Intermarriage with foreigners resulted in syncretism in their worship. In the post-exilic period Samaritans were looked on as not really being Jews, in regard to both their religion and race. Therefore, they were not permitted to join the Jews in the restoration of the Temple (Neh. 4:7, 8; cf. Ezra 4:1–3). They went on to build a rival temple on Mt. Gerizim, with their own priests, and develop their own version of the Pentateuch. They were so despised in Jesus' day that Jews had "no dealings with Samaritans" (John 4:9). Oddly enough, to teach on the duty of loving one's neighbor, Jesus made a Samaritan the hero of one of his parables (Luke 10).

Sanhedrin

A ruling council of Jewish elders, the exact origin of which is uncertain. Some have linked it to a governing council of elders in the time of Ezra (Ezra 5:5, 9; 7:7, 14; 10:8 cf. Neh. 2:16; 4:14, 19; 5:7). Others identify it with the *gerousia* ("senate") in the Greek period, mentioned by Josephus (*Antiq.*12.3.3). The Sanhedrin in Jesus' day was composed of the Pharisees, scribes, and Sadducees, and presided over by the High Priest. Within the Sanhedrin the Sadducess were the dominant party. It is this ruling council that tried, condemned, and turned Jesus over to the Romans for crucifixion (Luke 22:66–71).

Seleucid

A term describing something related to the Seleucid Dynasty. Seleucus, a general under Alexander the Great, took over part of his empire after his death, which included Syria and most of Asia Minor (modern Turkey).

Semitic

Describing a member of any of a number of peoples in ancient southwestern Asia, including the Akkadians, Phoenicians, Hebrews, and Arabs, also the culture and language of these people groups. In Scripture these groups are descendents of Shem, one of Noah's sons (Gen. 5:32).

Septuagint (Lat. *Sepuaginta,* "seventy")

An early Greek translation of the Hebrew OT. This version of the Jewish Scriptures was prepared and edited in the 3rd and 2nd centuries B.C. by Jewish scholars and later adopted by Greek-speaking Christians. If the ancient Letter to Aristeas is correct, the work began under the sponsorship of Ptolemy II (285–246 BC) with the translation of the Pentateuch by 70 Jewish scholars, hence the name Septuagint. A common designation is LXX, the Roman number for seventy.

Shekinah (fr. Heb. *shekan,* "to abide or dwell")

Not a biblical term but a Hebrew word used by Rabbis to refer to the radiance of God's presence manifested to Israel. His presence was often associated with the "glory" of God (Heb. *kabod*) revealed especially (but not exclusively) in the tabernacle and temple (Ex. 40:34–35; 1 Kings 8:11; 2 Chron. 5:14; cf. Ex. 40:36–38).

Southern Kingdom

The kingdom designated as such when the northern ten tribes of Israel broke away from Solomon's son, Rehoboam (1 Kings 12), resulting in two kingdoms. The Northern Kingdom is variously referred to as Israel (1 Kings 12:16); Ephraim, the largest tribe (Isa. 7:17); or Samaria, its capital city (1 Kings 13:32). The Southern Kingdom consisted of two tribes, Benjamin and Judah. It was referred to as "Judah," since it was the larger and more prominent of the two (2 Kings 23:27–28). The Southern Kingdom continued the kingly line of David. Its history, despite having seven[28] righteous kings, was marked by idolatry and spiritual decline. It fell to the Babylonians and was taken into captivity in 586 BC.

Synagogue (Gk. *sunagōgē*)

The Septuagint often uses the term as an assembly of Israel. However, by NT times it referred to a building where Jews regularly met for worship, education, and the administration of community affairs. It probably came into existence during the Exile. Israel, deprived of their temple, sought solidarity

---

[28] Eight, if you count Amaziah (2 Kings 14:1–3), of whom it is said that he "did right in the sight of the Lord, yet not like David his father." The account goes on to describe his accommodation of idolatry.

by regularly meeting and centering their religious life around prayer, worship, and the study of the Scriptures. In NT times synagogues were built wherever Jews lived. In Paul's missionary journeys, he often visited synagogues (Acts 13:14; 14:1; 17:1, 10). Luke tells us that it was Jesus' custom to attend synagogue services on the Sabbath (Luke 4:16) (C. Feinberg, *NBD*, 1227–29).

Syncretism / syncretistic

The blending of different forms of belief or practice from two or more distinct religions. A classic biblical example of syncretism is Israel's worship of the golden calf (Ex. 32:4–8). (In all probability, the calf was actually a bull, an idolatrous image borrowed from the worship of one of Egypt's many gods [e.g., Aphis, Mnevis, or Horus].) From the words of Aaron in Ex. 32:4–5, it seems clear that Israel was not replacing the Lord (Yahweh) with a foreign god but seeking to worship the God of their deliverance through this idol.

Synoptic Gospels (fr. Gk. *sun,* "together," and *optomai,* "to see")

Refers to the gospels of Matthew, Mark, and Luke. They are called "synoptic" because they present a similar view of the earthly life and ministry of Jesus.

Tabernacles, Feast of

Also called the Feast of Booths, or "Ingathering,"[29] this feast commemorated God's provision in Israel's wilderness journey from Egypt to Canaan. It celebrated the harvest and God's goodness in bringing them to a fruitful land. This feast is mentioned in John's gospel (7:2, 37).[30]

Teraphim

Probably refers to small objects or figurines. They appear throughout Israel's biblical history. It is translated "images" or sometimes "gods." It most often appears in contexts associated with idolatry: Micah's idolatrous shrine (Jud. 17:5–18:30), with Laban's idolatry (Gen. 31:19), with divination (Ezek. 21:21), and with Israelite practices that are condemned (1 Sam. 15:23; 2 Kings 23:24).

Testament (see COVENANT)

---

[29] See Ex. 23:16; 34:22; Lev. 23:33–36,39–43; Num. 29:12–34; Deut. 16:13–15; Zech. 14:16–19.

[30] Jesus used the celebration to point to himself as "living water" (v. 38). Just as Yahweh, the Lord, provided water from the rock that kept them alive, Jesus would offer himself as God's life-giving water, providing eternal life. Cf. 1 Cor. 10:1–4.

Trans-Euphrates

A term to describe the location of Palestine in the time of Ezra and Nehemiah. It means "across the Euphrates." It shows the perspective of one who is looking from Babylon toward Jerusalem. Normally, Jews would think of Babylon as being "beyond the river" (Euphrates), but Ezra and Nehemiah, looking from Babylon, refer to the Judah and Palestine as "beyond the river" (Ezra 4:10, 11, 16, 17, 20; Neh. 2:7, 9).

Urim and Thummin

Objects kept in the breastplate of the High Priest (Ex. 28:30; Lev. 8:8) which he used to "inquire of the Lord" and get divine counsel (Num. 27:21; 1 Sam. 28:6). Some have suggested that these were objects that could be cast out of a container like lots, which would yield a positive or negative answer (J. Motyer, *NBD*, 1306). However, such an interpretation does not fit other passages where the Urim and Thummin are in use.[31] It seems wise to conclude that Scripture does not give us enough details to know for certain what they were and how they were used.

Variant reading

A difference that appears when comparing two or more manuscripts of the same biblical text. See Textual criticism.

Zealots (Gk. *zēlōtēs*)

People involved in a violent political revolt against Rome in the time of Jesus. The name may have come from the story of Phineas's zeal for the Lord (Num. 25:1–11). Josephus mentions the group in connection with the Jewish War of AD 66.[32] In the Gospels, Simon the Canaanite (Matt. 10:4, Mark 3:18) was a Zealot (Luke 6:15, Acts 1:13). The Zealots believed that it was unlawful to pay taxes to Rome (Matt. 22:17) because God alone was Lord and Caesar's claim to be Lord was for them intolerable. The Sicarii were a radical wing of the Zealots, who were involved in assassination and terrorism against those who supported Rome. Eventually, their rebellion led to the Jewish War of AD 66–73 and the destruction of the Temple in AD 70.

---

[31] For example, Saul inquired of the Lord by using the Urim, but "the Lord did not answer him" (1 Sam. 28:6), an unlikely result if only a yes or no answer was required by the casting of lots. Again, David calls for Abiathar, the high priest, to bring the ephod and inquires of the Lord (1 Sam. 23:9–18), asks direct questions, and receives yes-no answers. However, in 2 Sam. 5:19,23 David twice inquires of the Lord and the answers given are anything but a simple yes or no, the latter giving elaborate battle strategy!

[32] See Josephus *Wars of the Jews* 4.3.9,13,14; 4.4,5ff; 4.5,1,5; 7.8,1.)

Zion

The name for both Jerusalem and the mount (raised plateau) it was built on, along with the Temple. In the Bible, Zion is associated with the Davidic covenant (2 Sam. 5:7; 1 Kings 8:1), serves as a symbol of God's presence (Ps. 9:11), his Lordship over Israel and the nations (Ps. 2:6; 48:2; cf. Matt. 21:5; John 12:15; Ps. 2:8), the source of salvation (Ps. 9:14; 14:7), the origin of Israel's Messiah-Savior (Zec. 9:9; Rom. 9:33; 11:26–27), and the place from which knowledge of God will fill the earth (Isa. 2:2–3; Micah 4:1–2). (See *PDBS*, 126.) In contrasting Jerusalem with Mount Sinai, Paul has Mount Zion in mind as the place where God has established the New Covenant (Gal. 4:24–31).

Biblical Theology (OT and NT)

Already—not yet

A theological expression that describes the believer's existence from a vantage point of eschatology. With the coming of Christ and God's provision of salvation a new age has dawned. This age is referred to as the *eschaton*, or the end-time epoch of redemptive history when God will make good his promises of salvation anticipated in the OT (see Acts 2:17). The expression here belongs to a largely Pauline view of what is called "inaugurated eschatology." That is, with the first coming of Christ the believer has been transferred into the age to come. The believer's status is often described from the divine perspective of "already" accomplished in Christ. However, because redemption is "not yet" fully realized until after the Christ's second coming (see PAROUSIA) and the believer's resurrection, the NT writers can present the status of the believer as in progress or awaiting completion. (See text box.)

> If any man destroys the temple of God, God will destroy him, for the temple of God is holy, and that is what you are. –1 Cor. 3:17, NASB
>
> ...so that He may establish your hearts unblamable in holiness before our God and Father at the coming of our Lord Jesus with all His saints. –1 Thess. 3:13, NASB

Amillennialism

The belief that the thousand-year earthly reign of Christ between His two comings is not to be understood literally. Instead this reference to a millennium is understood symbolically as the reign of Christ in heaven during the Church age. Christ's second coming is understood to occur at the end of history. Most often, of the two resurrections in Revelation 20, only the second is regarded as a bodily resurrection, the first being commonly seen as referring to the new birth.[33] This view is contrasted with PREMILLENNIALISM, which understands the thousand-year earthly reign of Christ to be literal and prior to the revelation of Christ at his second coming. Amillennialism shows similarities with POSTMILLENNIALISM by rejecting the millennium as a literal thousand year reign of Christ on earth. Rather, it holds that the millennial reign of Christ began with Christ's first coming and will continue through the Church age until the world is converted, after which Christ will literally return.

Antichrist (Gk. *antichristos,* "against [or "instead of"] Christ")

The Greek term is used five times by the apostle John in the NT. It more often describes the spiritual character and preaching content of those who oppose the truth of the gospel, particularly as it relates to the identity of Christ as the Messiah and incarnate Son of God (1 John 2:22–23; 4:3; 2 John 1:7). But John's use of this title also points to a particular individual (1 John 2:18; 2 John 1:7) whose end-time opposition to Christ makes for easy identification with the "lawless one" (2 Thess. 2:8) and the "beast" (Rev. 17:8) who wages war with the Lamb during the Tribulation.

Antinomian (Gk. *anti,* "against"; *nomos,* "law")

A term used to describe the doctrine of individuals in the early church who believed that because Christians were under grace and not under the law, they were under no obligation to keep the moral demands of God's law. This view led to the practical heresy of "libertinism." Here, the understanding of one's freedom in Christ is so radical as to trivialize moral failure and encourage sins of the flesh. Paul was aware of such antinomian views in the Church and addressed them in passages such as Rom. 6:1–11 and Gal. 5:1–13.[34]

Apologist (Gk. *apologia,* "defense")

One who makes a reasoned defense of the Christian faith before unbelievers. Apologia in secular Greek was a legal term and referred to a defense of a person or position, the verb *apologeisthai* signifying to defend, justify, give

[33] Millard Erickson not only provides a clear description of amillennialsim but discusses how amillennialists interpret Rev. 20 differently from other millennial views. See *Christian Theology*, 1218–22.

[34] Note that in both passages the spiritual freedom of the believer (Rom. 6:7,14; Gal. 5:1) and the status of not being under law (Rom. 6:14; Gal. 5:2–4) are acknowledged. However, Paul also makes it clear that such a freedom is not moral license or the unbridled freedom to sin (Rom. 6:12–15), or indulge the flesh. Rather it is freedom to serve one another in faith, love (Gal. 5:6,13), and the power of the Spirit (5:16–25).

account, or an answer. This sense of the *apologia* is found in reference to Paul's defense before the Roman magistrates and his opponents (Acts 22:1; 1 Cor. 9:3; 2 Tim. 4:16). It is also used in contexts where the gospel is being presented (Phil. 1:7, 16; 2 Peter 3:15).[35]

Apostasy (Gk. lit. "a standing away from")

Signifies an abandonment, breach of faith, or rebellion against an established system or authority (*BDAG*, 120). In the Bible it is used of a rebellion against God and a defection from his truth, both in the OT (Josh 22:22; 2 Chron. 29:19) and in the NT (Acts 21:21; 2 Thess. 2:3). Owing to different theological commitments and presuppositions, debate exists over the definition of apostasy. Roman Catholics tend to see it as abandonment of the "true church" of Rome. Calvinists, who teach the doctrine of eternal security (see PERSEVERANCE OF THE SAINTS), see it as a rejection of the truth by those who were never really believers (see CALVINISM). Arminians (see ARMINIANISM) define it as a falling away from salvation by those who had once experienced salvation (*PDTT*, 14).

Baptism (Gk. *baptismos*, "dipping, immersion")

A Christian sacrament[36] involving the ritual use of water, which in the NT marked the reception of God's deliverance from sin, or salvation in Christ (Acts 2:38, 40), and the believer's incorporation into the body of Christ as a member (1 Cor. 12:13). The mode of baptism is variously practiced in the Church (immersion, pouring, sprinkling), and its significance debated.[37] What the NT clearly teaches is that baptism depicts our identification with and participation in the death and resurrection of Christ and testifies to the saving effects of that union (Rom. 6:3–10; Cf Col. 2:11–12).

---

[35] Debate exists over the purpose and function of Christian apologetics as a science—whether it is essential to the presentation of the gospel or is simply a prelude to it. See *PDTT*, s.v. "apologetics." Apart from this debate we should note that in the NT the word *apologia* appears in evangelistic contexts. Certainly the apologetic treatises of early church fathers (e.g., Justin Martyr, Origen, Tertullian), while relying on logical arguments and philosophical reasoning, could not avoid presenting the gospel they were attempting to defend.

[36] I use the term "sacrament" to mean an outward sign of an inward or spiritual work of grace, not in the sense of sacramental theology, where the grace is bound to and imparted through the sacramental rite.

[37] Note that depending upon one's theological commitments and interpretation of key passages, baptism can be viewed as testifying to the saving act of God in Christ or the means by which one receives salvation and a new nature in Christ ("baptismal regeneration").

Baptism in the Holy Spirit

The expression is used of the spiritual experience predicted four times by John the Baptist (Matt. 3:11, Mark 1:8; Luke 3:16; John 1:33) and once by Jesus himself (Acts 1:5). The OT anticipates this experience in the numerous promises to Israel of spiritual restoration that include an outpouring of the Spirit.[38] The fulfillment of these predictions occurred at Pentecost. Acts refers to it by a number of different descriptions.[39] The NT evidence presents this experience as an empowerment of the Spirit (Luke 24:49, Acts 1:8) experienced by believers for Christian service and witness.[40] The testimony of Acts presents speaking in tongues (Gk. *glossalalia*) as the outward accompanying evidence of this experience.[41]

Charismatic (see also Charismatics)

From the Greek word *charisma*, which refers to a gracious endowment, or "gift," of the Spirit (cf. 1 Cor. 12:4). As an adjective, charismatic speaks of something that relates to or expresses the empowerment of the Holy Spirit in the life of the Church or Spirit-filled believer (Arrington, 85, 116, 471).

Christocentric

A theological perspective that places Christ at the center of its focus. For example, the speeches in Acts, as recorded by Luke, are Christocentic in their emphasis on Christ as God's Messiah and agent of salvation.

Coming of the Lord (see also Rapture)

An expression closely aligned with "the day of the Lord" in the OT, a day of divine visitation for deliverance and healing (Isa. 30:26) or judgment and

---

[38] See Isa. 32:15; 44:3; Ezek. 36:26–27; 37:14; 39:29; Joel 2:28–29; Zech. 12:10.

[39] It is called "the promise of the Father" (1:4), "the coming of the Holy Spirit" (1:8), being "filled with the Holy Spirit" (2:4; 9:17), a "pouring forth" of the Spirit (2:17,18), receiving "the promise of the Holy Spirit" (2:33), receiving "the gift of the Holy Spirit" (2:38), receiving the Holy Spirit (8:15,17; 10:46,47; 19:2); "the Holy Spirit falling upon" someone (10:44); "gift of the Spirit" being "poured out" (10:45), being "baptized in/with the Holy Spirit" (11:16), God "giving the Holy Spirit" (15:8), and the "Holy Spirit coming upon" someone (19:6).

[40] Pentecostals and Charismatics hold that the baptism in the Holy Spirit results in spiritual empowerment, not salvation. In this they distinguish between the baptism *in* the Holy Spirit, where Jesus is the baptizing agent and the Spirit is the medium into which the believer is immersed (Mark 1:8 etc.), and the baptism *by* the Spirit, where the Spirit is the agent baptizing the believer into the body of Christ (1 Cor. 12:13; cf. Gal. 3:27).

[41] See Acts 2:4; 10:46; and 19:6. Admittedly, other instances of Spirit-baptism in Acts appear without a reference to any accompanying phenomena (Acts 8:17,18; 9:17). However, where Luke pauses in his narrative to record such phenomena, tongues is present.

destruction (Joel 1:15), or both (Isa. 61:2). In the NT it most often refers to the 2nd Coming of Christ at the end of this age (Matt. 24:3). The Greek word *parousia* means "coming," "arrival," or "presence" and can refer to both the return of Christ that gathers believers in the so-called RAPTURE (1 Thess. 4:15, 2 Thess. 2:1) for deliverance and the revelation of Christ which results in final victory over Satan (2 Thess. 2:8–9; cf. 1 Peter 1:13).

Covenant (Heb. *berith*, Gk. *diathēkē*)

Basically denotes a solemn agreement between two parties outlining the promises, commitments, and obligations by one or both parties.[42] The term is widely used throughout the Bible to express God's sovereign initiative in establishing a special relationship with an individual and/or his people, making it one of the most important concepts in biblical theology. In the OT several covenants can be found to resemble two main types of covenants in the ancient Near East: (1) The royal grant covenant refers to a king's sovereign and unconditional commitment to a loyal servant.[43] (2) The suzerain-vassal covenant refers to a powerful king's pledging his provision and protection to one of his vassal kings in exchange for absolute loyalty and obedience to the terms of the covenant.[44] The NT expands the use of the term to refer to a "will" or "testament" that delivers an inheritance (Heb. 9:15–22).

Great Tribulation

The 3½ year (1,260 days [Rev. 11:3; 12:6; cf. Dan. 12:11]) period of ANTICHRIST rule on earth before the public and universal revelation of Christ at His second coming (Matt. 24:29–30; Rev. 19:11–21). It is a period of unprecedented tribulation and suffering (Matt. 24:21) during which the wrath of God falls on the world in the plagues of Revelation 6–18.

---

[42] Depending on one's theological commitments or system, covenants can be viewed differently. Reformed covenantal theologians, for example, often stress the sovereign nature of God's covenant and dispensation of grace, while minimizing the importance of reciprocal obligations. See John Murray, "Covenant" in *NBD*, 264–68. While God's sovereign and gracious action in establishing biblical covenants is undeniable, this is also true of the mutual or reciprocal responsibilities of those covenants. See P. R. Williamson, "Covenant," in *NDBT*, 422–26.

[43] God's covenants with Noah (Gen. 9:8–17), Abraham (Gen. 15:9–21), Phinehas (Num. 25:10–13), David (2 Sam. 7:5–16) and the "new covenant" to Israel (Jer. 31:31–34; cf Heb. 8:8–12) fall into the Royal Grant category.

[44] The conditional and reciprocal nature of this covenant finds parallels in the second covenant with Abraham (Gen. 17) and the Sinaitic, or Mosaic, covenant (Ex. 19–24).

Harmartiology (fr. Gk. *harmartia,* "sin")

The teachings (doctrine) of the Bible with respect to sin: its origin, nature, effects, and consequences for the human race. See Sin.

Heresy (Gk. *hairēsis,* "sect" or "heresy")

Can refer to a religious sect as it does in Acts 24:14. However, the term is used more commonly of a false teaching that does not conform to the accepted and authoritative standards of a religious community (Elwell and Yarbrough, 398). With regard to NT Christianity, heresy would be any teaching that contradicts the core beliefs of the apostolic gospel and essential doctrine of the Christian faith (cf. Apostolic fathers).

Historicist school (See Apocalypse, ch. 5)

Jacob's trouble

A time of intense suffering and persecution for Israel predicted by Jeremiah (30:5–7), followed by a day of deliverance. While Jeremiah seems to have Israel's restoration from exile in his prophetic sight (vv. 8, 18), the description of the time of trouble seems to resemble a future time of tribulation prophesied by Jesus (Matt. 24:21).[45] If Jeremiah is prophesying of the same tribulation as Jesus, Jacob's trouble refers to the 3½ year period known as the Great Tribulation mentioned in Rev. 6:17 (cf. Rev. 11:3; 12:6).

Mid-Tribulation (See also Pre-Tribulation and Post-Tribulation)

The belief that the Rapture of the Church described in 1 Thess. 4:13–17 will take place half-way (3½ years) through the seven years of the Tribulation and right before the Great Tribulation. (See also Jacob's trouble.) The latter is identified as the outpouring of the wrath of God from which the Church is spared[46] (Erickson, 1230).

Millennium

A thousand year period mentioned in Rev. 20:2–6 after the return of Christ with his saints to reign on earth and establish his kingdom. This kingdom will

---

[45] Jeremiah says of the day of trouble, "None will be like it." This parallels Jesus' words, "For then there will be great distress, unequaled from the beginning of the world until now—and never to be equaled again." This description also seems to echo Dan. 12:1 and Joel 2:2. While the devastation–tribulation prophesied by Joel has a reference to his day, the deliverance accompanying the Day of the Lord (1:15) certainly leaps forward to the messianic age. See Joel 2:23–31; cf. Acts 2:16–21.

[46] A popular treatment of this position can be found in Marvin Rosenthal, *The Pre-Wrath Rapture of the Church* (Nashville, Tenn.: Thomas Nelson, 1990).

be marked by righteousness, peace, and prosperity. To a large extent the nature of the Millennium is determined by one's particular view of Millennialism. See AMILLENNIALISM, POSTMILLIENNIALISM, and PREMILLENNIALISM.[47]

Mosaic Law

Refers to the body of instruction and laws that God gave to Moses for Israel and recorded in the Pentateuch. See also TORAH.

Oral Torah / Law

Another way to refer to the Jewish oral tradition behind the MISHNAH (ch. 2), a written compilation of oral law arranged topically. There are sixty-six tractates, or essays, grouped in six divisions: the holiness of the land of Israel, the holiness of time, the holiness of family life, the sanctification of property, the holy place, and the bounds of holiness.

Postmillennialism

The particular view of the MILLENNIUM (Rev. 20) that rejects the notion of a literal thousand-year reign of Christ on earth. It views the millennial reign of Christ as having begun with his first coming to establish his spiritual reign in human hearts. This reign continues to this day and no future reign of Christ is anticipated. Through the preaching of the gospel, peace and righteousness will gradually prevail and evil will be subdued. Finally, when the gospel has had its full impact on the world, Christ will return.

Post-Tribulation (see also MID-TRIBULATION and PRE-TRIBULATION)

The belief that the RAPTURE of the Church described in 1 Thess. 4:13–17 will take place after the seven years of Tribulation. This period is identified as the 70th week (i.e., of years) of Daniel (Dan. 9:25–27) and includes the 3½ years of the GREAT TRIBULATION (see also JACOB'S TROUBLE). Post-tribulationists see Christ's second coming as one event at the end of the Tribulation. Although the Church is saved from God's wrath (1 Thess. 1:10), it is not spared tribulation, which it will victoriously endure (Matt. 24:9–13).[48]

---

[47] For a very helpful survey of these three millennial views, see Robert G. Clouse, ed., *The Meaning of the Millennium* (Downers Grove, Ill.: InterVarsity Press, 1977). Clouse has four scholars discuss their positions on the Millennium (premillennialism is represented from both the historic premillennial and dispensational premillennial positions).

[48] A well-known proponent of this view of the Tribulation is Robert Gundry. See *The Church and the Tribulation* (Grand Rapids: Zondervan , 1973).

Premillennialism (see also AMILLENNIALSIM)

The particular view of the MILLENNIUM that understands the thousand year earthly reign of Christ mentioned in Rev. 20:2–6 to be literal and physical. It will be preceded by a terrible period of tribulation (see JACOB'S TROUBLE) prior to the revelation of Christ at his second coming.[49] The two resurrections mentioned in Rev. 20 are taken to be physical resurrections that are suggested in passages such as Dan. 12:2 and John 5:29.

Preterism (see APOCALYPSE, PRETERIST, ch 5)

Pre-Tribulation

The belief that the RAPTURE of the Church described in 1 Thess. 4:13–17 will take place prior to the seven years of the TRIBULATION. This period is identified as the 70th week (i.e., of years) of Daniel (Dan. 9:25–27) and includes the 3½ years of the GREAT TRIBULATION (see also JACOB'S TROUBLE). Pre-Tribulationists see the second coming of Christ in two parts: the RAPTURE, in which Christ comes to catch away his Church, and the Revelation of Christ, in which he comes to earth with his saints to bring judgment on the world (Rev. 19).[50]

Rapture (see also COMING OF THE LORD)

An event identified with the second coming of Christ depicted by Paul in 1Thess. 4:13–17. In it there is a resurrection of the believers who have died. They, along with those Christians that remain alive at his Coming (Gk. *parousia*), are caught up in the clouds to meet the Lord. It is often referred to in the Church as "the blessed hope" (Titus 2:13; 4:13).

Repent / repentance (Gk. *metanoeō* or *metanoia*)

To turn one's entire mind, affections, and will away from sin and toward God. In the context of salvation, repentance is something both that people are called to do in their response to God (Mark 1:4; 6:12) and that God grants to them (Acts 11:18) through the preaching of the gospel.

[49] Premillennial scholars disagree over whether the Church will be present on earth during the Tribulation, but all agree that the world immediately preceding the Millennium will be marked by trouble, turmoil, persecution, and suffering. See Erickson, *Christian Theology*, 1218.

[50] A classic presentation of this position is done by John F. Walvoord in *The Rapture Question* (Finlay, Ohio: Dunham, 1957).

Restitution

A principle of justice which speaks of making up for a wrong that was committed. Mosaic instruction in the OT prescribed different degrees of restitution, depending on the kind of wrong done or injury suffered (see Ex. 22:1–6; Lev. 6:5; Num. 5:7; cf. Ex. 21:22–36). A classic example of restitution in the NT is found in the case of Zacchaeus, whose life-changing encounter with Jesus resulted in a desire to pay back fourfold (Luke 19:8) the amount he defrauded (W. R. Thompson, *BDT*, 451).

Resurrection (Gk. *anastasis*)

In theology the term does not refer to a physical resuscitation from death, which occurs both in the OT (1 Kings 17:23) and the NT (Mark 5:42). The term more properly refers to either the resurrection of Jesus (Matt. 27:53) or an eschatological event (Matt. 22:23–31) in which both the righteous (Luke 14:14) and unrighteous dead are raised to either eternal life or God's eternal judgment (John 5:29; cf Dan. 12:2). Revelation 20 speaks of the two resurrections, "the first resurrection" at the beginning of the MILLENNIUM (v. 4) and a second resurrection thereafter (see vv. 7–15).

Retribution

Refers to an aspect of justice where punishment is meted out for a wrongdoing. In the OT, for example, capital punishment is the retribution prescribed for murder (Num. 35:33). With respect to salvation, the death of Christ is at the same time a merciful atonement and the working of divine justice in providing retribution for sin (Rom. 3:25–26) (Ockenga, *BDT*, 454).

Sacrifice

The act of offering something to God. In the OT numerous offerings were prescribed as a means of worship and maintaining or restoring relationship with God (see Lev. 1–7). In all but one of those offerings (grain offering) an animal was sacrificed and its blood poured out. In particular, the sin/guilt offering (Lev. 4:1–5:13) taught Israel the truth that the blood is necessary to provide an atonement (Heb. *kaphar,* "to cover") for sin and that without the shedding of blood there could be no forgiveness (Lev. 17:11; cf. Heb. 9:22). This pointed ahead to Christ, the "Lamb of God" (John 1:29), who would not just cover sins but remove them.

Saints (Heb. *Qadosh,* Gk. *hagioi,* "holy ones")

Used widely in the Bible for God's holy or consecrated people: Israel in the OT and Christian believers in the NT. It is one of Paul's favorite titles of address for Christians in the churches. In the NT the term does not carry any sense of an elite spiritual status or group of Christians but is used of all true followers of Christ.

Salvation (Heb. *yeshuah/yesha;* Gk. *soteria*)

A very broad term that expresses the ideas of deliverance, rescue, or preservation in and through a host of threatening circumstances. Theologically the term refers to the gracious action of God in delivering us from sin and its penalty of death and offering us eternal life by trusting in his Son, Jesus Christ, as our sin offering (John 1:29).

Salvific

An adjective that designates something as relating to salvation, having the power to save, or redeem, or salvation as its purpose. E.g., the Gospels contain a salvific message for all humanity.

Second Coming (see Coming of the Lord)

Second death

Revelation 20 speaks of the two resurrections, "the first resurrection" at the beginning of the Millennium (v. 5) and a second resurrection after the Millennium (see vv. 7–15). After the second resurrection those raised are judged, and anyone whose name is not found in the "book of life" is thrown into the lake of fire. "This," John says, "is the second death" (v.14).

Seventy weeks

A phrase occurring only in Dan. 9:24, in an obscure prophetic vision. Literally the Hebrew reads "seventy sevens," but since the context is one of historical sequence, most scholars see the "sevens" as referring to weeks. That being so, the verse identifies a 490 year period that is decreed for Israel in which the Messiah will accomplish six purposes: "to finish the transgression, to make an end of sin, to make atonement for iniquity, to bring in everlasting righteousness, to seal up vision and prophecy and to anoint the most holy place" (*NASB*). The start of this period is clearly stated as the decree to restore and rebuild Jerusalem. After 69 weeks (62+7), the Messiah (lit. "the Anointed one"), ruler, comes (v. 25) and is "cut off" (i.e., killed). Since the 70th week is mentioned in v. 27 in connection with "the end" and with war and desolation, some scholars see here a reference to the seven year period of tribulation that precedes the 2nd Coming of Christ (Matt. 24:29–30; Rev. 19:11–21).

Sin

May be summarized as any lack of conformity to or violation of God's nature and revealed will. The Bible has numerous terms that serve to define or describe the nature of sin.[51] The most common NT word translated "sin" is the Greek *hamartia*, which describes a "missing the mark," a coming up short of God's standards of moral perfection (see Rom. 3:23). On the relational side, sin is a failure to put one's faith in God and trust him by being obedient to his will (James 4:17; Rom. 14:23). Thus, from a biblical perspective, sin describes the condition of fallen humanity and the individual sinner; it involves not only what one does but also what one is (*PDTT*, 107).

Son of David

A phrase meaning "descendent of David." It became a title for the Jewish Messiah, probably in association with the Davidic covenant and God's promise to establish an everlasting kingdom through one of his descendents (2 Sam. 7:8–16).[52] The messianic expectation of the Jews was that the Messiah would be a descendent of David (see Isa. 11:1–2, 11; cf. Acts 13:22–23; Rom. 15:12).

Son of Man

Jesus' favorite title for himself. It has more than one sense and association in the history of Israel. Ezekiel used it of himself as a prophet agent standing in identification with humanity (Ezek. 2:2, 3, 6, 8). The Hebrew phrase (*ben adam*) could serve as a roundabout way of referring to "a man" (Jer. 50:40). Finally, the title is used by Daniel of a transcendent heavenly Son of Man who is granted dominion by God and an everlasting kingdom that will never be destroyed (Dan. 7:14). It is this latter use that gave the title its messianic overtones. Oddly, the post-resurrection Church did not use it as a christological title (see Christology), preferring less ambiguous titles.

Transgression (Heb. *pesha;* Gk. *paraptōma*)

One of the many biblical terms for Sin. It describes sin as a violation of God's laws and commandments (1 John 3:4). The Hebrew term carries the idea of a willful and rebellious act. The Greek word connotes a violation of a known moral standard, as in the case of Adam's sin (Rom. 5:15–20) (*DBAG*, 770).

---

[51] Biblical words dealing with sin convey such concepts as failure, error, iniquity, trespass, transgression, evil, unrighteousness, wickedness, lawlessness, wrongdoing, injustice, immorality, moral impurity.

[52] Matthew's genealogy of Jesus Christ is emphatic in pointing out the lineage of Jesus the Messiah from the line of David.

Tribulation (see Jacob's trouble)

Unpardonable sin

A term taken from Jesus' encounter with the Pharisees when they accused him of working with Beelzebul to cast out demons (Mark 3:22). Jesus informed them that they were blaspheming against the Holy Spirit, adding, "whoever blasphemes against the Holy Spirit never has forgiveness, but is guilty of an eternal sin" (v. 29). Although it is tempting to identify this sin, careful interpretation of this passage and parallel accounts indicates that Jesus is describing not an isolated incident of sin but a long-standing spiritual condition that has reached a final state of spiritual blindness.[53]

Vicarious

Describes something performed or suffered by one person as a substitute for another, or in their place. The term is often used in Christian theology to describe the substitutionary nature of Jesus' death on the cross releasing us from the penalty for sins. In the OT a picture of the vicarious nature of the sin offering is given in the ritual sacrifice of one goat and the release of the "scapegoat" (Lev. 16).

Yahweh Yireh ("Yahweh provides," also Jehovah Jireh)

A Hebrew expression that depicts God's faithfulness in providing a ram as a substitute sacrifice for Isaac (Gen. 22:8–14). Abraham named the mountain location of that sacrifice "the Lord will provide." See also Vicarious.

Systematic / Historical Theology

Adoption (Gk. *huiothesia,* "adoption")

The gracious act of God whereby he takes estranged sinners and places them in his family, making them his children and heirs of an eternal inheritance in heaven

---

[53] Note in particular that those who blaspheme are not ignorant of the Scriptures ("scribes . . . from Jerusalem" [v.22]). They knew what the Messiah would do from passages like Isa. 61:1. Their sin was not a single act. The Greek of Mark 3:22 should be translated, "and they kept saying." Luke (11:16) indicates that they were demanding a sign so that they could believe. Jesus had just indicated that the Holy Spirit would be given to those who ask the Father (11:13). The Spirit working through Jesus (4:1,14) then gave them a sign—deliverance from demonic bondage. Not only did they reject the sign, but rather than interpreting the source of power as divine, they saw it as evidence that Jesus was working with Satan. How great was the darkness that enveloped their hearts such that they could not distinguish God's work from the Devil's!

(Heb. 9:15; 1 Peter 1:4).[54] This adoption is granted to those who believe in/receive Christ (John 1:12; cf. John 3:15–16), who are born again by the Spirit (John 3:5–6) and have received the "Spirit of adoption" (Rom. 8:15–16), who is the down payment, pledge, and seal of their future inheritance (Rom. 8:23; Eph. 1:13–14; 4:30).

Arminianism

A system of theology named after James Arminius, a sixteenth-century Dutch theologian. Arminius developed his theology largely in debate with Calvinists over the doctrine of predestination, rejecting the teaching that people are unconditionally predestined to salvation or damnation.[55] Instead Arminius held that human freedom is considered by God in the process and appropriation of his free gift of salvation (J. Grider, *BDT*, 51). God's grace enables people to repent and believe. While he did not totally deny the predestination of individuals, he held that it was based on God foreknowing what individuals would freely decide. Furthermore, since salvation is freely received, it can be freely forfeited through unbelief and disobedience—a notion alien to both Luther and Calvin (*PDTT*, 15). See also Calvinism.

Calvinism

A system of theology named after John Calvin (1509–64), a French reformer and arguably the greatest theologian and biblical scholar of the Reformation. Calvin's theology, expounded in his *Institutes of the Christian Religion*, emphasized the sovereignty of God to the extent that human will plays no part in the process of appropriating God's gracious offer of salvation. Instead, salvation of individuals is grounded in God's divine decree to elect and predestine some to salvation and others to damnation. Calvinism is the formal development of Calvin's theology by his successors. It was articulated by the Synod of Dort (1619) and summarized by the acronym TULIP, which stands for five interlocking and interdependent doctrines: total depravity, unconditional election, limited atonement, irresistible grace, and perseverance of the saints (Taylor, *BDT*, 85–88). See also John Calvin.

---

[54] Note that the "already-not yet" motif appears in connection with this inheritance: Christians have already received an inheritance, the pledge of which is the Holy Spirit (Eph. 1:11,13–14, 18; Col. 1:12), and they will receive a future inheritance (Col. 3:24; Heb. 9:15; 1 Peter 1:4). In the same way, Paul presents adoption as something believers have already received (Rom. 8:15; Gal. 4:5,6) and something they wait for, at least for the fullness of its benefits (Rom. 8:23).

[55] The debate between Calvin and Arminius begins with contrasting views over God's sovereign decrees relative to creation and redemption. It is far too complex to summarize herein. One excellent overview of the debate can be found in J. K. Grider, "Arminianism", in *Evangelical Dictionary of Theology*, Walter A. Elwell, ed., (Grand Rapids: Baker Book House, 1984), 79.

Charismatics

Believers in the Charismatic Movement, which began in America ca. 1960 among the historic Christian churches. The term comes from the Greek word *charismata*, referring to the "gifts of the Spirit" (cf. 1 Cor. 12:4), which Charismatics believe are to be experienced in the Church today. These gifts are viewed as part of the Spirit-filled Christian life and available through the baptism in the Holy Spirit. Spirit-baptism is a distinct Christian experience that follows conversion in which the believer is immersed in the presence and power of the Holy Spirit. Charismatics differ from classical Pentecostals not over the nature and practice of tongues (Gk. *glossalalia*), but over its significance in relation to Spirit-baptism. Charismatics generally view tongues as one of many accompanying evidences of being filled with the Spirit, whereas Pentecostals see it as the initial outward sign that a believer has been baptized in the Holy Spirit (J.R. Williams, *EDT*, 204–208).

Christendom

Can refer to the religion of Christianity itself or that part of the world where Christianity prevails or exerts a major influence.

Christology (Gk. *Christos,* "anointed one"; *logos,* "word")

A term used in theology to denote the doctrinal study devoted to the person and work of Jesus Christ. This includes his identity and all aspects of his divine and human natures before, during, and after his incarnation and the significance of his life, death, and resurrection to God's plan of salvation for the world.

Church Fathers

A term that refers to church leaders (usually prominent bishops) in the post-apostolic Church (cf. Apostolic fathers) who championed the orthodox teaching of the Church as taught by the apostles of Christ (*PDTT*, 25).

Deism (also deist, deistic)

The belief that although God created the world, he did so by making it self-sustaining. I.e., God does not providentially support his creation, nor does he intervene so as to set aside the laws that govern it. It is derived from an 18th century philosophy of religion that emphasized natural religion guided by reason (cf. Rationalism), not by an appeal to divine Revelation (as in the Scriptures) (*PDAP*, 32).

Depravity

A theological term that refers to the state of moral and spiritual corruption. This condition shows itself in humanity in the tendency to sin. The

Calvinist doctrine of total depravity contends that due to original sin every part of human nature was corrupted so that no human being is capable of knowing or obeying God, or capable of doing anything that would secure personal salvation (*PDTT*, 37).

> The heart is more deceitful than all else and is desperately sick; Who can understand it?
> —Jer. 17:9, NASB

Dialectic

The existence of opposing or contradictory ideas or positions within a rational system of thought, reasoning, or argumentation.[56] Such a system usually seeks to resolve the conflict. In theology a dialectical tension is sometimes created when human language or experience has no adequate terms to rationally explain divine mystery, e.g., the incarnation.

Dispensationalism (fr. Gk. *oikonomia,* "household management")

A theological system that attempts to understand the history of salvation as revealed in the Bible. It sees God as working out his plan progressively through successive periods, or dispensations (e.g., innocence [Garden of Eden], human conscience [the Fall to the Flood], human government [the Flood to Abraham]). While the ultimate goal of restoring the kingdom of God remains singular and the means of salvation remains the same (by grace through faith), the terms of obedience and the way God works with humanity differ in each dispensation. Dispensationalism is also commonly identified as a way of interpreting the Scriptures. It emphasizes the literal interpretation of Scripture, especially prophecy. Theologically it is noted for its commitment to PREMILLENNIALISM (see also AMILLENNIALSIM) and maintaining an eternal distinction between Israel and the Church.

Ecclesiastical (fr. Gk. *ecclesia,* "church / assembly")

Of or relating to the church, its clergy and ministry, as an established institution. In theology "ecclesiology" refers to the doctrine of the Church as taught in the Scriptures.

---

[56] The philosopher who is most often associated with the "dialectic" is G. W. F. Hegel (1770–1831). He described the process of change as an evolutionary development of thought called "dialectical materialism." Hegel believed an idea (thesis) generated a counterpoint (antithesis) which created a "dialectical tension" that called for a resolution, or synthesis. Adolf von Harnack (1851–1930) used this theory to explain the history of theological development in the Early Church.

Ecumenical / Ecumenism / Ecumenical Movement

From the Greek term *oikoumenē*, "the whole inhabited earth." Thus the term "ecumenical" was used to describe those councils and their creeds that expressed the universal faith of the church. Of the numerous ancient church councils, only seven were recognized by the Roman Catholic and Eastern Church as being ecumenical. These seven, ending with the 2nd Council of Nicea in AD 787, are called the Ecumenical Councils (Childers, *BDT*, 180). Today "ecumenical" is used to describe a movement that seeks unity and cooperation for the Christian church throughout the world. The emphasis is on shared spiritual heritage and common goals. Critics of this movement point out that the unity envisioned is institutional, which remains minimal because of variant commitments to world evangelization and failure to reach doctrinal agreement as to what constitutes the gospel and the faith of the Church (Weber, *EDT*, 340–42).

Election (Gk. *eklektos,* "chosen")

Most commonly refers to God's choice of a redeemed people (see Rom. 8:33; 1 Peter 1:1). The doctrine is the object of intense debate, especially among Calvinists (see Calvinism) and Arminians (see Arminianism). The debate is not over whether God chooses, but the nature, object, and purpose of his choice. Most Calvinists combine the doctrines of predestination and election to refer to his sovereign choice of individuals for either salvation or damnation. As such, election is unconditional. Arminians usually respond that God's predestination, and therefore his election, is based on his "foreknowledge" of how people will respond to the gospel (*BDT*, 221).[57]

Eschatology (fr. Gk *eschatos,* "last, final")

That branch of theology that attempts to understand the entire scope of redemptive history and God's ultimate destiny for humanity. Human history is called "this age"[58] and is contrasted in the NT with "the age to come."[59] It

[57] A more satisfactory Arminian position is articulated by Robert Shank. He points out first of all that predestination and election are not synonymous. Election has reference to who is chosen; predestination has to do with the purpose for which the Elect were chose. Furthermore, he demonstrates that God's election is "in Christ" (Eph. 1:4) and is primarily corporate; God has chosen for himself a redeemed people in Christ. Therefore, while his election comprehends all people potentially, it comprehends no person unconditionally. Faith is a necessary response that results in incorporation into Christ as the Elect of God. See Shank, *Elect in the Son* (Springfield, Mo.: Westcott Publishers, 1970), 45–55, 99–108.

[58] See Luke 16:8; 20:34; 1 Cor. 1:20; 2:6,8.

[59] See Matt. 12:32; Luke 18:29,30. Moreover, "this present age" is characterized as "evil," and Christians have been rescued or delivered from it by Christ (Gal. 1:4; cf. Col. 1:13).

focuses on the final events that will happen at the "end of the age,"[60] especially at the climactic end of human history prior to Christ's second coming. It also is concerned with following the culminating events that will follow Christ's return (e.g., resurrection, the millennium, judgment) leading into the eternal age to come (Luke 18:30) and his eternal kingdom (2 Peter 1:11).

Eternal security

The Calvinistic doctrine that no true believer can fall from grace and lose his or her salvation (also called PERSEVERANCE OF THE SAINTS). The doctrine flows out of and is grounded in God's eternal decree to unconditionally elect and predestine every individual to salvation or damnation. If "the elect" are saved by a decree of God, then they will be saved regardless of what they do or do not do after conversion.[61]

Ethics / ethical

Refers to that branch of philosophical (and theological) inquiry that seeks to determine what is right and wrong. It also seeks to determine the basis (e.g., principles or criteria) for making moral judgments as to what is good and evil, moral and immoral, in the contexts of human or societal behavior (*PDTT*, 47).

Evangelical (Gk. *euaggelion,* "gospel / good news")

As a noun the term usually refers to a Christian who emphasizes salvation through a personal conversion ("being born again") that comes by believing in Christ and God's work of redemption as proclaimed in "the gospel." Historically, Evangelicals are known for their commitment to the inspiration, authority, and infallibility of Scripture. The adjective describes something that relates to, or expresses the proclamation of the Christian gospel as presented in the NT, especially the four Gospels.

Evangelism

The preaching of the Christian gospel to those who are unbelievers, in need of God's salvation provided through the life, death, and resurrection of Jesus Christ (1 Cor. 15:1–4).[62]

---

[60] See Matt. 13:39–40,49,50; 24:3; 28:19,20.

[61] The debate over eternal security is complex and hinges on the interpretation of multiple texts. For a balanced presentation of Arminian and Calvinistic positions, see W. T. Purkiser, "Eternal Security," in *BDT*, 192–93, and J. H. Gerstner, "Perseverance" in *BDT*, 403–4. A very helpful work which deals exegetically with nearly all relevant texts is Shank, *Life in the Son.*

[62] Some might argue that evangelism should be defined to include the making of disciples and point to the Great Commission (Matt. 28:18–20) as support for their position. Certainly the tasks are related in the work of the Church. However, the words "gospel (Gk. *euaggelion*) and

Evolution

The process of change seen to take place within species of animals and plants; however, it more often refers to the theory that attempts to explain the origin of human life via forces operating according to natural law.[63] As such, evolution most often leads to atheism. By positing that all life forms evolved from simpler forms there is no need for a personal Creator.

Ex nihilo (Lat., "out of nothing")

Speaks of God's original creation of the world / universe (Gen. 1:1). His creation is declared to be a fiat act where he creates without the aid of any previously existing matter.[64]

Expiation (see Propitiation)

Closely related to the word Propitiation, both being derived from the Greek verb *hilaskomai* and its cognate nouns *hilasmos* and *hilastērion*. Scholars debate whether the noun describes a sacrifice that "satisfies the wrath of God" or one that provides "a covering for sin." Paul describes Christ's death as a *hilasterion*, "in his blood" (Rom. 3:25). Given the predominant theme of God's wrath against sin in the OT[65] and Paul's recognition of the same (Rom. 1:18, 24, 26, 28), it is difficult to imagine that the satisfaction of God's wrath was not part of Paul's thinking concerning what Christ's death accomplished.

"to preach the gospel" (Gk *euaggelizomai*) do not appear in the text of Matt. From a linguistical stand point, then, it seems better to view the work of evangelism as directed toward lost sinners and the work of discipleship toward the believing Christian.

[63] Those laws were identified by Charles Darwin in his *Origin of the Species* (1859). He saw the change-producing agent as random mutations and the change mechanism as "natural selection." Today many scientists have serious doubts and problems with Darwin's explanation, but few deny that Darwinian evolution makes the existence of God unnecessary. For a concise clarification of how the theory of evolution leads to atheism, see Lee Strobel's interview with Jonathan Wells concerning "Doubts About Darwinism" in *The Case for a Creator* (Grand Rapids: Zondervan, 2004), 31–68. Perhaps the most scholarly critique of Darwinian evolution to date is Philip Johnson, *Darwin On Trial*, 2nd ed. (Downers Grove, Ill.: InterVarsity Press, 1993).

[64] We should note that the biblical account of and references to creation emphasize the fact that the world is a creation of God. They are not given for the purpose of telling us the manner in which God created it. Nevertheless, the many references to the beginning of the world or creation before there was a material creation certainly suggest that the original act was *ex nihilo*. See Matt. 13:35; 25:34; Mark 10:6; 13:19; Luke 11:50; John 1:1; 8:44; Rom. 1:20; Eph. 1:4; 1 Peter 1:20; 1 John 1:1; Rev. 3:14; 13:8; 17:8, et al. (Erickson, *Christian Theology*, 395).

[65] See Leon Morris, "Propitiation," in *Evangelical Dictionary*, ed., Elwell, 888. Cf. Leon Morris, "The Use of *Hilaskesthai* in Biblical Greek," *Expository Times* (May 1951), 227–33.

There is no good reason to conclude that the Greek word group above does not refer to a sacrifice that both covers or cancels one's sin and at the same time satisfies God's wrath (Erickson, 828–29).[66]

Foreknowledge (fr. Gk. *proginōskō,* "to know beforehand")

That aspect of God's total knowledge (omniscience) that allows him to know something before it happens.[67]

Humanism (Christian, secular)

Refers to a movement or philosophy that emphasizes the supreme and inherent worth of human beings. In one sense, Christianity can be called humanistic because human worth is established by the doctrine of creation. Humans derive their worth because they are created in the divine image (Gen. 1:26–27) and are the objects of his redemptive love (John 3:16). Secular humanism, on the other hand, removes God from the picture, and human worth is derived apart from any notion of God (*PDTT*, 61). Thus, in the search for truth there is no higher appeal than to natural human reason and experience. Cf. Rationalism.

Hypothesis (fr. Gk. *hupotithenai,* "to place under, suppose")

An unproven assumption or concession granted for the sake of argument. It is accepted in order to draw out and test the validity of a theory either by logic or empirical experimentation.[68]

Immanence / immanent

God's presence in, nearness to, and involvement with his creation and its creatures. God's active participation in human history is clearly seen in the history of redemption as chronicled in Scripture. Immanence is a byproduct of God's omnipresence, but it does not result in God's being inseparable from

---

66 For some, the hesitancy to think of Christ death as "appeasing" the wrath of God, is based on the faulty assumption that such a view would make God a reluctant party to redemption. As the NT clearly teaches, Christ is not in opposition to the will of the Father who would judge the sinner if not for Christ's atoning sacrifice. Rather, "God was in Christ reconciling the world to himself" (2 Cor. 5:19). The paradox of this doctrine is that God provides what his justice demands. He satisfies the demands of his wrath by sending His own Son to be an atoning sacrifice.

67 Debate and theological controversy exists over who or what it is that God knows and what results from his foreknowledge. See Arminianism. The NT uses the verb and noun sparingly. See Rom. 8:29; 11:2; 1 Peter 1:2, 20; Acts 2:23.

68 For example, in the debate of creation vs. evolution, the hypothesis of God's existence or nonexistence could be granted by those in the debate. Once accepted the legitimacy or

his creation. In Scripture the Creator is never confused with his creation but remains distinct from it (see Rom. 1:25), which is one reason why all forms of idolatry are forbidden (see Isa. 40:26–41:7). See also TRANSCENDENCE.

Imminence / imminent

That quality or state of being that describes something that is ready to take place. In a negative context it could describe an impending danger, crisis, or disaster. The term is used in connection with the second coming of Christ, as an event that could occur at any time. Some theologians argue that Christ's coming is imminent, or near, because it is the next major event on God's redemptive calendar (*PDTT*, 64).

Immutability / immutable

The quality or state of being unchangeable or insusceptible to change. This quality is attributed to God by theologians. God affirms this of himself when he states, "I, the LORD, do not change" (Mal 3:6). Although Scripture clearly indicates that God is unchanging in his essential character and nature,[69] immutability should not be interpreted so that God loses the dynamic freedom to act in accordance with the changing circumstances of human existence.[70]

Incarnation (fr. Lat. *in carne,* "in flesh")

Refers to the wondrous and unfathomable act of God the Son's taking on a sinless human nature in the person of Jesus Christ for the purpose of redeeming humanity. Historic Christian ORTHODOXY has always maintained that Christ possessed both human and divine natures, distinct and separate, without reduction of either or transformation into a new third nature that is neither.

Inerrancy / inerrant

The condition of being free from error. When applied to Scripture it means that the Bible is without error in what it teaches and absolutely trustworthy

---

plausibility of the two positions can be discussed by examining the evidence from empirical sciences. That is, if God does (or does not) exist, what kind of world would we expect to find? What kind of world do we find?

[69] See Num. 23:19; 1 Sam. 15:29; Ps. 55:19; 110:4; Jer. 4:28; Mal 3:6; Heb. 7:21.

[70] See Ex. 32:12; 2 Sam. 24:17; Jer. 26:3,13. A classic illustration of this is found in the Book of Jonah. God delivers an unconditional statement of judgment: "Yet forty days and Nineveh will be overthrown" (3:4). It looks like God did not make good on his prophecy or changed his mind. Actually, God's character of mercy is responsible for his delay of judgment until the time of Nahum (some 150 years later). It is also consistent with what he revealed elsewhere.

in the truth claims it makes. Some theologians limit the scope of the Bible's inerrancy to the areas of Christian faith and practice (called "limited inerrancy"). However, the Scriptures themselves make no such limitation.[71]

Infallible / infallibility

Being free from or incapable of error. These terms are near synonyms to the previous pair above. Some, however, have redefined infallibility in applying it to the Scriptures. They take it to mean that Scripture is incapable of failing in its predetermined purpose of revealing God and his plan of salvation (*PDTT*, 66). While this statement is true, it seems to avoid the debate about inerrancy by importing meaning that is not resident in the words themselves.

Justification

The gracious act of God whereby he acquits guilty sinners (Rom. 4:7–8) and declares them righteous on the basis of their faith in Christ (Rom. 4:5–6). This act brings sinners into right relationship with God and allows him to bestow on them all the blessings of his redemptive grace (Rom. 5:1–2; cf. Eph. 1:3).

Kenosis (fr. Gk. *kenoō,* "to empty")

A theological term derived from the Greek verb of Phil. 2:7 in Paul's description of the Incarnation. Scholars see here a sacrificial self-emptying by Christ and have sought to understand how that applies to his divine and human natures on earth. The basic question posed is, What did Christ empty himself of? Orthodox Christianity, while admitting to the full humanity of Christ, has been careful that the answer does not diminish his full deity.[72] Many understand the term to mean that for the purpose of accomplishing the work of redemption, Christ on earth surrendered not only his heavenly glory but also the independent use of certain divine attributes (e.g., omniscience).

God is free to change his actions toward both the righteous (who abandon righteousness) and the unrighteous who repent and begin practicing righteousness (Ezek. 18:23–32).

[71] Wayne Grudem conducts a comprehensive inductive study of what the Bible teaches about itself and concludes that Scripture presents a uniform testimony: "Hundreds of texts encourage God's people to trust Scripture completely, but no text encourages any doubt or even slight mistrust of Scripture. . . . To rely on the 'inerrancy' of every historical detail affirmed in Scripture is . . . to follow the teaching and practice of the biblical authors themselves. . . . All the words of the Bible are God's words and that God cannot speak untruthfully." See Wayne Grudem, "Scripture's Self-Attestation and the Problem of Formulating a Doctrine of Scripture," in *Scripture and Truth*, ed. D. A. Carson and John D. Woodbridge (Grand Rapids: Zondervan, 1983), 59.

[72] Theologians have often interpreted the *kenosis* as an addition of humanity, but not a subtraction from His deity.

Libertinism

A view of Christian living characterized by an abandonment of all moral restraint or a perverse freedom from acceptable standards of morality. Both Paul and Peter encountered a form of libertine teaching and practice in some of the churches. See Rom. 6:1, 15–15; Gal. 5:13, 16–21; 1 Peter 2:16–19. The teaching probably came as a result of a Greek notion from the time of Plato, i.e., that matter is evil and spirit is good. Moreover, the two domains are separate. Libertines may have reasoned that if we are spiritually resurrected with Christ and sit in heavenly places with him (Eph. 1:3), then what we do with our physical bodies has little relevance to the Christian life.

Linear thinking

An ordering of thought that moves in a patterned sequence of cause and effect or in a progression of time from beginning to end. This pattern of thought is often considered more characteristic of Western than Eastern cultures. While there is some validity in this observation, it must be pointed out that historical sequence is hardly absent from OT narratives. Furthermore, in one sense the Hebrew understanding of human history is linear since it is bracketed by creation at one end and final judgment at the other. The progress of God's redemptive dealings with humanity is moving history toward a definitive and climactic end (Carson, 1996, 500–501).

Marcion (ca. AD 150)

A heretical 2nd century teacher in the church of Rome whose writings parallel elements in Gnosticism. Marcion, like the later Gnostics, was anti-Jewish. He rejected the OT Scriptures, believing that the God of the OT was not God the NT, who sent the Lord Jesus Christ. He rejected most of the writings of the NT, accepting only Luke's gospel and ten epistles of Paul. His closure and reduction of the NT CANON incited the development of an orthodox NT canon (the MURATORIAN CANON ca. AD 170).[73]

Modalism (see SABELLIUS)

Monotheism (Gk. *monos,* "one"; *theos,* "god / God")

The belief in one God, in contrast to many gods (polytheism). There are three monotheistic religions in the world: Judaism, Christianity, and Islam.

[73] For a concise but informative description of Marcion's "contribution" to the formation of the NT canon, see David Dunbar, "The Biblical Canon," in *Hermeneutics, Authority and Canon*, ed. Carson, D. A. and John D. Woodbridge (Grand Rapids: Academie Books, 1986), 331–32.

All three affirm the existence of one true, eternally self-existent divine being. However, they differ significantly concerning how this God has revealed himself to humanity and what he has revealed concerning his plan of salvation.

Muratorian Canon

An ancient list of NT books named after its first editor, Ludivico Muratori. Its date of composition is disputed,[74] but most scholars place it around AD 170. In all probability, it was compiled to provide an orthodox list to contrast the one produced by MARICON, which contained only Luke's Gospel and ten letters of Paul.

Ordo salutis (Lat., "order of salvation")

This phrase describes how salvation comes to an individual by tracing a series of events that take place within God's plan of salvation. Roman Catholics view the church as God's instrument for dispensing grace through the sacraments. Reformed theologians view the order of salvation as descriptive of the logical order of experiences: (1) effectual calling, (2) regeneration, (3) faith, (4) justification, (5) sanctification, (6) glorification (Collins, EDT, 802). Arminian theologians (see ARMENIANISM) place a response of faith before regeneration, making God's regenerating work contingent upon this response and preserving the freedom of human will. This faith is not mere human effort but a result of God's grace working through Word and Spirit (Williams, 23–28).

Paradox (Gk. *paradoxos,* "contrary to what one thinks or supposes")

A statement that seems to be contradictory, illogical, or opposed to common sense, and yet is perhaps true. When applied to theology or biblical revelation, it refers to a statement that presents truth with two incompatible elements. Jesus spoke of life proceeding from death (John 12:24–25), of becoming great in the kingdom by becoming the least (Luke 9:48). Paul taught that Jesus was exalted by being humbled (Phil. 2:8–9). Jesus, in his incarnation, was both God and man (John 1:1, 14). These, and many others, are examples of theological paradoxes.

Perseverance of the saints (see ETERNAL SECURITY)

---

[74] Some scholars, like A. C. Sundberg, have argued for a fourth century date (ca. AD 350). However, this late date is unlikely and the evidence used in support of this dating is inconclusive. See Everett Ferguson, "Canon Muratori: Date and Provenance," *Studia Patristica* 18, no. 2 (1982): 677–83.

Plenary inspiration

> All Scripture is inspired by God and profitable for teaching, for reproof, for correction, for training in righteousness.
> –2 Tim. 3:16, NASB

Refers to the divine inspiration of the entire content of the Bible. See Inspiration.

Pneumatology (Gk. *pneuma,* "spirit"; *logos,* "word")

That branch of Christian theology that deals with the person and work of the Holy Spirit. In the OT it focuses largely on the activity of God's Spirit among Israel's prophets, kings, and judges. In the NT the focus is on how the Spirit relates to God the Father, Christ, salvation, and the ministry of the Church (Horton, *DPCM*, 410–417).

Predestination (see Calvinism)

A doctrinal position associated mainly with Calvinism. It holds that God sovereignly decreed to elect and predestine those who will be saved and those who will be damned or lost.[75]

Preincarnate

A theological term that applies to the time prior to Christ taking upon himself a human nature (John 1:14) through his miraculous conception (Luke 1:35) and birth (Matt. 1:23–25).

Prevenient grace

The grace extended through the work of the Holy Spirit upon human hearts whereby people are enabled to respond to God's offer of salvation presented in the gospel. Wesley (and Arminians in general) understood this grace as extended to all of humanity, while Calvin understood it as granted only to those whom God has chosen to be saved (*PDTT*, 95).

Propitiation (Gk. *hilasmos* or *hilasterion*, "propitiation")

A blood sacrifice, or sin offering (Rom. 3:25), that satisfies the wrath of God, restores fellowship, and allows him to grant us His divine favor and blessing (*DBAG*, 474). The Book of Hebrews uses the term to represent the sin

[75] This is also known as "double predestination," which Luther rejected, holding that predestination applies only to those chosen for salvation. Two basic problems exist with this doctrine. One, it equates election with predestination while the relevant NT texts suggest otherwise. Two, it ignores the NT use of the verb "predestine" as to its objects. Robert Shank

offering (2:17) and the Mercy Seat, or place where the blood of the atoning sacrifice was put (9:5). The NT is clear in presenting Christ as the propitiation for our sins (1 John 2:2; 4:10).

Reconciliation (Gk. *katallagē*)

One facet of God's work of salvation. In reconciliation God restores sinners to fellowship with himself by removing the enmity that stands between them because of sin. He does this by allowing Christ to become their sin offering (Rom. 3:25) and by punishing their sins through his death on the cross (Eph. 2:15–16). That death secures not only the forgiveness of their sins (Eph. 2:15–16) but establishes their "peace" with God (Eph. 2:17).[76]

Redeem / redemption

Both the Hebrew (*gaal, padah*) and the Greek (*lutroō, exagoradzō*) verbs mean "to redeem, purchase, buy back." In the OT the doctrine of redemption refers to the gracious action of God whereby he saves, delivers, or frees his people (Ex. 6:6; Jer. 15:21; Isa. 49:26; 60:16). In the NT the doctrine focuses on God's action of purchasing (1 Cor. 6:20) us from sin's penalty (Eph. 1:7; Gal. 3:13), bondage, and power (Heb. 9:12–14; cf. Rom. 6:6–9) through the death and resurrection of Jesus.

Regeneration (Gk. *Palingenesia,* "regeneration, renewal")

Commonly refers to the new birth, or being "born again"[77] by the Spirit of God (John 3:3–8; cf. Titus 3:5). Related concepts are the "new creation" (2 Cor. 5:17), taking on a "divine nature" (2 Peter 1:4), and being spiritually resurrected and "made alive" in Christ (Eph. 2:5; Col. 2:13; cf. Rom. 6:11).

---

has clearly shown that the two terms are not equivalent. First, he admits that "election" has to do with who will be saved but demonstrates exegetically that it is a primarily a "corporate" election "in Christ" in which people individually participate by faith. Second, the six uses of the Greek *prooridzō* ("predetermine, predestine, foreordain") reveal that predestination focuses on, in Shank's words, the "circumstance" (purposes or goals) of that election: (1) the goal of believers being conformed to the image of God's Son and glorified with him (Rom. 8:29,30; Eph. 1:11,12); (2) the hidden wisdom of God being revealed in the Gospel (1 Cor. 2:7); (3) the goal of adoption—to be children of God through Christ (Eph. 1:5). See Shank, *Elect in the Son*, 21–55, 155–58.

[76] Note how often in his epistles Paul greets the churches with a salutation such as "Grace and peace to you from God our Father and the Lord Jesus Christ." As a Jew, Paul undoubtedly had in mind the Hebrew word *shalom*, a word that recalls the peace and total well-being of one who stands in covenant relationship to God.

[77] The Greek phrase can also be translated being "born from above."

Sabbatarianism (Heb. *sabbat,* "Sabbath")

A religious conviction within the Christian church that seeks to establish Saturday as the Christian day of worship in place of Sunday and / or to reestablish the OT Sabbath regulations (esp. its prohibition against work) in the Church (Lyons, *BDT*, 464).

Sabellius

A third-century teacher in the Church who struggled with the doctrine of the Trinity. In an attempt to guard against tritheism (belief in three gods), he taught that the Father, Son, and Holy Ghost were three different manifestations of God, or modes of being. Alhtough God is essentially one, Sabellius taught that in his self-revelation to humans he takes the form of Father, Son, and Holy Spirit. This error is called MODALISM or Sabellianism and was condemned by the orthodox church at a council in Rome in AD 263 (W. Kelly, *BDOT*, 465).

Sacraments (Lat. *sacramentum,* "something set apart")

Formal religious rites that symbolize a spiritual reality. Early Latin fathers of the Church used the term to translate the Greek word *musterion* ("mystery") to signify a special sacred rite or ordinance through which the believer received some blessing from God. Today theologians commonly refer to a sacrament as an outward and visible sign of an inward and spiritual grace given to believers. The rite itself has been ordained by Christ. Protestants recognize two such sacraments (BAPTISM and the Lord's Supper), while the Roman Catholic and Eastern Orthodox churches recognize seven (baptism, the Lord's Supper, confirmation, penance, extreme unction, ordination, and matrimony). The term "sacramentalism" is used when the sacramental rite itself is viewed as the means by which grace is conveyed (R.Wallace, *BDOT*, 465–66; A. Peisker, *BDT*, 465).

Sanctification

Relates to both the believer's status of being "holy" before God and the process of becoming holy, i.e., partaking of God's holy nature. Both the Hebrew (*qadash*) and Greek (*hagiadzō*) verbs, translated "to sanctify" or "make holy," carry the idea being "set apart" or "consecrated" for God's holy use or purpose. Thus, Paul addresses believers as saints (*hagioi*) because they have been set apart by God for his service in accordance with his will.[78] This declares their redeemed status and position before God. However, believers are also engaged in a process of spiritual

[78]See Rom. 1:7; 8:27; 1 Cor. 1:2; 2 Cor. 1:1; Eph. 1:1; Phil. 1:1; Col. 1:2, etc.

transformation (Rom. 8:2; cf. Heb. 12:14) into conformity with the image of God's Son (Rom. 8:29). This process is the work of the Holy Spirit and has as its goal our glorification (2 Cor. 3:18), i.e., "being transformed into the same image [of Christ] from glory to glory, just as from the Lord, the Spirit."[79]

Soteriology (Gk. *sōtēria,* "salvation")

That branch of Christian theology that focuses on the divine work of salvation through Jesus Christ. See SALVATION.

Sovereignty

A term used in Christian theology to describe God in his supreme and absolute power, freedom, and authority to do whatever he wills in regard to his creation (Ps. 115:3). Theologians debate not the right of God to act sovereignly but the exercise of that right and how it impacts his dealings with humans, who as moral agents are accountable for their choices and actions (N. Oke, *BDT*, 171).

Synergistic (fr. Gk. *sunergos,* "fellow, co-worker")

A term often used in Christian theology to describe the cooperation between Divinity and humanity in the salvation and spiritual development of the individual (R. Price *BDT*, 510). As understood by Arminians, this does not cancel salvation by grace, as they do not see the response of the human will as a work that merits salvation; it is, rather, a necessary response of consent and acceptance that results in God's saving grace being imparted. Calvinists would disagree, arguing that there is only one divine worker in salvation—God; human will is involved only in the sense that God's irresistible grace acts upon that will, effectively causing a response of faith.

Teleological (Gk. *telos,* "goal" or "end")

Relating to or giving evidence of purposeful design, especially in nature or the physical universe. Theologians often point to the intricate and incredible design of that universe as evidence of an intelligent Designer or Creator.[80]

Theism (fr. Gk. *theos,* "god")

The term literally means "belief in god" (or gods) and can be discussed in various religious contexts. Christian theism refers to the belief in the one true

---

[79] For a very helpful work devoted to this doctrine, Donald L. Alexander, *Christian Spirituality: Five Views of Sanctification* (Downers Grove, Ill.: InterVarsity Press, 1988).

[80] See Lee Stobel's discussion with Michael Behe concerning the evidence for a purposeful Designer gleaned from the field of biochemistry. See Strobel, *Case for a Creator*, 193–218.

God of the Bible—the God who is infinite, eternal, and self-existent.[81] This God is the un-caused first cause, the transcendent and sovereign Creator—Sustainer of the universe and the author of humankind's salvation through his Son, Jesus Christ.

Theodicy (Gk. *theos,* "god"; *dikē,* "justice")

Refers to a reasoned defense of God's goodness / righteousness or an attempt to vindicate his justice in view of the presence of evil or circumstances that call his justice and goodness into question.[82]

Theology (Gk. *theos,* "God"; *logos,* "word")

That branch of Christian doctrine that focuses on the person and work of God and his relations to the world and creation, especially as revealed in the Scriptures.[83] In popular usage, the term "theology" becomes an all-inclusive term for the study of the Bible and its doctrine. E.g., "Jack came for supper last night and we talked 'theology' until midnight."

Theophany (Gk. *theos,* "God"; *phainō,* "appear")

A visible manifestation of deity or God. OT theophanies took a variety of forms. This includes the burning bush that appeared to Moses (Ex. 3), God's appearance to Moses and the 70 elders of Israel (Ex. 24:1), and the Angel of the Lord who appeared to Jacob (Gen. 32:24–28), Gideon (Jud. 6:11–23), and Joshua (Josh. 5:13–15). On one occasion God's visible presence was promised to Moses in the form of a "thick cloud" (Ex. 19:9). The greatest theophany is found in the incarnation of Christ (John 1:14), which fully revealed the very essence of God's glory, nature, and being (John 1:18; Heb. 1:3; Col. 1:19; 2:9).

Transcendence

In theology this term speaks of the relationship between God and his creation. Transcendence is the state of being separate and distinct from his creation.

---

[81] Any definition of God is imperfect and incomplete. Here are merely given some essential attributes of God that characterize Christian theism.

[82] For example, Paul embarks on a theodicy in Romans 9–11. Jewish Christians have come to a crisis of faith over the fact that Israel as a nation is not embracing the gospel. The fallout is that the promises of God remain unfulfilled and some Jews are calling into question the faithful character of God to make good his promises to Israel. Paul takes these three chapters to argue that there is no injustice with God (9:14). For a very illuminating interpretation of Rom. 9–11 in view of this theodicy, see Shank, *Elect in the Son*, 108–19.

[83] Systematic theology also employs philosophy, history, social anthropology (human conscience), and even natural science to explore certain evidences of God's existence and providential presence in the world.

In the words of Kierkegaard, it speaks of God being "wholly other" than anything he has created. It is not to be equated with being "remote" or uninvolved in this world (see Deism). God can be both Immanent (near, present) and transcendent with regard to this world without contradiction.

Trichotomy

A theological term that describes a human being as composed of three basic parts: body, soul, and spirit (Heb. 4:12; 1 Thess. 5:23). Trichotomists draw a distinction between the soul (Gk. *pseuchē*) and spirit (Gk. *pneuma*) within a person. They view the soul as that part that houses human personality, while the spirit is that part that can know and relate to God. Dichotomists contend that there are only two parts to human nature (Gen. 2:7; Matt. 10:28; 1 Cor. 7:34): the body (its physical dimension) and the soul (its non-physical dimension). Within the latter dimension are many functions and capacities described with terms like soul, spirit, heart, mind, will, etc.[84]

Popular Terms and Expressions

Classical Pentecostals

In addition to the doctrinal commitments of Pentecostals, classical Pentecostals traditionally believe that the reception of the Baptism in the Holy Spirit is accompanied by tongues (Gk. *glossalalia*), which serves as the initial sign–evidence of its reception (cf. Acts 2:4) (Synan, *DPCM*, 220).

Conservative Scholarship

A phrase generally used to describe scholarship by individuals who hold to the divine inspiration and authority of Scripture,[85] and have a commitment to the Orthodox doctrines of the historic Christian church. See also Liberal scholarship.

Great Commission Christians

Refers to believers who take seriously the commands of Jesus in Mark 16:15 to preach the gospel to all creation, and in Matt. 28:18–19 to make disciples of all nations.

---

[84] One of the better treatments of the debate over whether humans are a "dichotomy" or a "trichotomy" is found in James O. Buswell Jr., *A Systematic Theology of the Christian Religion*, vol. 1 (Grand Rapids: Zondervan, 1962), 231–51.

[85] This is sometimes referred to as having a "high view" of Scripture and often this includes the belief in the "inerrancy" or "infallibility" of Scripture.

Legalism

A negative term used in the Church to refer to Christianity that defines itself by or emphasizes certain prescribed rules, behavioral practices, and / or rituals. The biblical example most often given is of the Pharisees, whose strict adherence to the Law and tradition narrowly defined what was acceptable Judaism.[86]

Liberal scholarship

A phrase generally used to describe scholarship by individuals who are not bound by authoritative creeds, traditions, or accepted standards of doctrinal Orthodoxy. (See also R. V. Pierard, *EDT*, 631–32.)

Oneness

An abbreviated term used mostly to describe the doctrine of Oneness Pentecostals, who reject the traditional doctrine of the Trinity: that God is one in essence but eternally exists as three distinct persons, the Father, Son, and Holy Spirit, who are co-equal in every respect as to divine nature and glory. Instead, Oneness Pentecostals contend that these names represent three ways God reveals himself to humanity as recorded in Scripture. Furthermore, they hold that the divine reality / essence is manifested uniquely in the person of Jesus, who is the Son, who as transcendent deity is the Spirit, who in his revelation of God is the Father (D. Reed, *DPCM*, 648–49).[87] See Modalism.

Pentecostals

Christians who believe that there is a post-conversion experience called the Baptism in the Holy Spirit available to every believer. Taking their cue from the Book of Acts, Pentecostals contend that this experience provides spiritual empowerment for Christian service and gospel witness (1:8), which includes all the spiritual gifts (Gk. *charismata* [1 Cor. 12]) mentioned in the Pauline epistles, including miraculous signs and wonders necessary to fully preach the gospel to the world (Rom. 15:19). The underlying theological assumption is that the same experience of Spirit-baptism that empowered the disciples on the Day of Pentecost is a "gift" available to believers of every age (Acts 2:38) (Arrington, 19–20, 115–144).

---

[86] Jesus rebuked them and showed how this kind of legalism can undermine the great moral principles contained in the law. The irony was that the Pharisees in their zeal to keep the Law through their traditions wound up setting aside the Law, thus violating it (Mark 7:6–13).

[87] David Reed calls Oneness Pentecostalism "a form of simultaneous modalism that, unlike Sabellianism, regards all three manifestations as present at the same time, not in successive revelatory periods." See *DPCM*, s.v. "Oneness Pentecostalism," 649.

Plead the blood

The "blood" is a NT metaphor for the death of Christ on the cross. Some use the expression meaning to verbally confess and affirm the significance of Christ's death for salvation (e.g., atonement for our sins [Matt. 26:28]; justification [Rom. 5:9; et al.], reconciliation [Eph. 2:13; et al.]) and the powerful work of God in destroying the works of Satan through the cross (Col.:13–20, cf. 1 John 3:8).[88]

[88] Unfortunately, some use the expression assuming that the words themselves carry some intrinsic power and that by merely reciting the words that power is released. This parallels the pagan use of magical formulas in the Greco-Roman world and is condemned in Scripture. See Matt. 6:7; Acts 19:13–16.

Selected Bibliography

Alexander, Donald L. *Christian Spirituality: Five Views of Sanctification.* Downers Grove, Ill.: InterVarsity Press, 1988.

Anderson, Gordon L. "Pentecostal Hermeneutics." *Conference Papers*, Vol. 2 of the 22nd Annual Meeting of the Society for Pentecostal Studies, Springfield, Mo., November 12–14, 1992, 1–21.

Archer, Gleason L., Jr. *A Survey of Old Testament Introduction.* Rev. ed. Chicago: Moody Press, 1974.

Arnold, Bill T., and Bryan E. Beyer. *Encountering the Old Testament.* Grand Rapids: Baker Books, 1999.

Arrington, French L. *Encountering the Holy Spirit: Paths of Christian Growth and Service.* Cleveland, Tenn.: Pathway Press, 2003.

Aune, David E. *The New Testament in Its Literary Environment.* Philadelphia: Westminster Press, 1987.

———. "The Gospels: Biography or Theology?" *Bible Review* 6, no. 1 (February 1990): 15–37.

Bauman, Michael, and David Hall, eds. *Evangelical Hermeneutics.* Camp Hill, Pa.: Christian Publications, 1995.

Berkhof, Louis. *Principles of Biblical Interpretation.* Grand Rapids: Baker Book House, 1950.

Braaten, Carl E. *New Directions in Theology Today.* Edited by William Hordern. Vol. 2, *History and Hermeneutics.* Philadelphia: Westminster Press, 1966.

Bray, Gerald. *Biblical Interpretation: Past and Present.* Downers Grove, Ill.: InterVarsity Press, 1996.

Brinsmead, Bernard Hungerford. *Galatians—Dialogical Response to Opponents.* Chico, Calif.: Scholars Press, 1982.

Brown, Raymond E. "Parable and Allegory Reconsidered." *Novum Testamentum* 5 (January 1962): 36–45.

Bruce, F. F. *The Canon of Scripture.* Downers Grove, Ill.: InterVarsity Press, 1988.

———. *The New Testament Documents: Are They Reliable?* Leicester, England: InterVarsity Press, 1988.

Bullinger, E. W. *Figures of Speech in the Bible: Explained and Illustrated.* Reprint, Grand Rapids: Baker Book House, 1968.

Bullock, C. Hassell. *Encountering the Book of Psalms*. Grand Rapids, MI: Baker Academic, 2001.

Bultmann, Rudolf. *New Testament and Mythology and Other Basic Works*. Edited and translated by Schubert M. Ogden. Philadelphia: Fortress Press, 1984.

Buswell, James O., Jr. *A Systematic Theology of the Christian Religion*. Vol. 1. Grand Rapids: Zondervan, 1962.

Caldwell, Larry W. "Third Horizon Ethnohermeneutics: Reevaluating New Testament Hermeneutical Models for Intercultural Bible Interpreters Today." *Asian Journal of Theology* 1 (1987): 314–33.

Carson, D. A. *Exegetical Fallacies*. Grand Rapids: Baker Book House, 1984a.

_____. *The Gagging of God: Christianity Confronts Pluralism*. Grand Rapids: Zondervan, 1996).

_____. "Redaction Criticism: On the Legitimacy and Illegitimacy of a Literary Tool." In *Scripture and Truth*, edited by D. A. Carson and J. D. Woodbridge, 119–46. Grand Rapids: Zondervan, Academie Books, 1983.

_____ . "A Sketch of the Factors Determining Current Hermeneutical Debate in Cross-Cultural Contexts." In *Biblical Interpretation and the Church: The Problem of Contextualization*, edited by D. A. Carson. Nashville, Tenn.: Thomas Nelson, 1984b.

_____. "Unity and Diversity in the New Testament: The Possibility of Systematic Theology." In *Scripture and Truth*, edited by D. A. Carson and J. D. Woodbridge, 65–100. Grand Rapids: Zondervan, Academie Books, 1983.

Childs, Brevard. *Introduction to the Old Testament as Scripture*. Philadelphia: Fortress Press, 1979.

Clouse, Robert G.. ed. *The Meaning of the Millennium*. Downers Grove, Ill.: Inter-Varsity Press, 1977.

Collins, J. J. *Daniel: With an Introduction to Apocalyptic Literature*. FOTL 20. Grand Rapids: Wm. B. Eerdmans, 1984.

Daly, Mary. *Quintessence: Realizing the Archaic Future—A Radical Elemental Feminist Manifesto*. Boston: Beacon, 1998.

Dockery, David S. *Biblical Interpretation Then and Now: Contemporary Hermeneutics in the Light of the Early Church*. Grand Rapids: Baker Book House, 1992.

Dodd, C. H. *The Parables of the Kingdom*. Rev. ed. London: Nisbet, 1955.

Donner, Theodore. "Some Thoughts on the History of the New Testament Canon." *Themelios* 7 (1982): 23–27.

Dowley, Timothy, ed. *Introduction to the History of Christianity*. Minneapolis: Fortress Press, 1985.

Dunbar, David. "The Biblical Canon." In *Hermeneutics, Authority and Canon*, edited by D. A. Carson and J. D. Woodbridge. Grand Rapids: Zondervan, Academie Books, 1986.

Dunn, James. "Demythologizing: The Problem of Myth in the New Testament." In *New Testament Interpretation: Essays on Principles and Methods*, edited by I. Howard Marshall, 285–88. Grand Rapids: Wm. B. Eerdmans, 1977.

Duvall, J. Scott, and J. Daniel Hays. *Grasping God's Word: A Hands-On Approach to Reading, Interpreting, and Applying the Bible.* Grand Rapids: Zondervan, 2001.

Efird, James M. *How to Interpret the Bible.* Atlanta: John Knox Press, 1984.

Ellis, E. E. "How the New Testament Uses the Old." In *New Testament Interpretation: Essays on Principles and Methods*, edited by I. Howard Marshall, 199–219. Grand Rapids: Wm. B. Eerdmans, 1977.

Elwell, Walter A., ed. *Evangelical Dictionary of Theology.* Grand Rapids: Baker Book House, 1984.

Elwell, Walter A., and Robert W. Yarbrough. *Encountering the New Testament: A Historical and Theological Survey.* Grand Rapids: Baker Book House, 1998.

Erickson, Millard. *Christian Theology.* 2d ed. Grand Rapids: Baker Book House, 1999.

Evans, C. Stephen. *Pocket Dictionary of Apologetics and Philosophy of Religion.* Downers Grove, Ill.: InterVarsity Press, 2002.

Farrar, Frederic W. *History of Interpretation.* Grand Rapids: Baker Book House, 1961.

Fee, Gordon D. "The Textual Criticism of the New Testament." In *The Expositor's Bible Commentary*, edited by F. E. Gaebelein, 1:419–33. Grand Rapids: Zondervan, 1979.

Fee, Gordon D., and Douglas Stuart. *How to Read the Bible for All Its Worth.* Grand Rapids: Zondervan, Academie Books, 1982.

———. *How to Read the Bible for All Its Worth.* 2d ed. Grand Rapids: Zondervan, 1993.

Ferguson, Duncan. *Biblical Hermeneutics: An Introduction.* Atlanta, Ga.: John Knox Press, 1986.

Ferguson, Everett. *Backgrounds of Early Christianity.* 2d ed. Grand Rapids: Wm. B. Eerdmans, 1993.

Fiorenza, Elizabeth Schüssler. *In Memory of Her: A Feminist Theological Reconstruction of Christian Origins.* New York: Crossroad, 1983.

Garland, David E. "Background Studies and New Testament Interpretation." In *New Testament Criticism and Interpretation*, edited by David Alan Black and David S. Dockery. Grand Rapids: Zondervan, 1991.

Geisler, Norman, and William E. Nix. *A General Introduction to the Bible.* Chicago: Moody Press, 1980.

Goldsworthy, Graeme. *Preaching the Whole Bible as Christian Scripture.* Grand Rapids: Wm. B. Eerdmans, 2000.

Grant, Robert M., and David Tracy. *A Short History of the Interpretation of the Bible.* Philadelphia: Fortress Press, 1984.

Grenz, Stanley, David Guretzki, and Cherith Fee Nordling. *Pocket Dictionary of Theological Terms.* Downers Grove, Ill.: InterVarsity Press, 1999.

Grider, J. Kenneth. "Arminianism." In *Evangelical Dictionary of Theology*, edited by Walter A. Elwell, 79–81. Grand Rapids: Baker Book House, 1984.

———. "Scholasticism." In *Beacon Dictionary of Theology*, 473–74. Kansas City: Beacon Hill Press, 1983.

Grudem, Wayne. "Scripture's Self-Attestation and the Problem of Formulating a Doctrine of Scripture." In *Scripture and Truth*, edited by D. A Carson and J. D. Woodbridge, 19–64. Grand Rapids: Zondervan, Academie Books, 1983.

Gundry, Robert. *The Church and the Tribulation*. Grand Rapids: Zondervan , 1973.

Guthrie, Donald. *New Testament Introduction*. 3d ed. Downers Grove, Ill.: Inter-Varsity Press, 1970.

Harris, Stephen L. *Understanding the Bible*. 4th ed. Mountain View, Calif.: Mayfield, 1997.

Hasselgrave, David J. "Contextualization and Revelational Epistemology." In *Hermeneutics Inerrancy and the Bible*, edited by E. D. Radmacher and R. D. Preus. Grand Rapids: Zondervan, 1984.

Hernando, James D. "Irenaeus and the Apostolic Fathers: Inquiry in the Development of the New Testament Canon." PhD diss., Drew University, Madison, N.J., 1990.

______. "2 Corinthians." In *Life in the Spirit New Testament Commentary*, edited by French L. Arrington and Roger Stronstad. Grand Rapids: Zondervan, 1999.

Hirsch, E. D., Jr. *Validity in Interpretation*. New Haven, Conn.: Yale University Press, 1967.

Holmes, Michael. "Textual Criticism." In *New Testament Criticism and Interpretation*, edited by D. A. Black and D. S. Dockery, 101–34. Grand Rapids: Zondervan, 1991.

Jewett, Robert. "Romans as an Ambassadorial Letter." *Interpretation* 36 (1982): 5–20.

Johnson, Marshall D. *Making Sense of the Bible: Literary Approach as an Approach to Understanding*. Grand Rapids: Wm. B. Eerdmans, 2002.

Kaiser, Walter C., Jr. *Toward An Exegetical Theology: Biblical Exegesis for Preaching and Teaching*. Grand Rapids: Baker Book House, 1981.

———. *The Old Testament Documents: Are They Reliable and Relevant?* Downers Grove, Ill.: InterVarsity Press, 2001.

——— and Moisés Silva. *An Introduction to Biblical Hermeneutics: The Search for Meaning*. Grand Rapids: Zondervan, 1994.

Kee, H. C. "Aretalogy and Gospel." *Journal of Biblical Literature*. 92 (1973): 402–22.

Keener, Craig. *The IVP Bible Background Commentary: New Testament*. Downers Grove, Ill.: InterVarsity Press, 1993.

Kennedy, G. A. *New Testament Interpretation through Rhetorical Criticism*. Chapel Hill: University of North Carolina Press, 1994.

Klein, William W., Craig L. Blomberg, and Robert L. Hubbard. *Introduction to Biblical Interpretation*. Waco, Tex.: Word Publishing, 1993.

———. *Introduction to Biblical Interpretation*. Rev. ed. Nashville, Tenn.: Thomas Nelson, 1993.

Köstenberger, A. J., T. R. Schreiner, and H. S. Baldwin. *Women in the Church: A Fresh Analysis of 1 Timothy 2:9–15*. Grand Rapids: Baker Book House, 1995.

Kroger, C. C., and R. C. Kroger. *I Suffer Not a Woman: Rethinking 1 Timothy 2:11–15 in Light of Ancient Evidence*. Grand Rapids: Baker Book House, 1992.

Lawson, John. *Historical and Theological Introduction to the Apostolic Fathers.* New York: Macmillan, 1961.

Lehmann, Paul. "The Reformers' Use of the Bible." *Theology Today* 3 (1946): 328–48.

Livingston, James C. *Modern Christian Thought from the Enlightenment to Vatican II.* New York: Macmillan, 1971.

Longenecker, Richard N. *Biblical Exegesis in the Apostolic Period.* Grand Rapids: Wm. B. Eerdmans, 1975.

Longman, Tremper. *Literary Approaches to Biblical Interpretation.* Grand Rapids: Zondervan, 1987.

Mack, Burton. *Rhetoric and the New Testament.* Guides to Biblical Scholarship. Minneapolis: Fortress Press, 1990.

Marshall, I. Howard. "Historical Criticism." In *New Testament Interpretation: Essays on Principles and Methods,* edited by I. Howard Marshall, 126–38. Grand Rapids: Wm. B. Eerdmans, 1977.

McKim, Donald K., ed. *A Guide to Contemporary Hermeneutics: Major Trends in Biblical Interpretation.* Grand Rapids: Wm. B. Eerdmans, 1986.

———, ed. *Historical Handbook of Major Biblical Interpreters.* Downers Grove, Ill.: InterVarsity Press, 1998.

_____. *Westminster Dictionary of Theological Terms.* Louisville, Ky.: Westminster/John Knox Press, 1996.

McKnight, Edgar V. *Postmodern Use of the Bible: The Emergence of Reader-Oriented Criticism.* Nashville, Tenn.: Abingdon Press, 1988.

McQuilken, Robertson. *Understanding and Applying the Bible.* Rev. ed. Chicago: Moody Press, 1992.

Mickelsen, A. Berkeley. *Interpreting the Bible.* 1963. Reprint, Grand Rapids: Wm B. Eerdmans, 1974.

Moo, Douglas J. "The Problem of *Sensus Plenior.*" In *Hermeneutics, Authority and Canon,* edited by D. A. Carson and J. D. Woodbridge. Grand Rapids: Zondervan, Academie Books, 1986.

Morris, Leon. "The Use of Hilaskesthai in Biblical Greek." *Expository Times* (May 1951): 227–33.

Mulholland, M. Robert., Jr. "Sociological Criticism." In *New Testament Criticism and Interpretation,* ed. D. A. Black and D. S. Dockery, 296–316. Grand Rapids: Zondervan, 1991.

Nash, Ronald H. *Christianity and the Hellenistic World.* Grand Rapids: Zondervan, 1984.

Osborne, Grant R. *The Hermeneutical Spiral: A Comprehensive Introduction to Biblical Interpretation.* Downers Grove, Ill.: InterVarsity Press, 1991.

Padilla, Rene. "The Interpreted Word: Reflections of Contextual Hermeneutics." In *A Guide to Contemporary Hermeneutics: Major Trends in Biblical Interpretation,* edited by Donald McKim. Grand Rapids: Wm. B. Eerdmans, 1986.

Payne, J. Barton. *Encyclopedia of Biblical Prophecy: The Complete Guide to Scriptural Predictions.* New York: Harper and Row, 1973.

Poythress, Vern S. "Analysing a Biblical Text: Some Important Linguistic Distinctions." *Scottish Journal of Theology* 32 (1979).

Puckett, D. L. "Calvin, John." In *Historical Handbook of Major Biblical Interpreters*, edited by Donald K. McKim, 171–79. Downers Grove, Ill.: InterVarsity Press, 1998.

Radmacher, Earl D., and Robert D. Preus, eds. *Hermeneutics, Inerrancy and the Bible*. Grand Rapids: Zondervan, Academie Books, 1984.

Ramm, Bernard L. "The New Hermeneutic." In *Hermeneutics*, by Bernard L Ramm and others. Grand Rapids: Baker Book House, 1952.

______. *Protestant Biblical Interpretation*. 3d. ed. Grand Rapids: Baker Book House, 1970.

______. *Varieties of Christian Apologetics*. Grand Rapids: Baker Book House, 1966.

Robinson, James M. "Hermeneutics Since Barth." In The New Hermeneutic, edited by James M. Robinson and John B. Cobb, Jr., 1–77. New York: Harper and Row, 1964.

Rosas III, L. J. "Kierkegaard, Søren Aabe." In *Historical Handbook of Major Biblical Interpreters*, edited by Donald K. McKim, 330–36. Downers Grove, Ill.: InterVarsity Press, 1998.

Rosenthal, Marvin. *The Pre-Wrath Rapture of the Church*. Nashville, Tenn.: Thomas Nelson, 1990.

Ryken, Leland. *How to Read the Bible as Literature*. Grand Rapids: Zondervan, Academie Books, 1984.

Ryrie, Charles C. *Dispensationalism Today*. Chicago: Moody Press, 1965.

Sandmel, Samuel. "Parallelomania." *Journal of Biblical Literature* 81 (1962): 2–13.

Scharlemann, Robert P. "Deconstruction: What Is It?" *Dialog* 26, no. 3 (Fall 1978): 184–88.

Shank, Robert. *Elect in the Son*. Springfield, Mo.: Westcott Publishers, 1970.

Silva, Moisés, ed. *Foundations of Contemporary Interpretation*. Grand Rapids: Zondervan, 1996.

Soulen, Richard, N. *Handbook of Biblical Criticism*. 2d ed. Atlanta, Ga.: John Knox Press, 1981.

Soulen, Richard N., and R. Kendall Soulen. *Handbook of Biblical Criticism*. 3d ed. Atlanta, Ga.: John Knox Press, 2001.

Stanton, Graham N. "Presuppositions in New Testament Interpretation." In *New Testament Interpretation: Essays on Principles and Methods*, edited by I. Howard Marshall, 60–70. Grand Rapids: Wm. B. Eerdmans, 1977.

Stein, Robert H. *A Basic Guide to Interpreting the Bible: Playing by the Rules*. Grand Rapids: Baker Book House, 1994.

______ "The Benefits of an Author-Oriented Approach to Hermeneutics." *Journal of the Evangelical Theological Society* 44, no. 3 (September 2001): 451–66.

Strobel, Lee. *The Case for Christ: A Journalist's Personal Investigation of the Evidence for Jesus*. Grand Rapids: Zondervan, 1998.

Stronstad, Roger. *The Prophethood of All Believers: A Study in Luke's Charismatic Theology*. Sheffield, England: Sheffield Academic Press, 2003.

______. *Spirit, Scripture and Theology: A Pentecostal Perspective*. Bagio City, Philippines: APTS Press, 1995.

Tate, W. Randolph. *Biblical Hermeneutics: An Integrated Approach*. Peabody, Mass.: Hendrickson Publishers, 1991.

Terry, Milton S. *Biblical Hermeneutics: A Treatise on the Interpretation of the Old and New Testaments*. New York: Hunt and Eaton, 1890.

Thiselton, Anthony C. *The Two Horizons: New Testament Hermeneutics and Philosophical Description with Special Reference to Heidegger, Bultmann, Gadamer and Wittgenstein*. Grand Rapids: Wm. B. Eerdmans, 1980.

Travis, Stephen H. "Form Criticism." In *New Testament Interpretation: Essays on Principles and Methods*, edited by I. Howard Marshall, 153–64. Grand Rapids: Wm. B. Eerdmans, 1977.

Virkler, Henry A. *Hermeneutics: Principles and Processes of Biblical Interpretation*. Grand Rapids: Baker Book House, 1981.

Walvoord, John F. *The Rapture Question*. Finlay, Ohio: Dunham, 1957.

Wenham, David. "Source Criticism." In *New Testament Interpretation: Essays on Principles and Methods*, edited by I. Howard Marshall, 139–49. Grand Rapids: Wm. B. Eerdmans, 1977.

Westerholm, Stephen. *Israel's Law and the Church's Faith: Paul and His Recent Interpreters*. Grand Rapids: Wm. B. Eerdmans, 1988.

Williams, J. Rodman. *Renewal Theology*. Vol. 2. Grand Rapids: Zondervan, 1990.

Woodbridge, J. D., and T. E. McComiskey, *Doing Theology in Today's World*. Grand Rapids: Zondervan, 1991.

Zuck, Roy B., ed. *Rightly Divided: Readings in Biblical Hermeneutics*. Grand Rapids: Kregel Publications, 1996.

Term Index

Additional Terms Request

As in the development of any book of this nature, there may be terms that you feel should have been included. If you feel that there is a term you would like to see included in the next edition of this *Dictionary of Hermeneutics*, write the term(s) on a 3 x 5 card and mail it with your name and address to:

Dictionary of Hermeneutics
Gospel Publishing House
1445 N. Boonville Avenue
Springfield, Missouri 65802

Or send an e-mail to us with your suggested term(s).

hermeneutics@gph.org

The names of anyone whose suggestions this author uses in future editions of *Dictionary of Hermeneutics* will be added to the list of acknowledgements.